Dr. Stephen L. Snover is currently an assistant professor at the University of Hartford, and was formerly on the faculty at Babson College and a writer for the Boston University Mathematics Project.

Dr. Mark A. Spikell is an associate professor at Lesley College and an adjunct professor at Boston University. He has co-authored two other books, *Problem Solving in the Mathematics Laboratory* and *Multibase Activities*.

HOW TO PROGRAM YOUR
PROGRAMMABLE CALCULATOR

Stephen L. Snover
Mark A. Spikell

Prentice-Hall, Inc., Englewood Cliffs, New Jersey 07632

Library of Congress Cataloging in Publication Data

Snover, Stephen L.
How to program your programmable calculator.

(A Spectrum Book)
1.–Programmable calculators, I.–Spikell, Mark A., joint author. II.–Title.
QA75.S557 001.6'42 78-11701
ISBN 0-13-429365-7
ISBN 0-13-429357-6 pbk.

A SPECTRUM BOOK

Printed in the United States of America

10 9 8 7 6 5 4 3 2

Editorial/production supervision by
Maria Carella and Shirley Covington
Interior design by Shirley Covington
Cover design by Richard Pacifico
Manufacturing buyer: Cathie Lenard

PRENTICE-HALL INTERNATIONAL, INC., *London*
PRENTICE-HALL OF AUSTRALIA PTY., LIMITED, *Sydney*
PRENTICE-HALL OF CANADA, LTD., *Toronto*
PRENTICE-HALL OF INDIA PRIVATE, LIMITED, *New Delhi*
PRENTICE-HALL OF JAPAN, INC., *Tokyo*
PRENTICE-HALL OF SOUTHEAST ASIA PTE., LTD., *Singapore*
WHITEHALL BOOKS, LIMITED, *Wellington, New Zealand*

Preface

Over 100 million hand-held calculators are estimated to be in the United States alone. Generally, these calculators fall into three broad categories—arithmetic, advanced function, and programmable calculators. The most powerful of these are the programmable ones.

Recent technological breakthroughs have made these hand-held, computer-like calculators available at very inexpensive prices. Programmable calculators have a wide range of exciting uses, from performing everyday arithmetic to evaluating functions and solving advanced problems requiring decision-making.

If you are considering purchasing a more advanced calculator (or even your first one), perhaps one of the inexpensive programmable calculators is just for you. Programmable calculators have all the features of nonprogrammable calculators and much more, as summarized in the following table:

Calculators	*Ability* Perform Arithmetic Computations	Evaluate Advanced Functions	Solves Problems Requiring Decision-making
Arithmetic	X		
Advanced function	X	X	
Programmable	X	X	X

Who is this Book For?

Any person who wants to learn about programmable calculators and how to program them to solve problems will benefit from this book, especially:

- college students in engineering, business, science and mathematics,
- high school students interested in the mathematical sciences,
- teachers and professors who want a reference of problems that can be done on programmable calculators or minicomputers,
- calculator enthusiasts who want to extend their problem solving ability, and
- persons interested in pre-experience for learning eventually to program computers.

What is the Purpose of this Book?

When you buy a programmable calculator, you receive an owner's manual or text designed to show how to use the calculator, what its various special features are, and other relevant technical information. But you receive hardly any instruction on how to program the calculator or how to design programs to solve problems. Furthermore, you receive very few exercises and problems on which you can practice and develop programming skills. This book is carefully designed to complement the owner's manual by providing you with:

- information on how to design programs to solve problems on any programmable calculator,
- over 160 carefully sequenced examples, exercises, and problems solvable on any programmable calculator or minicomputer, and
- insight on what programmable calculators can do and how they are used as problem-solving tools.

How Can You Use this Book?

If you own an appropriate programmable calculator, you might use this book:

- as a self-study manual,
- as a text in a mini-course or continuing education course, or
- as a resource in a math club setting.

Even if you do not own a programmable calculator, you might use this book:

- as a self-study manual,
- as an aid in deciding whether to buy a programmable calculator and, if so, which one,
- as a reference of exercises and problems solvable on any programmable calculator or minicomputer, or
- as a library reference.

Which Programmable Calculator Should I Have to Get the Most Out of this Book?

Since the authors believe you can learn most rapidly by doing rather than by just reading, this book is written with a "hands on" approach. That is, if you have a programmable calculator at hand, you can follow the text and work through the examples on your calculator while you read. Because it is impossible to design a "hands on" book to be used with every one of the many programmable calculators presently available, this book is designed specifically to be used with the least expensive of the major manufacturer types of programmable calculators, namely:

- Texas Instruments TI 57 (Parts 1 and 2 of this book).
- Radio Shack EC-4000 (Parts 1 and 2 of this book).
- Hewlett-Packard HP 33E (Parts 3 and 4 of this book).

An important feature of this book is its adaptability. Both the programming techniques discussed in the text and the solutions to the problems are easily adapted to these other programmable calculators:

- Texas Instruments SR 56 and SR 52
- Texas Instruments TI 58 and TI 59
- Hewlett-Packard HP 29C and HP 19C
- Hewlett-Packard HP 67 and HP 97
- Sharp PC 1201
- Hewlett-Packard HP 25 and HP 25C

We authors wish to thank Ralph Oliva and William Kernahan of Texas Instruments, and Hugh Field and Scott Eaton of Hewlett-Packard for providing calculators at crucial times in the preparation of this manuscript; Karl West of the Needham Public School System and Stephen Krulik of Temple University for reading selected early chapters; and Janet Manter for her fine typing. We would also like to thank Laurie and Ans for their patience—they must have thought we would never finish!

STEPHEN L. SNOVER
Newton, Massachusetts

MARK A. SPIKELL
Wayland, Massachusetts

Contents

I

EVALUATING FUNCTIONS— TI 57 AND EC 4000

LOOPING AND DECISION MAKING—TI 57 AND EC 4000

Programming Finite Loops 97

EVALUATING FUNCTIONS—HP 33E

Writing Your First Programs to Compute Answers 111

Using Preprogrammed Functions in Writing Programs 121

Checking and Editing Programs 133

Introduction

SECTION 1: WHAT IS A PROGRAMMABLE CALCULATOR?

Today's hand-held calculators come in all sizes and types, but basically they can be grouped into three categories:

1. four-function calculators,
2. advanced-function calculators, like scientific and business calculators, and
3. programmable calculators.

In order to distinguish among these calculators, imagine that each is a "black box" with buttons and a display on the outside. Inside is a little man with a scratch pad and pencil who knows how to add, subtract, multiply, and divide.

The Four-Function Calculator

The cheapest of all the calculators, the four-function calculator is simply the black box already described. With this calculator you can perform the four arithmetic operations—addition, subtraction, multiplication, and division.

Introduction

Since more functions, such as [$\sqrt{x}$] [log] [x^2] and [e^x] appear on the advanced-function calculator, you might guess that it contains specially designed, or "hard-wired," circuitry inside the calculator for computing each such function. The little man inside the black box, you might guess, has been trained to compute each of these functions. Actually this is not the case. Building special circuitry for each additional function is far too expensive.

Instead, what really happens can be best described by extending the analogy of the little man in the black box. Because you pay more for your advanced-function calculator, the little man inside is provided with a helpful instruction booklet that tells him how to perform each advanced function, not directly, but as a sequence of the four arithmetic functions he already knows.

For example, suppose the square root function, [$\sqrt{x}$], is pressed. The little man inside sees the button pressed, but on the inside the button reads "Page 2." He then opens the instruction booklet to page 2 and reads:

- *Step 1*: Copy the number from the display onto line 1 of the scratch pad. Then write a 1 on line 2.
- *Step 2*: Divide the number on line 2 into the number on line 1 and put the quotient on line 3.
- *Step 3*: Add the number on line 2 to the number on line 3 and then divide the sum by 2. Place the result on line 2 (erasing any number that was there before).
- *Step 4*: If the numbers on lines 2 and 3 are equal, put that value in the display and stop. Otherwise, go back to step 2 and repeat.

In the analogy, the little man in the box has no idea that he is calculating a square root, but that hardly matters. It is only necessary that page 2 is written properly and that he follows the steps letter perfect.

Each other function on the advanced function calculator is computed in a similar fashion, although its instructions are different and they appear on a separate page of the booklet.

The Programmable Calculator

When you purchase a programmable calculator, you buy most of the features of an advanced-function calculator plus the flexibility of being able to create (or program) your own functions.

The little man in the black box receives an instruction booklet with one page for each advanced function and with one additional *blank* page. The little man does either of two things with this blank page. If the calculator is in the so-called "learn" or "program" mode, he records on the blank page any sequence of buttons that are pressed. Or if the calculator is in the "run" mode, he considers this page just like any other page and follows its instructions when the [R/S] or run/stop button is pushed.

While the little man analogy may seem simplistic, it does indicate in nontechnical terms what a programmable calculator is. With a programmable calculator, you can perform most functions available on any advanced-function calculator with a single button. Furthermore, you can create or program your own functions and access them by just pressing the R/S key.

SECTION 2: WHAT PROBLEMS CAN PROGRAMMABLE CALCULATORS SOLVE?

To illustrate the wide range and variety of problems that can be solved on a programmable calculator, the following representative problems have been selected. You can find each of these problems together with their solutions in the text.

Programmable calculators can solve:

- from simple arithmetic:

$$24(1 + .05)^{300} = ?$$

  to complex calculations:

$$\sum_{n=1}^{\infty} \frac{n^2}{2^n} = \frac{1}{2} + \frac{4}{4} + \frac{9}{8} + \frac{16}{16} + \frac{25}{32} + \frac{49}{64} + \cdots = ?$$

- from relatively straightforward computations:
  Convert a temperature in degrees Fahrenheit to degrees Celsius
  to very indirect computations:
  Find the smallest positive whole number that has a remainder of 5 when divided by 6 and a remainder of 8 when divided by 11.
- from simple decisions:
  The United Parcel Service will not ship any package if the length plus the girth exceeds 108 inches. Can a particular package with given dimensions be sent by the United Parcel Service?
  to complex decisions:
  At a special fund raising banquet, 100 senators, and representatives, and lobbyests showed up. Senators paid $75 each; congresspersons paid $99; and lobbyests, $40 each. If $7,869 was collected, how many of each came to the banquet?
- from applications in business:
  If a new car dealer advertises an automobile at a delivery price of $5,272.50, how much does this car cost the dealer and how much profit is the dealer making?
  to applications in science:
  Suppose you have a large collection of n bricks, all the same size. Say each has unit length. If you stack them so that the top brick extends as far to the right of the bottom one as possible, can the top one overhang more than one unit length to the right of the bottom brick?
  to applications in recreational mathematics:
  Imagine a square-based pyramid of cannonballs with one cannonball on top and a square number of cannonballs on each layer. How many cannonballs are there in the top 10 layers? How many layers can be made from 10,000 cannonballs?

SECTION 3: THE EVOLUTION OF CALCULATING MACHINES

Introduction

Incredible as it may seem, man has been on earth for more than a million years while the programmable hand-held calculator has been here only since 1973! Man invented the first calculating machines some 5,000 years ago, but almost all advances leading to calculators as we know them today have occurred in the last 30 years.

To place the evolution of calculating machines in perspective, some of the major historical developments have been placed on the following time line, interspersed with other notable historical events:[1]

pre-3,000 B.C.	Abacus (performs +, −)
1456 A.D.	Movable type printing press
1617	Napier's bones (performs ×, ÷)
1642	Pascal calculating machine (+, −)
late1600 s	Leibnitz calculator (+, −, ×, ÷, $\sqrt{\ }$)
about1760	Industrial Revolution
1820	First reliable commercial calculating machine
1835	Mechanical programmable computing machine
1890	Electrical input reading computers
1939	Fully automatic calculator
1946	First digital computer, ENIAC
1957	Sputnik satellite
1958	Integrated circuit chip
1963	Desk-top computer, PDP-5
1969	First person to walk on the moon
1971	First hand-held calculator, Bowmar Brain
1973	First hand-held programmable calculator, HP 65
1975	HP 25
1976	HP 25C
1977	TI 57, 58, and 59
1977	Radio Shack EC 4000
1978	HP 33E

SECTION 4: AOS AND RPN CALCULATORS

One way of distinguishing the types of programmable hand calculators is to scan the keyboard for an "equal" key. If there is one, your calculator is an Algebraic Operating System (AOS) calculator. Otherwise, it is most likely a Reverse Polish Notation (RPN) calculator.

What does it mean to say that a calculator is an AOS or RPN calculator? An AOS calculator allows you to enter calculations as they are generally written. For example, the computation of 3 + 4 is done by

[1]For a detailed historical presentation, you may consult the TI 57 owner's manual, *Making Tracks into Programming* (TI Learning Center, 1977), Chapter 12.

pressing the keys [3] [+] [4] and [=] in that order. With an AOS calculator, the + operation is not performed until the equal key is pressed.

An RPN calculator, in contrast, uses the key stroke sequence [3] [↑] [4] [+] to perform the same calculation. In other words, RPN calculators perform the operations at the same time as the appropriate operation key is pressed.

Most persons prefer one type of calculator or the other; each has certain unique characteristics. AOS calculators allow you to enter arithmetic calculations from left to right as they are written algebraically. With RPN calculators, all data is entered before pressing any operation key. All programmable AOS calculators have parentheses while programmable RPN calculators do not. Some people feel that parentheses make programs more readable. Others feel that programs without parentheses are more efficient, that is, the programs often take fewer steps.

Two major American manufacturers, Texas Instruments and Hewlett-Packard, produce hand programmable calculators. Texas Instruments produces AOS calculators while Hewlett-Packard produces RPN calculators.

SECTION 5: THE TEXAS INSTRUMENTS FAMILY OF CALCULATORS

The Texas Instruments family of calculators includes five programmables: SR 56, SR 52, TI 57, TI 58, and TI 59. The SR 56 and SR 52, no longer manufactured, were the first programmables produced by Texas Instruments.

The SR 56 initially sold for about $100 and eventually fell in price to about $65. Features of this machine included 100 program memory steps, 10 memory registers, decision-making tests, and even subroutine capability. The SR 52 initially sold for about $295 and eventually fell in price to about $150. In addition to all of the features of the SR 56, this machine has 224 program memory steps, 20 memory registers, insert and delete editing capability, and magnetic cards for program storage.

The TI 57, 58, and 59 programmables have been designed for a wide range of users. The TI 57, selling for less than $65, is the best beginner's calculator because of its low cost and its capability of meeting most programming needs. Features of this calculator include 8 memory registers, 50 merged program steps (nearly the same as 100 nonmerged steps), the equivalent of 8 decision tests, insert and delete editing, labels, and subroutines.

The TI 58 and 59 programmables are more advanced and come equipped with programmable read only memory chips, called PROMs, which contain numerous programs already written. Both machines can be attached to the TI PC 100A printer, which sells for about $175. The TI 59, selling for about $250, has effectively twice the number of memory registers and program steps as the TI 58, selling for about $125. Furthermore, the TI 59 can be used with magnetic cards.

SECTION 6: THE HEWLETT-PACKARD FAMILY OF CALCULATORS

Hewlett-Packard was the first to come out with a programmable hand-held calculator, the HP 65, costing initially $800. With 100 program memory steps, the HP 65 was fully programmable and used magnetic cards. Shortly thereafter Hewlett-Packard introduced the HP 55 for $400 and then the HP 25 for only $200. Not only did the price drop, but the technology advanced, making the HP 25 almost as powerful as the other machines for much less cost. Some of the features of the HP 25 include 8 memory registers, 50 merged program memory steps (nearly equivalent to 100 nonmerged steps), and 8 decision tests.

Next, Hewlett-Packard improved upon their most expensive model, replacing the HP 65 with a pair of machines, the HP 67 for about $400 and the HP 97, the same calculator with a built-in printer and selling for about $700. Some of the features of these machines included 224 merged program memory steps, 30 memory registers, and such advanced programming tools as insert and delete editing, labels, indirect addressing, and subroutines.

Hewlett-Packard revised the HP 25 by introducing the HP 25C, selling for about $150. It has a continuous memory permitting the storage of a program for recall even when the calculator is turned off.

Next Hewlett-Packard came out with a pair of middle price range calculators, the HP 19C and HP 29C. These machines not only have a continuous memory, but also 30 memory registers (16 of which are continuous memories), 98 merged program steps, labels, insert and delete editing capability, subroutines, and indirect addressing. The HP 29C sells for less than $160. Its companion, the HP 19C has the same features plus a built-in printer and retails for under $300.

Most recently Hewlett-Packard has introduced two programmables, the HP 33E and the HP 38E. The HP 33E replaces the HP 25 and HP 25C calculators and is the best beginner's calculator because of its low cost (about $80) and capability of meeting most programming needs. The HP 38E is an advanced financial calculator with programmability features.

SECTION 7: THE CALCULATORS CHOSEN FOR THIS BOOK

Even the least expensive calculators are powerful enough to satisfy most programming needs. Consequently, any of them could serve as ideal beginning machines on which to learn programming. This book is designed around the least expensive models of the Texas Instruments and Hewlett-

Packard families of programmable calculators. As revealed by the summary chart in Table 1-1, these least expensive models are the TI 57 and its twin, the Radio Shack EC 4000, and the HP 33E. While this book is written specifically for these three calculators, the text and the programs presented as the solutions to the problems are easily adapted for all the other programmable calculators listed in the summary chart.

TABLE I–1. Old and New Programmables

Texas Instruments	*Early Models*	*Current Models*	
Least expensive	SR 56	TI 57[a]	
		TI 58[b]	
Most expensive	SR 52	TI 59[b]	
Hewlett-Packard	*Early Models*	*Current Models*	
Least expensive	HP 25	HP 33E	HP 38E
	HP 55	HP 29C	HP 19C[c]
Most expensive	HP 65	HP 67	HP 97[c]

[a]Identical to the Radio Shack EC 4000
[b]With attachable printer
[c]With built-in printer

SECTION 8: POSSIBLE EFFECTS OF PROGRAMMABLE CALCULATORS ON THE TEACHING OF MATHEMATICS

In June of 1976, the National Science Foundation and the National Institute of Education jointly sponsored a conference on badly needed research and development on hand-held calculators in school mathematics. The following observation from the conference report is significant: "Microelectronic technology is changing at an astonishing pace. Today's four-function calculator will soon be replaced, at the same price, by one with many more functions. Today's scientific calculator will be replaced soon by comparably priced programmable calculators . . . ".[2]

The observation has already been prophetic. Presently, programmable calculators are indeed available at remarkably low prices—prices so low, in fact, that teachers can give serious attention to considering the use of these machines in the school mathematics curriculum at every level.

Because the availability of inexpensive programmable calculators is such a recent phenomenon, educators have not yet been able to arrive at a consensus on what to do with these machines in the school curriculum.

[2]National Science Foundation and National Institute of Education, *Report of the Conference on Needed Research and Development on Hand-Held Calculators in School Mathematics*, (Washington, D. C., 20208: U.S. Department of Health, Education and Welfare, June, 1976).

However, programmables could have an impact on the teaching of mathematics in a number of important ways.

- Topics from numerical methods, previously considered too advanced, can now be brought down to the level of high school mathematics. For example, programmable calculators greatly facilitate the study of limits of sequences and sums of series.
- Reading logarithm, trigonometric, power, and root tables is no longer necessary. Programmable calculators, in addition to having built-in function keys for obtaining this information, can be programmed to generate tables of related data for use as needed.
- The slide rule, long a significant tool for performing calculations, is now obsolete, because programmable calculators do everything a slide rule does —and much more. Programmable calculators also provide a degree of accuracy and a speed of computation not possible with slide rules.
- "Exhaustive searches" to generate data are now practical. The calculator can be programmed to search (or test) hundreds or thousands of special cases—a chore essentially impossible to do by hand. For example, consider the problem of finding all integer Pythagorean triples, $a^2 + b^2 = c^2$, with the hypotenuses, c, less than 100. Finding such triples by hand would be quite tedious and time-consuming. However, the calculator can find all such triples accurately and quickly.

In addition, the educational community can and should address other broader issues. The entire mathematics curriculum must be examined and, where appropriate, redesigned to utilize the power of programmable calculators and minicomputers. Among the pertinent issues are:

- How does the availability of programmable calculators affect the teaching of algebra? Geometry? Trigonometry? And other mathematics courses, especially calculus?
- Would teaching programming on programmable calculators be a useful topic for a senior level mathematics course?
- Could a unit on logic be designed around the decision-making capability of programmable calculators?
- At what age and in what course experiences should iterative techniques for solving equations (for example, the Newton–Raphson method) be introduced on programmable calculators?
- Is it possible for an exhaustive search to become an integral part of a mathematical proof? For example, is it permissible to combine an exhaustive search for $n \leqslant 10{,}000$ together with an analytical proof (valid only) for $n > 10{,}000$ to establish a proof for all positive integers, n?

SECTION 9: PROGRAMMABLE CALCULATORS AND PERSONAL COMPUTERS

Scarcely a decade ago a four-function desk-top adding machine cost many hundreds of dollars. Now the cost of an equivalent four-function calculator is close to \$5. In the near future, however, the prices need not continue to drop. Instead, the capabilities and flexibilities will increase in calculators that remain at certain price levels.

With the advent of the ROM or Read Only Memory, calculators became cheap. With the RAM or Random Access Memory, calculators could memorize many locations worth of information—so programmable calculators became likewise inexpensive. Next the PROM, or Programmable Read Only Memory, was introduced allowing much greater programmable flexibility.

In the next few years, man will witness a vast broadening of the flexibility and power of the hand-held calculator. With the bubble memory, a hand-held calculator will be able to memorize and process vast amounts of information. With the new varieties of I/O, or input/output, interfaces, the programmable calculator will be able to display its results on one's home television screen. In essence, the programmable calculator, available for a moderately low cost, will become a personal computer with almost all the power and flexibility of today's expensive computers.

The 1950s constituted the decade of the beginning computer. The 60s were the decade of time-sharing. The 70s comprise the decade of the hand-held calculator. The 80s will likely be the decade of the hand-held personal computer.

1

EVALUATING FUNCTIONS— TI 57 AND EC 4000

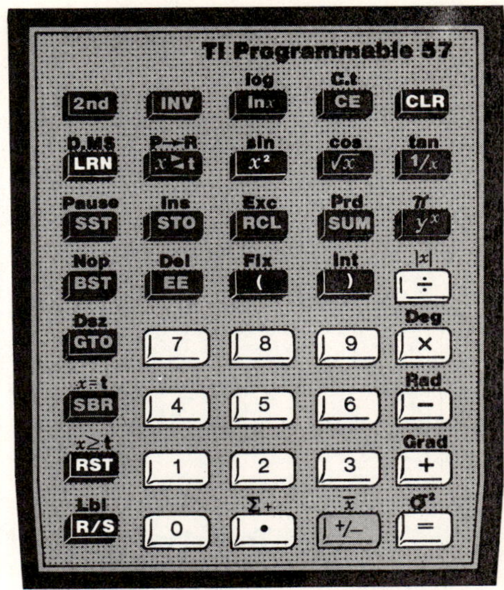

1

Writing Your First Programs to Compute Answers

Section 1: Calculating $2(n + 1)^2$ in the Run Mode

Turn on your calculator and press the sequence of key strokes indicated in the middle column:

STEP	KEY STROKE	DISPLAY SHOWS
00	2	2
01	×	2.
02	(	2.
03	4	4
04	+	4.
05	1	1
06	)	5.
07	x^2	25.
08	=	50.

You have just computed the value of $2(4 + 1)^2$ on your calculator. Using a similar sequence of key strokes, compute the value of $2(9 + 1)^2$ to obtain 200.

You have been using your calculator in what is called the *run mode*. In this mode the calculator's primary purpose is to perform basic arithmetic operations.

Suppose you want to compute $2(7 + 1)^2$, $2(11 + 1)^2$, $2(16 + 1)^2$, and $(25 + 1)^2$. You could do so in the run mode by using a sequence of key strokes almost identical to that described in steps 00 through 08. The only difference for each computation would be the number entered in step 03 after the left parenthesis in step 02.

Section 2: Programming $2(n + 1)^2$ in the Learn or Program Mode

When you find it necessary to use a particular sequence of key strokes repeatedly, you can avoid a great deal of work by using an important feature of your calculator called the *learn mode*. In this mode, the calculator is able to "memorize" sequences of key strokes, called a program. This program can then be executed (run) in the run mode of the calculator.

In Section 1 you considered the computation of $2(n + 1)^2$, where n could be any number. Using this computation, you will now program your calculator to memorize the appropriate sequence of key strokes to perform the calculation.

First, turn your calculator off, then on. Now press the LRN (learn) key; this key switches your calculator from the run mode to the learn mode. You should see "00 00" in the display.[1] Now press the sequence of key strokes that follows:

STEP	KEYSTROKES	DISPLAY SHOWS
00	2	01 00
01	×	02 00
02	(	03 00
03	R/S	04 00
04	+	05 00
05	1	06 00
06	)	07 00
07	x^2	08 00
08	=	09 00
09	R/S	10 00

Press the LRN key. This returns your calculator to the run mode where the program can be executed. To initialize (start) the program, press CLR

[1]When the calculator is "memorizing" a key stroke, you see a different display from when the calculator is performing the instruction represented by the key stroke. See your owner's manual for details.

(clear registers), RST (reset), R/S. You will see "2." in the display. Then enter any value for n, say 3, and press R/S. The quantity "32." should appear in the display. To run the program to compute $2(n + 1)^2$ for other values of n, merely press CLR RST R/S, enter the desired value of n, and press R/S each time. Doing so for n equaling 7, 11, 16, and 25, the display should show "128., 288., 578., 1352.," respectively.

You have just entered and executed your first program. It was entered and memorized in the learn mode when you pressed the sequence of keys in steps 00–09. It was executed in the run mode after being initialized.

Your calculator has exactly two modes of operation, the learn mode and the run mode. In the learn mode the calculator can only memorize a sequence of key strokes. In the run mode the calculator can either perform any key stroke sequence that is pressed or execute a memorized key stroke sequence.

When your calculator is first turned on, it is automatically in the run mode. Thereafter, whenever the LRN key is pressed, the calculator switches from one mode to the other.

Section 3: Using $2(n + 1)^2$ to Solve a Problem

You may wonder why you would ever want to program your calculator to compute $2(n + 1)^2$. There might be any number of reasons, but this particular computation was selected because it happens to provide the answer to an interesting question suggested by the American flag.

Have you ever noticed how the 50 stars are arranged on the present-day American flag? There are 4 short rows of 5 stars in each row and 5 longer rows of 6 stars in each. (See Figure 1–1.)

Similar patterns of stars can be formed with 8, 18, and 32 stars. See Figures 1–2, 1–3, and 1–4, respectively. Notice that the 8-star pattern uses 1 short row of 2 stars and 2 longer rows of 3 stars; the 18-star pattern uses 2 short rows of 3 stars and 3 longer rows of 4 stars; the 32-star pattern has

Figure 1–1

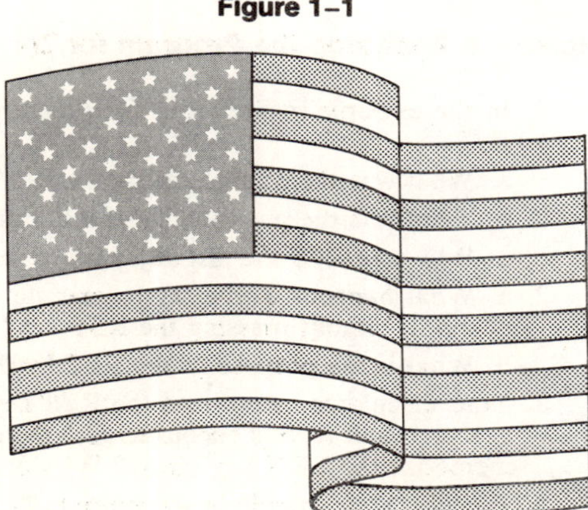

Figure 1–2

Figure 1–3

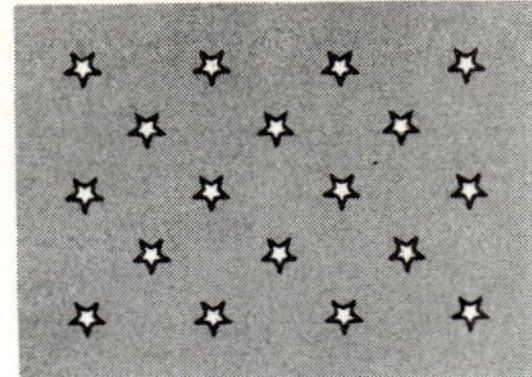

Figure 1–4

3 short rows of 4 stars and 4 longer rows of 5 stars. What other numbers of states would have to be in the United States for this specific type of star pattern to be used on the flag?

There would have to be n short rows of $(n + 1)$ stars and $(n + 1)$ longer rows of $(n + 2)$ stars. So in total there would be $n(n + 1) + (n + 1)(n + 2) = 2(n + 1)^2$ stars. Since each star represents one state, there would have to be $2(n + 1)^2$ states in the United States for the same type of star pattern to be used.

Using the program in Section 2 for computing $2(n + 1)^2$ you can find all the numbers of states for which the stars could be arranged in the same type of pattern as the 50-star pattern.

Section 4: Exercises in Analyzing the Program for $2(n + 1)^2$

1. In the example in Section 2 the program was 2, ×, (, R/S, +, 1,), x^2, = , R/S.
   a. What was the purpose of the first R/S in the program?
   b. What was the purpose of the left and right parentheses?
   c. Why was R/S the last key pressed in the program?
2. a. What happens if you try to execute the program in Section 2 in the run mode without pressing the RST key?
   b. What is the purpose of the RST key?
3. Your calculator memorized the R/S key so that when the program is being executed and R/S is encountered, the program stops. Can your calculator memorize the LRN key stroke? Why or why not?
4. Program your calculator to compute $2n^2 + 1$ for any value of n.

The program to compute $2(n + 1)^2$ is summarized by the two diagrams in Figure 1–5, called flow charts. One, the *general flow chart*, presents an overview of what the program is designed to do. The other, the *detailed flow chart* presents step-by-step instructions (based on the general flow chart) for writing the actual program.

By comparing the flow charts to the program, you can see that each rectangle in either flow chart corresponds to one or more key strokes in the program. The brackets between the flow charts and the program indicate this correspondence. The vertical arrows in the general flow chart indicate the order in which instructions are to be carried out.

Figure 1–5

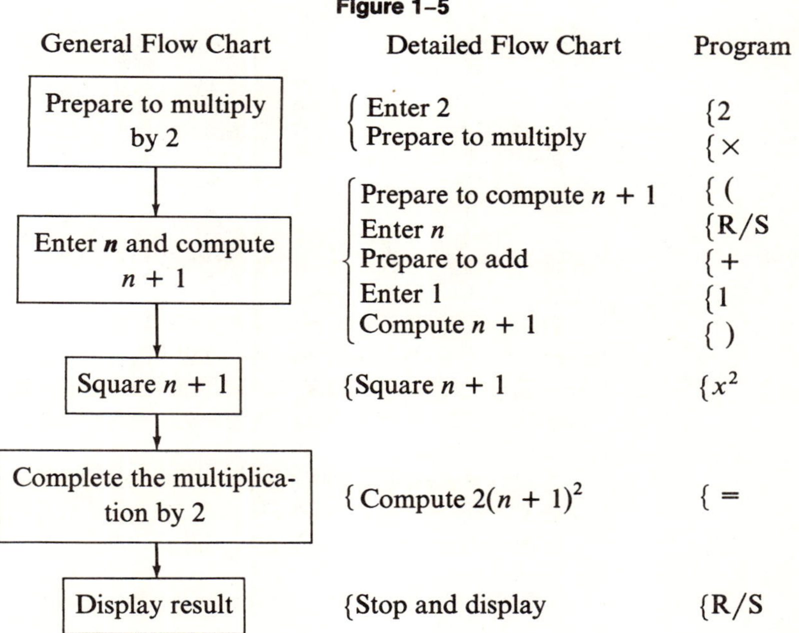

Making flow charts can help you organize your thoughts when writing programs. The general flow chart should consist of a few instructions to make it clear at a glance what a program is designed to accomplish. The detailed flow chart should show how to do each instruction in the general flow chart. From the detailed flow chart it should be easy to write the actual program. You may find it helpful to make one or both of the flow charts before writing a program. As you become better at writing programs, you may find less of a need for the detailed flow chart.

As another example of the use of flow charts, consider writing a program to compute the area of a triangle according to the formula:

$$A = \frac{b \cdot h}{2}$$

where b is the base length and h is the height of the triangle. Starting from the general flow chart, the detailed flow chart and program can be prepared as shown in Figure 1–6.

Figure 1–6

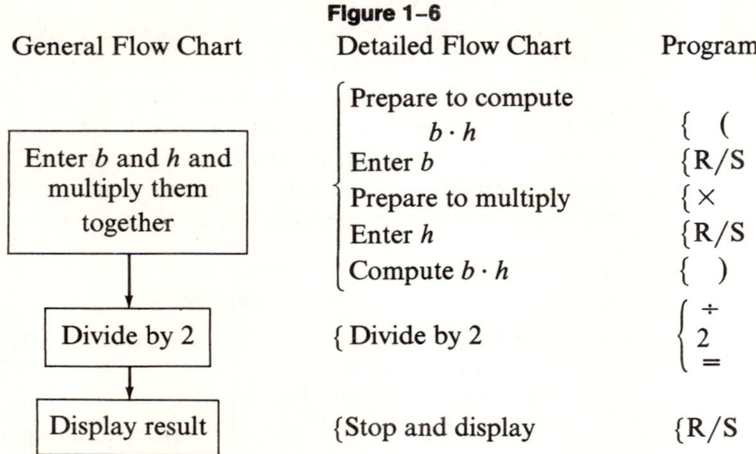

Section 6: Exercises Using Flow Charts When Writing Programs

Here are a few helpful hints that you may need to know in order to proceed with the problems in this section.

Before entering any program, you should clear (or erase) any program previously in the calculator. Clearing can be done by turning the calculator off, then back on.

If you find that you have entered a step of your program incorrectly, you can correct the error in a variety of ways. For now, you should simply clear your calculator and re-enter the program. Ways to edit a program without erasing it will be described in Chapter 3, Section 4.

1. In some states there is a special tax on food served in restaurants. If the tax is 8 percent and the cost of the dinner is \$5.00, then \$5.40 is the cost of the dinner plus tax. The general flow chart in Figure 1–7 describes a program that computes the total cost of a dinner (including tax) with the formula, Total cost of the dinner = 1.08 · Dinner cost.

Figure 1–7

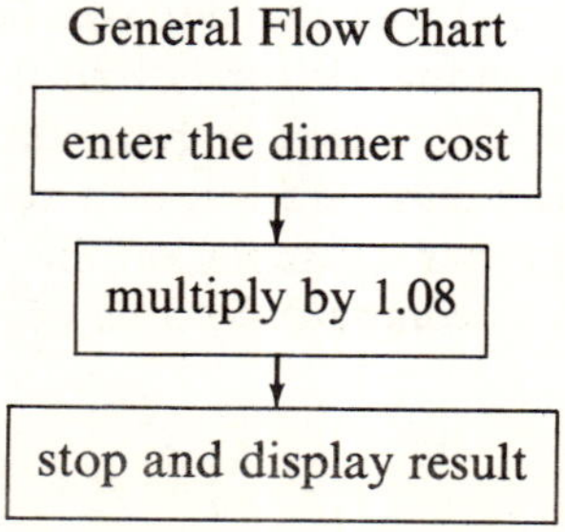

General Flow Chart

enter the dinner cost

↓

multiply by 1.08

↓

stop and display result

a. Make a detailed flow chart for this program.
b. Write the corresponding program from the detailed flow chart.

2. Make a detailed flow chart for a program that converts measurements in feet to meters according to the formula,

$$\text{Number of meters} = \frac{\text{Number of feet}}{3.28}$$

3. In order to convert temperatures from Fahrenheit to Celsius (centigrade), you may use the formula, $C = \frac{F - 32}{1.8}$, where F is the Fahrenheit temperature and C is the Celsius. A detailed flow chart for a program to make the conversions is given in Figure 1–8.

Figure 1–8

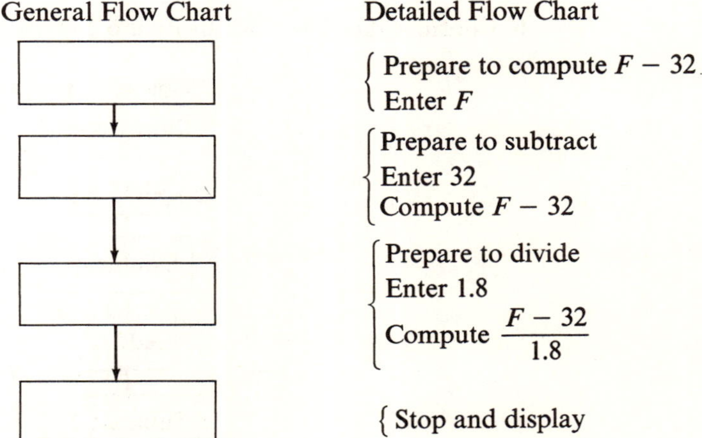

a. Complete the corresponding general flow chart in that figure.
b. Write the corresponding program.

4. The average of two numbers is found by adding the two numbers together and then dividing by two. The general flow chart in Figure 1–9 describes a program for averaging two numbers.

Figure 1–9

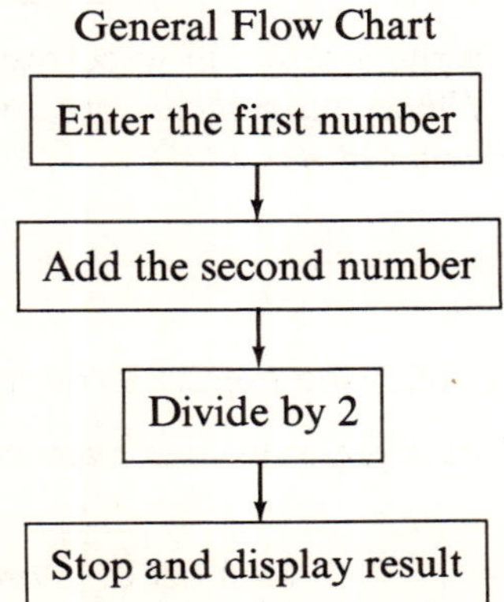

a. Make the corresponding detailed flow chart.

b. Write the corresponding program.

5. You can find the volume of a box in Figure 1–10 by multiplying the length, times the width times the height of the box. Make flow charts for a program that calculates the volume of a box. Now write the program.

Figure 1–10

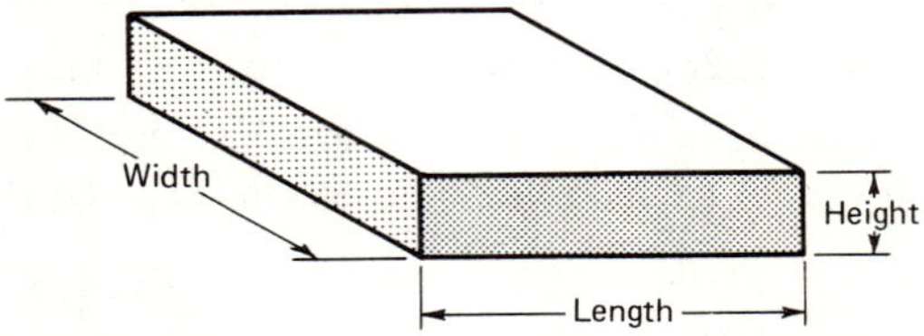

Width
Height
Length

6. Consider the flow chart in Figure 1–11.

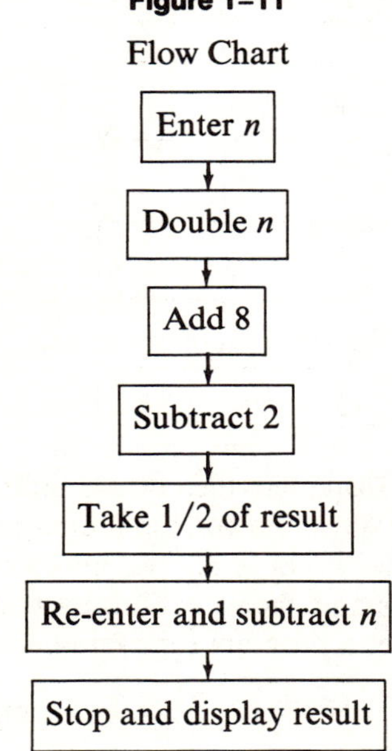

Figure 1–11
Flow Chart

a. Write a program to correspond to the flow chart.

b. When you run this program, what is always displayed, regardless of the value of n?

Section 7: Problems

For the following exercises you may find it helpful to use flow charts.

1. Write a program to convert miles to kilometers using the formula,

$$\text{Number of kilometers} = \frac{\text{(Number of miles)}}{.62}$$

How many kilometers is 5 miles, 8 miles, 31 miles, 500 miles, and 3,000 miles?

2. Write a program to compute the weekly salaries of someone who works part-time for $2.85 per hour and works 12 hours, 18 hours, 14 hours, and 22 hours. Use the formula, Salary = Number of hours · Hourly wage.
3. The following two formulas work for converting Celsius to Fahrenheit temperatures and vice versa:
   a. $C = (F + 40) \cdot \frac{5}{9} - 40$
   b. $F = (C + 40) \cdot \frac{9}{5} - 40$

   Write a program for each conversion.
4. A company is selling cardboard in rectangular sheets at 3¢ a square unit. Write a program to compute the cost of any rectangular sheet using the formula, Cost in dollars = $.03(l \cdot w)$, where l and w are the length and width of any rectangle. For $l = 10$ and $w = 8$, the cost is $2.40.
5. A dog owner wants to build a fence around a rectangular piece of land that measures l by w meters. Her choice of fencing costs $5.89 per meter. Write a program to determine the cost of the fencing with the formula, Cost = $5.89(2l + 2w)$. For $l = 5$ and $w = 4$, the cost is $106.02.
6. a. Write a program to average three numbers, a, b, and c.
   b. How would you adapt this program to average four numbers?
7. The area, A, of a trapezoid is given by,

$$A = h \cdot \frac{(b_1 + b_2)}{2},$$

   where h is the height and b_1 and b_2 are the two base lengths. (See Figure 1–12.)

Figure 1–12

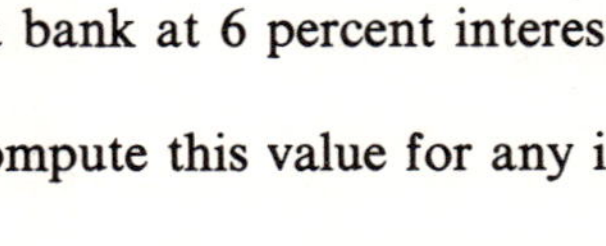

   Write a program for computing the area of a trapezoid: For $b_1 = 8$, $b_2 = 10$, and $h = 3$, $A = 27$.
8. When $\$n$ is invested in a bank at 6 percent interest, the value after 1 year will be $\$n(1 + .06)$.
   a. Write a program to compute this value for any invested number of dollars, n.
   b. Run your program once starting with $100 and see what will be in the bank at the end of one year.
   c. What will be in the bank at the end of the second year if you start with $100?

d. What will be in the bank at the end of 5 years if you start with $100?

9. A rectangle has area, $A = l \cdot w$.
   a. Write a program to compute the width of a rectangle, w, with length l and area 360.
   b. What are the widths of the rectangles when l is 5, 8, 10, and 15?
   c. Use your program to find the values of l and w when the area of the rectangle is 360 and the length is two more than the width.

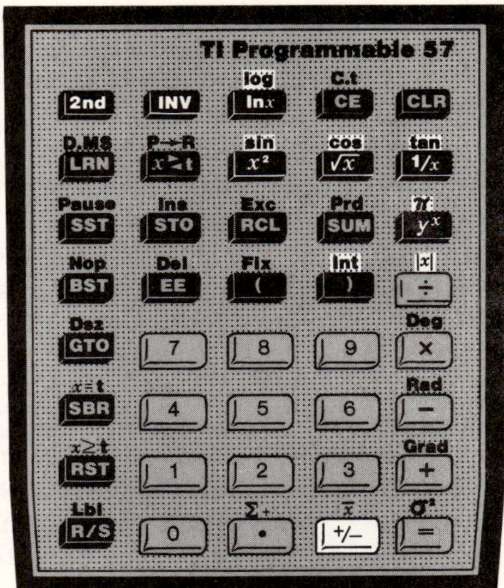

2

Using Preprogrammed Functions in Writing Programs

Section 1: An Investment Problem Introducing the Function y^x

Pieter Minuit, a Dutch colonist, bought Manhatten Island from the Indians in 1626 for a few trinkets, thought to be worth about \$24. If instead, Pieter Minuit had invested \$24 in a bank at 5 percent interest per year, what would he have earned after 1 year? After 2 years? By the end of 1638 when he moved to Delaware? Or by 1641 when he died? For that matter, how much would be in his account now, assuming nothing had ever been removed?

Clearly, after one year Minuit would have earned \$24 × .05 = \$1.20 interest. Thus his account would have had a total of \$25.20. At the end of the second year he would have earned \$25.20 × .05 in interest. Using your calculator, compute this value and determine the total amount in the bank account. Do the calculations in the run mode.

To answer the rest of the questions, a well known financial formula for computing compound interest is helpful. The formula is $t = p \cdot (1 + i)^n$, where p is the original amount invested, i is the yearly interest rate expressed as a decimal, and t is the total at the end of n years. Specifically, in the Minuit problem, the total becomes $\$24(1 + .05)^n$ or, simply, $\$24(1.05)^n$.

When Minuit moved to Delaware in 1638, twelve years had passed. So the total in the bank would have been the value of $\$24(1.05)^{12}$ or, \$43.10 to the nearest penny.

The goal here is to develop a program to compute $\$24(1.05)^n$ for any n. Before doing so, you need to know how to compute $24(1.05)^n$ for specific values of n. This requires the use of the preprogrammed (built-in) function key on your calculator, identified by the symbol, y^x.

Turn your calculator on and press the following sequence of keys: [2] [4] [×] [1] [·] [0] [5] [y^x] [1] [2] [=]. Your display should show 43.100552, or 43.10 rounded to the nearest hundredth. Therefore, $\$24(1.05)^{12}$ represents \$43.10. Using the key sequence [2nd] [Fix] [2] you can get your calculator to show the display rounded off to the nearest hundredth. You can return the display to the original quantity by pressing [2nd] [Fix] [9].

Essentially the same sequence of key strokes can be used to compute $\$24(1.05)^n$ for any value of n. Enter the program shown in Figure 2–1 in your calculator and try it out.

Figure 2–1

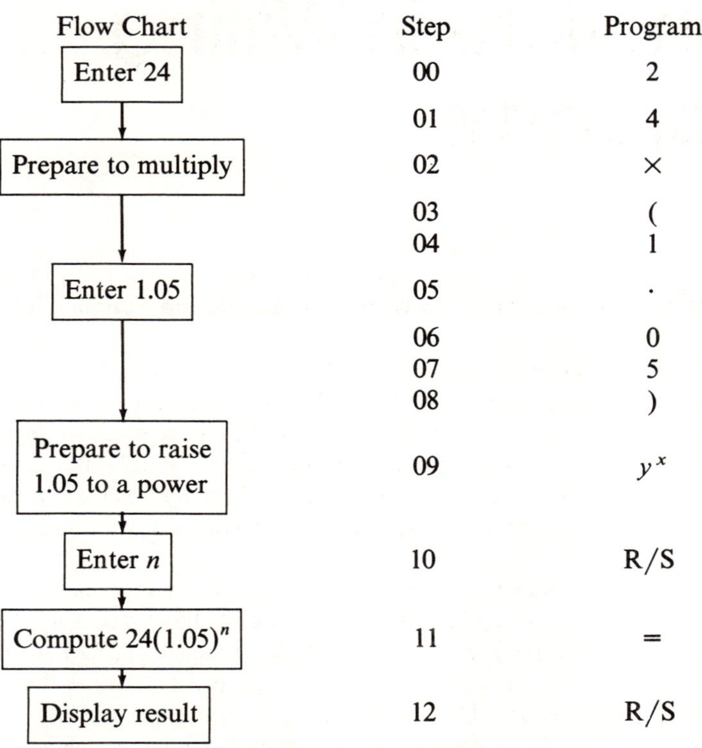

Step	Program
00	2
01	4
02	×
03	(
04	1
05	·
06	0
07	5
08	)
09	y^x
10	R/S
11	=
12	R/S

Initialize: [CLR] [RST] [R/S] enter n [R/S].

To test the program, use 20 for n and you should obtain 63.679145 in the display.

Notice that step 10 is the key stroke [R/S], which stops the program so you can enter the value of n. Step 12 is also the key stroke [R/S]. However, in this case, it stops the program to display the result of the computation $24(1.05)^n$.

Using this program you can answer each of the questions raised at the beginning of the section concerning the $24 investment, since each of the questions is answered by essentially the same key stroke sequence. Running the program is easier than entering the key stroke sequence over and over again. Furthermore, the program is easily adaptable for solving similar investment problems requiring the use of the formula $p \cdot (1 + i)^n$.

Section 2: Exercises Relating to the Investment Problem

1. Enter the program shown in Figure 2–1 in the previous section and check to see if the totals in the bank after one year and after twelve years agree with the information in the section. Such checking is a good technique to insure that you have entered a program correctly.
2. How much money would have been in the bank when Minuit died at the end of 1641, fifteen years after he bought the island?
3. How much money would have been there at the end of 1664 ($n = 38$) when Peter Stuyvesant surrendered Manhattan to the British?
4. How much would be in the bank after 300 years?
5. Write a program to compute the value of $100 invested at 6 percent for any number of years, n.

Section 3: Single and Double Variable Preprogrammed Functions

Your calculator comes equipped with many preprogrammed functions, most of which are accessed with one or two key punches. You have already used some of these functions, such as [x^2] [y^x] [+] [×] etc. These functions can be classified according to two types—single variable functions and double variable functions. There are important differences in how your calculator uses each type.

All single variable functions are computed immediately as the key stroke(s) is (are) pressed; they are computed immediately using the x-register, or quantity in the display. For example, consider the single variable function [x^2]. If you enter [4] and press [x^2] you discover that the squaring is done immediately as the [x^2] key is punched.

On the other hand, no double variable function is computed immediately when its key stroke(s) is (are) pressed, because the second of the two values necessary for the computation is not yet entered. The computation for a double variable function is completed when an equal sign, a right parenthesis, or a subsequent double variable function is pressed. Consider [y^x] for example. If you enter [2] [y^x] [3] your calculator is prepared to compute 2^3. However, you will not see the computed value of 8 until you press, say, the equals key.

Remember the following general rule: All single variable functions are computed immediately, where as all double variable functions merely prepare the calculator for a subsequent computation.

For your interest, most of the preprogrammed functions available with your calculator are listed in Tables 2–1 and 2–2. (See your owner's manual for a complete list.)

TABLE 2–1 Single Variable Functions

Key Strokes	*Description of the Function*
[x^2]	squares the number in the display
[+/−]	changes the sign of the number in the display
[2nd] [sin]	computes the sin of the angle in the display
[2nd] [cos]	computes the cos of the angle in the display
[2nd] [tan]	computes the tan of the angle in the display
[INV] [ln x]	raises $e = 2.7182818$ to the power of the number in the display
[ln x]	takes the natural logarithm of the number in the display
[INV] [2nd] [log]	raises 10 to the power of the number in the display
[2nd] [log]	takes the base 10 logarithm of the number in the display
[$1/x$]	computes the reciprocal of the number in the display
[2nd] [$\|x\|$]	computes the absolute value of the number in the display
[2nd] [π]	inserts $\pi = 3.1415927$ in the display
[$\sqrt{x}$]	takes the square root of the number in the display
[2nd] [Int]	deletes fractional part of number in display, keeping integer part
[INV] [2nd] [sin]	computes the angle whose sin is in the display
[INV] [2nd] [cos]	computes the angle whose cos is in the display
[INV] [2nd] [tan]	computes the angle whose tan is in the display
[INV] [2nd] [Int]	deletes integer part of number in display, keeping the fractional part

[a]y is the value in the display prior to pressing the [y^x] and x is the next value entered in the display.

TABLE 2–2 Double Variable Functions

Key Strokes	*Description of the Function*
[+]	prepares to add
[−]	prepares to subtract
[×]	prepares to multiply
[÷]	prepares to divide
[y^x]	prepares to raise to a power[a]
[INV] [y^x]	prepares to take a root[a]

[a]y is the value in the display prior to pressing the [y^x] and x is the next value entered in the display.

1. Which of the following programs correctly computes cos(θ) with the initialization: [RST] [R/S] enter θ [R/S]. For $\theta = 60°$, cos(θ) = 0.5; for $\theta = 45°$ cos(θ) = 0.7071068.

PROGRAM 1	PROGRAM 2
2nd cos	(
(	R/S
R/S	)
)	2nd cos
R/S	R/S

2. Which of these programs correctly computes $\sqrt{1 + n}$?

PROGRAM 1	PROGRAM 2	PROGRAM 3
$\sqrt{x}$	1	1
1	+	+
+	R/S	R/S
R/S	=	$\sqrt{x}$
=	$\sqrt{x}$	=
R/S	R/S	R/S

Each initializes with [CLR] [RST] [R/S] enter n [R/S]. When $n = 24$, $\sqrt{1 + n} = 5$.

3. What is the algebraic expression that each of the following key sequences evaluates? Hint: each sequence evaluates a different expression (computation).

SEQUENCE 1	SEQUENCE 2	SEQUENCE 3
1	1	1
+	+	+
enter n	enter n	INV 2nd log
=	INV 2nd log	enter n
INV 2nd log	=	=

4. The following program is designed to compute y^x when values for x and y are entered.

STEP	PROGRAM
00	y^x
01	R/S
02	=
03	R/S

In order to compute $3^5 = 243$, which of the following initialization sequences works?

a. [CLR] [RST] enter 3 [R/S] enter 5 [R/S].
b. [CLR] [RST] enter 5 [R/S] enter 3 [R/S].

Section 5: Sample Programs with Flow Charts

In this section examples of programs illustrate how various preprogrammed functions may be used. With each program there are general and detailed flow charts. As you will see, they are useful for reading and understanding programs that are already written.

Example 1. Finding the Hypotenuse of a Right Triangle

The hypotenuse, c, of a right triangle is related to the two legs, a and b, by the formula, $c = \sqrt{a^2 + b^2}$. (See Figure 2–2.)

If you are programming your calculator to compute c, you could proceed as shown in Figure 2–3.

Figure 2–2

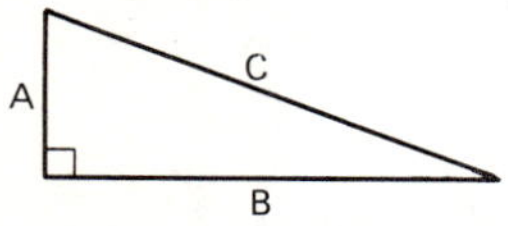

A
C
B

Figure 2–3

General Flow Chart	Detailed Flow Chart	Program
Enter and square a	{ Enter a	{R/S
	{ Square a	{x^2
Prepare to add	{ Prepare to add	{+
Enter and square b	{ Enter b	{R/S
	{ Square b	{x^2
Complete addition	{ Complete addition	{=
Take square root and display	{ Take square root	{$\sqrt{x}$
	{ Stop and display	{R/S

Initialize this program with [CLR] [RST] [R/S] enter a [R/S] enter b [R/S]. For $a = 5$, $b = 12$, you should obtain 13 for c.

Notice in this program that the square root is taken at the end of the program. Since $\boxed{\sqrt{x}}$ is a single variable function and operates on the number in the display, the sum, $a^2 + b^2$, *must* be computed before the $\boxed{\sqrt{x}}$ key is encountered.

Example 2. A Ladder Problem Using Trigonometry

Suppose you have a 4-meter long ladder and rest it against a wall so that the bottom of the ladder is d meters out from the wall, as shown in Figure 2–4. What angle does the ladder make with the ground?

In order to solve this problem, label the unknown angle as θ and use the fact that cosine of θ is $d/4$, that is, $\cos\theta = d/4$. Since θ is to be found, you can solve for θ algebraically and program your calculator with the resulting formula:

$$\theta = \text{INV} \cos \frac{d}{4}$$

The flow charts are shown in Figure 2–5.

Figure 2–4

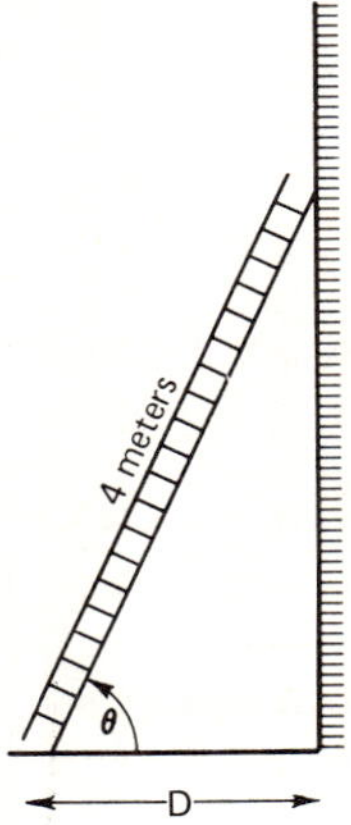

Figure 2–5

General Flow Chart	Detailed Flow Chart	Program
Enter d and compute $\frac{d}{4}$	Enter d	{R/S
	Prepare to divide	{÷
	Enter 4	{4
	Complete division	{=
↓		
Find inverse cosine and display result	Take inverse cosine	{INV 2nd cos
	Stop and display	{R/S

Initialize this program by pressing [CLR] [RST] [R/S] enter the value of d [R/S].

If you wish to verify that this program works, you may use the data below:

d IN METERS	θ IN DEGREES
0	90.
1	75.522488
1.5	67.975687
2	60.

Example 3. The Volume of a Barrel

The volume of a barrel (with a congruent top and bottom as shown in Figure 2–6) is given by the formula:

$$V = (r^2 + 2s^2)\frac{\pi h}{3}$$

Figure 2–6

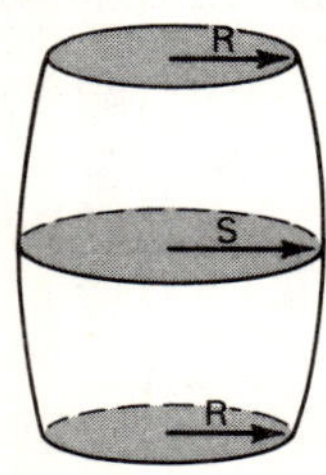

The flow charts are given in Figure 2–7.

Figure 2–7

General Flow Chart	Detailed Flow Chart	Program
	Prepare to compute $r^2 + 2s^2$	{(
	Enter r	{R/S
	Square r	{x^2
	Prepare to add	{+
Enter r and s and compute $r^2 + 2s^2$	Enter 2	{2
	Prepare to multiply	{×
	Enter s	{R/S
	Square s	{x^2
	Compute $r^2 + 2s^2$	{)
Prepare to multiply	{Prepare to multiply by $\frac{\pi h}{3}$}	{×

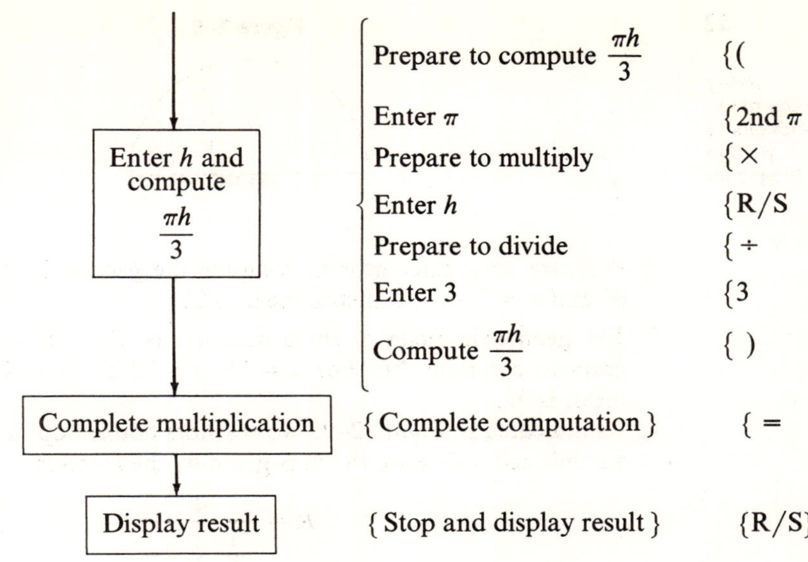

Initialize: [CLR] [RST] [R/S] enter r [R/S] enter s [R/S] enter h [R/S].

Verify that a rain barrel with r = 40 cm., s = 25 cm., and h = 90 cm. has a volume of 268606.17 cubic centimeters; that is, the rain barrel can hold about 268 liters.

Section 6: Problems

When doing these exercises, remember that each single variable function operates immediately on the value that is already in the display. For example, if you want to compute

$$1 + \tan(45°)$$

the sequence

1, +, 45, 2nd tan, =

gives the correct answer of 2. The sequence

1, +, 2nd tan, 45, =

gives an incorrect answer of 46.

1. Program your calculator to find the arithmetic mean of three numbers, a, b, and c. Use the formula,

$$\text{arithmetic mean} = \frac{a + b + c}{3}.$$

The mean for 10, 20, and 30 is 20.

2. Suppose the point P lies on the diameter of a semicircle and divides that diameter into two segments of lengths a and b, respectively. (See Figure 2–8.) Then the height from p to the circumference of the circle is the geometric mean of a and b. The geometric mean $= \sqrt{a \times b}$.

Figure 2–8

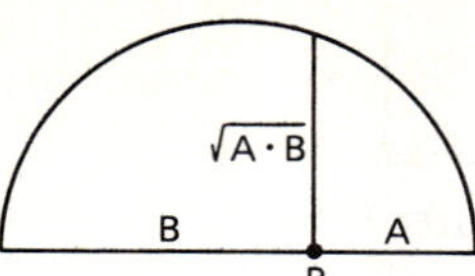

Program your calculator to compute the geometric mean. When a = 63 and b = 7, the geometric mean is 21.

3. The geometric mean of three numbers is $\sqrt[3]{a \times b \times c}$. Write a program to compute this. For a = 11, b = 22 and c = 44, the geometric mean is 22.
4. As indicated in Figure 2–9, two resistors hooked up in parallel produce a combined resistance in ohms given by the formula:

$$R = \frac{1}{\frac{1}{R_1} + \frac{1}{R_2}}.$$

Program your calculator to find this combined resistance. When R_1 = 36 ohms and R_2 = 45 ohms, you should obtain R = 20.

Figure 2–9

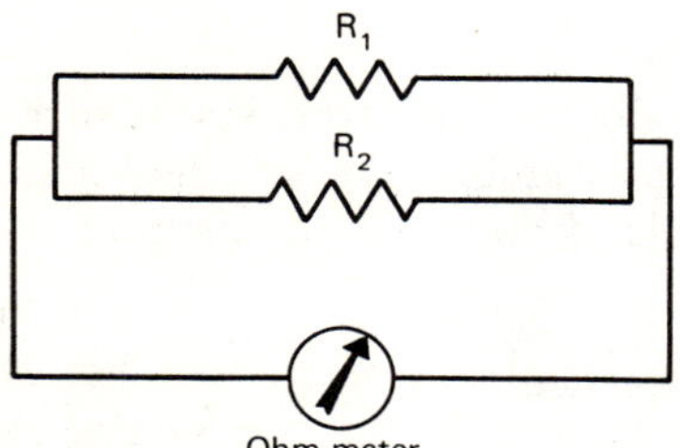

5. Your calculator has the trigonometric functions sine, cosine, and tangent but not their reciprocal functions, cosecant, secant and cotangent, respectively.
   a. Program your calculator to compute one or more of the following

$$\text{cosec}(\theta) = \frac{1}{\sin(\theta)} \qquad \text{For } \theta = 30°, \ \text{cosec}(\theta) = 2$$

$$\sec(\theta) = \frac{1}{\cos(\theta)} \qquad \text{For } \theta = 30°, \ \sec(\theta) = 1.1547005$$

$$\text{cotan}(\theta) = \frac{1}{\tan(\theta)} \qquad \text{For } \theta = 30°, \ \text{cotan}(\theta) = 1.7320508$$

b. An alternate method of calculating cotan (θ) is by cotan (θ) = tan (90° − θ).
Program your calculator for this formula. If θ = 20°, then the cotan (θ) = 2.7474774.

6. An ancient puzzle, depicted in Figure 2–10, called the Towers of Hanoi puzzle, has n discs of increasing size and three pillars. The object is to move the entire tower of discs from one pillar to another in the fewest possible moves given these two conditions:
a. move only one disc at a time,
b. never place a larger disc on top of a smaller one.

Figure 2–10

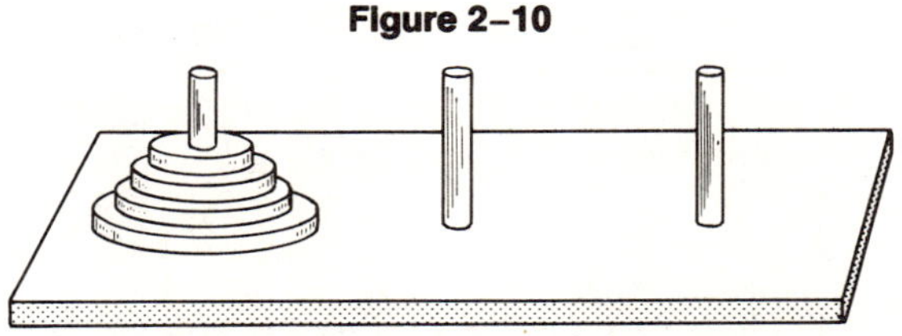

It is known that the fewest possible number of moves is $2^n - 1$. Program your calculator to compute this number for any number, n, of discs. For $n = 10$, $2^n - 1 = 1{,}023$.

7. At the time of the printing of this book, the first class postal rate was 15¢ for the first ounce. At the rate of 15¢ per ounce, the cost of sending a letter that weighs n ounces (where n is less than 32) can be computed by the formula:

$$\text{Charge} = .15[32 + \text{Int}(n - 32)] \text{ dollars}$$

Program your calculator to determine the postal charges for various letters. For a letter weighing 12 ounces, for example, $1.80 in postage would be sufficient.

8. If you want to find the number of years between two dates, you can take their difference. However, if the first date is smaller than the second, the difference will be negative. Using the absolute value function, you can make this difference positive regardless of what it was. In other words, the number of years between two dates equals the absolute value of their difference. Write a program to compute the number of years between two dates. For example, between 1930 and 1810 there were 120 years.

9. How many digits does a whole number have? You can count this number easily by eye when you look at any particular integer, n. For example, 3,269 has four digits. You can also have your calculator determine the number of digits by the formula: Number of digits = 1 + Integer part of the base 10 log of n. Program this formula and try it out for various values of n.

10. Suppose you blow a volume of 1,000 cubic centimeters (1 liter) of air into a spherically shaped balloon. (See Figure 2–11.) What will the

radius of the balloon be? From the formula for the volume of a sphere,

$$V = \frac{4}{3}\pi r^3,$$

you can algebraically solve for the radius, r. It is

$$r = \sqrt[3]{\frac{3V}{4\pi}}\ .$$

Program this formula and compute r. When $V = 1000$, $r = 6.2035049$.

Figure 2–11

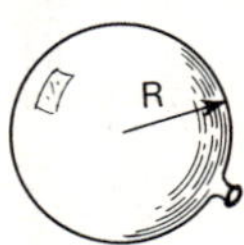

11. The formula for finding the volume of a barrel used in this section is a special case of a more general formula known as the prismoidal formula. It is

$$V = (T + 4M + B)\frac{h}{6}$$

where T, M, and B are the areas of the top, middle, and bottom cross sections of the object while h is its height. This formula works for any sphere, cylinder, cone, pyramid, or prism, as well as for many other solids including a barrel, a donut, and a bead. Write a program to find the volume for each of the following solids using the prismoidal formula. (See Figure 2–12.)

Figure 2–12a

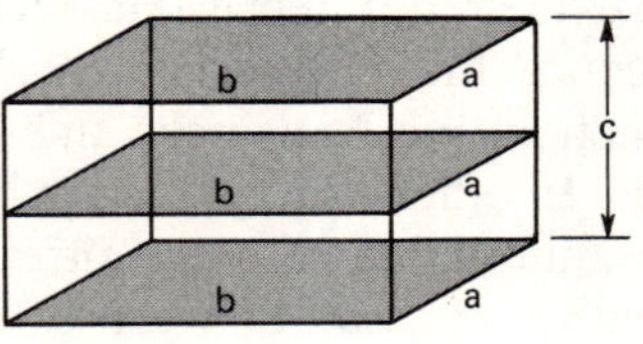

Figure 2–12b

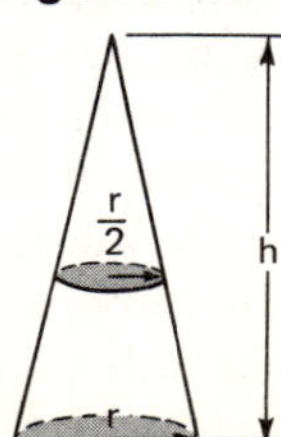

Figure 2–12c

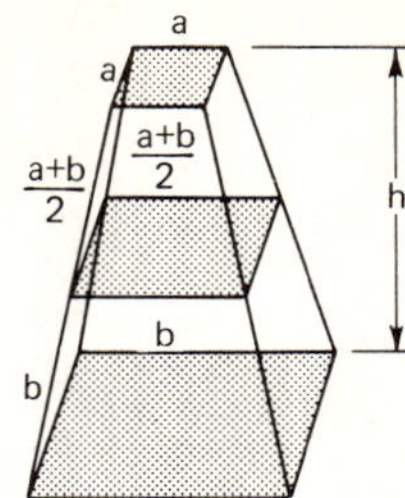

a. Rectangular prism—for $a = 2$, $b = 3$, and $c = 4$, the volume is 24.
b. Circular cone—for $r = 2$ and $h = 6$, the volume is 25.132741.
c. Frustum of a square pyramid—for $a = 3$, $b = 5$ and $c = 6$, the volume is 98.

12. When a baseball is thrown from the ground (assuming no air resistance and a constant gravitational attraction throughout flight) with an initial velocity of V_0 ft./sec. and angle θ, it will land back on the ground at a distance d from its starting position where

$$d = \frac{V_0^2 \sin(2\theta)}{32}.$$

a. Write a program to compute d.
b. Verify that for $V_0 = 90$ ft./sec. and $\theta = 60°$, $d = 219.2$ feet to the nearest tenth of a foot.
c. For what angle, θ, will a baseball thrown at 90 ft./sec. go the farthest? How many feet will it travel? (See Figure 2–13.)

Figure 2–13

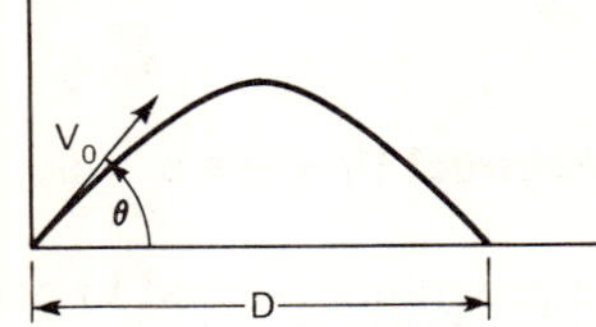

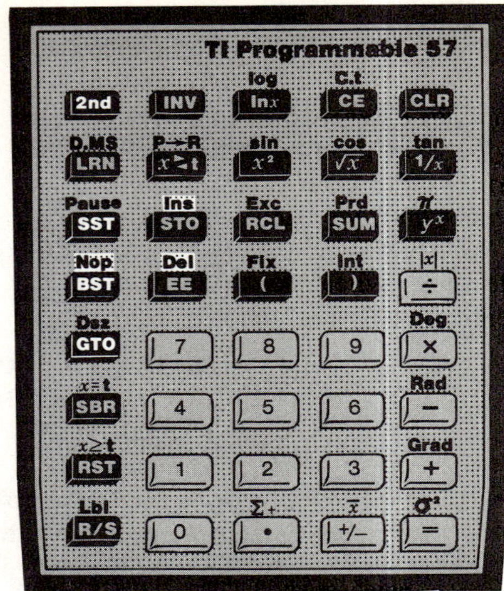

3

Checking and Editing Programs

Section 1: Detecting Incorrect Programs

Here is a program designed to compute $(n + 1)/2$. Enter the program and press [CLR] [RST] [R/S] enter 99 [R/S].

STEP	PROGRAM
00	(
01	R/S
02	+
03	)
04	÷
05	2
06	=
07	R/S

If you entered the program as written, you should see a flashing "99" in the display. A flashing display always indicates that an error has been made. In this case the error is that the number 1 is missing between the addition [+] step 02 and the right parenthesis [)] in step 03. Programs can be in error in lots of ways. To name a few, your program could be entered, written, or initialized incorrectly.

After you enter any program, you should always check it to see whether it is correct. A good way to do so is to enter input data for which you know (or can easily determine) the correct output. For example, in the previous program to compute $(n + 1)/2$, the input value $n = 99$ should have given an output of $(99 + 1)/2 = 50$.

When you check a program, the calculator may discover an error for you and give a flashing display. Or, the calculator may compute some result other than what you intended. For example, consider a program to solve the problem shown in Figure 3–1: 9 glass panels, each of side length s, fit together to form a square window of area A. Find the side length, s, of each glass panel.

Figure 3–1

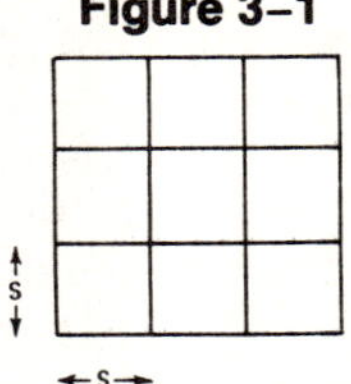

Since $A = 9s^2$, solving for s algebraically gives the formula

$$s = \sqrt{\frac{A}{9}}\ .$$

The following program was designed to evaluate this formula; enter it into your calculator.

STEP	PROGRAM
00	÷
01	9
02	$\sqrt{x}$
03	R/S

Upon checking this program with the initialization [CLR] [RST] enter 9 [R/S] you will discover an incorrect result. The side length should be 1 rather than 3. Why is there an error?

To answer the question, recall that [$\sqrt{x}$] is a single variable preprogrammed function. Consequently, as soon as it is pressed, the value in the display is square-rooted. In the program, [$\sqrt{x}$] immediately follows [9]. Hence, $\sqrt{9}$ is calculated rather than $\sqrt{9/9}$.

Whenever you check your program and find that there is an error, you will need to discover what the error is and then correct it. Sections 2, 3, and 4 of this chapter discuss features of your calculator that you can use to locate and correct program errors. Section 5 provides some exercises on editing programs.

Section 2: Reading a Program

A good first step toward locating and changing program errors is to read the program that your calculator has memorized. Some features on your calculator facilitate the reading of a program in the learn mode, including program memory location codes, program instruction codes, and forward-backward single stepping. These features are explained in this section.

Here is a program to find the volume, V, of a cube given the side length, s, using the formula $V = s^3$. Enter this program into your calculator.

STEP	PROGRAM
00	y^x
01	3
02	=
03	R/S

Check the program with the initialization [CLR] [RST] enter 3 [R/S]. You should obtain a volume of 27 for this side length of 3.

Press the [RST] and [LRN] keys to switch your calculator to the learn mode. The display should show "00 35." Each of these two-digit numbers, 00 and 35, is a special code.

The two-digit number 00 on the left names the program memory location where the first program step is memorized. There are 50 such locations, each identified by one of the code numbers 00 through 49.

The two-digit number 35 on the right indicates that the instruction y^x has been memorized. In Section 3 you will learn which instructions correspond to specific program instruction codes that appear in the display.

Remain in the learn mode and press [SST]. This key stroke advances the calculator to the next step of the program. You should see "01 03" in the display. The 01 on the left represents the next program memory location; the 03 is the instruction code for the "enter the digit 3" key stroke.

Pressing [SST] twice more will show first "02 85" and then "03 81" in the display.

As you have seen, the program consists of codes:

00	35
01	03
02	85
03	81

Now remain in the learn mode and press [BST]. This key stroke instruction causes the calculator to backstep the program so that the previous program memory location is displayed. Now press [BST] two more times so that "00 35" again appears in the display.

By using [SST] and [BST] in the learn mode you can move the program to any program memory location you wish.

Switch your calculator back to the run mode. It is possible to relocate your program to any memory location when in the run mode, but not with the [SST] and [BST] instructions. [BST] does nothing in the run mode.

By using the key sequence [GTO] [2nd] *n*, *n*, you can relocate the program to any program memory location. Here "*n*, *n*" represents any pair of digits between 00 and 49, that is, any one of the 50 program memory locations.

Key in the instruction sequence [GTO] [2nd] 02. Switch to the learn mode. You should see "02 85" showing that the program is now located at program memory location 02.

In summary, with [SST] and [BST] in the learn mode, you can go to and display any program memory location. In the run mode, however, the sequence [GTO] [2nd] *n*, *n*, where *n*, *n* is any program memory location between 00 and 49, will relocate the program to any particular memory location. Using these features you can read all or any of the memorized program steps.

Section 3: Interpreting Program Instruction Codes

When you are in the learn mode and see program codes, you need to interpet the codes to know the instructions they represent. In the three examples that follow, the program instruction codes are presented and explained in terms of five broad categories.

Example 1. Row-Column Codes and Digit Codes

Re-enter the program from Section 2 for computing the volume of a cube from its side length. The steps are:

STEP	CODE	PROGRAM
00	35	y^x
01	03	3
02	85	=
03	81	R/S

In step 00 the code 35 refers to the instruction [y^x] which can be located on the face of your calculator in the third row from the top and the fifth column from the left. Thus, the code 35 is a row-column code. In steps 02 and 03 the codes 85 and 81 are also row-column codes codes referring to [=] (row 8, column 5) and [R/S] (row 8, column 1), respectively.

Notice the program code 03 in step 01. The code 03 is a digit code and does not refer to the row and column location of a key. Instead, the code 03 refers to the digit 3 itself. Each of the digits (0, 1, 2, 3, . . . , 9) is similarly identified; that is, the code for each digit is the same digit preceded by 0. Hence 00, 01, 02, 03, 04, . . . , 09 are the codes for 0, 1, 2, 3, 4, . . . , 9, repsectively.

Example 2: 2nd Codes

Now enter this program into your calculator.

00	2nd log
01	2nd Int
02	+
03	1
04	=
05	R/S

The program determines how many digits are in a number placed in the display. Verify that the program gives 4 when 5,678 is placed in the display. Do so by pressing [CLR] [RST], 5, 6, 7, 8, [R/S].

If you press [RST] [LRN] you will see "00 18" in the display. The code 18 and others like it that end with 6, 7, 8, 9, or 0, (except for the digit key codes 06, 07, 08, 09, and 00) identify instructions that begin with 2nd. This means they refer to instructions printed *above* a particular key rather than *on* it. The left digit of the code 18, 1 in this case, still identifies the row in which the key is located. The right digit, 8 in this case, still identifies the column but according to this correspondence:

DIGIT	6	7	8	9	0
COLUMN FROM THE LEFT	1	2	3	4	5

Thus, the program instruction code 18 identifies the key stroke sequence [2nd] [log].

If you press the [SST] key five more times, you will see in the display the codes shown in the first two columns that follow. For your convenience the last column names the corresponding program instruction. Note that step 01 gives another illustration of an instruction code with a second digit of 6, 7, 8, 9, or 0.

STEP	CODE	PROGRAM
01	49	2nd Int
02	75	+
03	01	1
04	85	=
05	81	R/S

Each of two more types of program instruction codes uses the row-column identification already described but introduces an additional symbol. Both are illustrated in the following program.

Example 3: INV codes and Multiple Codes

Enter the following program and verify that it gives .857 when initialized with [CLR] [RST] enter 888 [R/S].

STEP	CODE	PROGRAM
00	45	÷
01	07	7
02	85	=
03	−49	INV 2nd Int
04	48 3	2nd Fix 3
05	81	R/S

This program divides any number by 7 and shows the decimal remainder in the display rounded to 3 digits.

Notice in step 03 that the instruction code is −49 which indicates that the [2nd] [Int] is part of the memorized instruction. Further, the − symbol indicates that the [INV] key is also part of it. Any time the [INV] key is part of the memorized key stroke sequence the − symbol will precede the two-digit program instruction code.

Notice in step 04 that the display shows "04 48 3." This is a multiple code. The 48 indicates that [2nd] [Fix] is in the memorized instruction. The single digit 3 is also part of the memorized key stroke sequence. In this case it is an instruction that tells the calculator to round the number in the display to 3 digits after the decimal.

There are other times when a single digit appears as part of a program instruction code. Generally, the single digit refers to one of your calculators eight memory registers or ten program labels. How these memory registers and program labels can be used is explained in later chapters.

Section 4: Editing a Program

Enter into your calculator the program (with the error) given in Section 1, namely:

STEP	CODE	PROGRAM
00	45	÷
01	09	9
02	24	$\sqrt{x}$
03	81	R/S

This program fails to compute s correctly from $s = \sqrt{A/9}$ because the division by 9 is not completed before the square root is taken. There should be an equals sign between the [9] (in step 01) and the [√x] (in step 02).

Your calculator has a special feature that permits you to insert the equals instruction between the [9] and [√x]. First use either [SST] and [BST] in the learn mode or [GTO] [2nd] [02] in the run mode in order to get "02 24" in the display. Then in the learn mode press [2nd] [Ins]. This pushes the instruction, [√x] at step 02 (and all subsequent instructions) down one location, leaving step 02 empty. Now press the equals instruction and it will be memorized at step 02. Now the program is corrected and looks like:

STEP	CODE	PROGRAM
00	45	÷
01	09	9
02	85	=
03	24	$\sqrt{x}$
04	81	R/S

In general [2nd] [Ins] works in the learn mode by taking the program instruction shown in the display and all subsequent instructions and pushing them down one location. This leaves the location shown in the display empty and ready to receive a new instruction.

In addition to being able to insert program steps, you can also delete program steps using the [2nd] [Del] instruction. As with the [2nd] [Ins] instruction, relocate the program (using [SST] and [BST] in the learn mode or [GTO] [2nd] *n, n* in the run mode) so that the step you want to eliminate is in the display. Press [2nd] [Del] and the instruction at that location is deleted. All subsequent instructions move up one location. The display shows the same step number, but that location now contains the new code of the instruction.

To illustrate how to delete an unwanted program step, enter the following (incorrect) program to compute the area of a circle from $A = \pi \cdot r^2$.

STEP	CODE	PROGRAM
00	30	2nd π
01	55	×
02	55	×
03	81	R/S
04	23	x^2
05	85	=
06	81	R/S

In the run mode, try this program with the initialization CLR RST R/S enter 2 R/S. Clearly, you do not obtain the correct answer, 12.566371, because the multiplication operation was erroneously entered twice in the program (steps 01 and 02).

To delete one of the extra multiplication operations, switch to the learn mode and use the SST or BST keys until "02 55" appears in the display. You go to step 02 since that is the step to be deleted. (Of course, you could choose to delete step 01 instead in this case.) Now press 2nd Del. Using the SST and BST keys verify that the program in your calculator is now as follows:

STEP	CODE	PROGRAM
00	30	2nd π
01	55	$\times$
02	81	R/S
03	23	x^2
04	85	=
05	81	R/S

There are other ways to edit a program in the learn mode. You can, for instance, simply re-enter an entire program or write over incorrect steps. You do the latter by going to the location of the incorrect step(s) and pressing the desired key stroke sequence(s). Also, you can render any step in a program inoperative with the 2nd Nop (No Operation) instruction. The effect of pressing 2nd Nop at a program location is to have the calculator pass through that location without doing anything.

Section 5: Exercises

1. The following program should compute the hypotenuse of a right triangle according to the formula $c = \sqrt{a^2 + b^2}$.

STEP	CODE	PROGRAM
00	81	R/S
01	23	x^2
02	75	+
03	81	R/S
04	23	x^2
05	24	$\sqrt{x}$
06	81	R/S

It is initialized with CLR RST R/S enter a R/S enter b R/S.

a. Run this program for $a = 3$, $b = 4$. Do you get 5?

b. In the program the addition operation is not computed before the square root is taken. Correct this error by inserting [=] between the instruction [x^2] (currently in step 04) and the instruction [$\sqrt{x}$] (currently in step 05).

c. Now use [SST] and [BST] in the learn mode to verify that the program has become:

STEP	CODE	PROGRAM
00	81	R/S
01	23	x^2
02	75	+
03	81	R/S
04	23	x^2
05	85	=
06	24	$\sqrt{x}$
07	81	R/S

d. Now initialize and run the program for $a = 3$ and $b = 4$ and obtain the correct answer $c = 5$.

2. The following program was written incorrectly to compute

$$\frac{(n^2 + 1)}{2}.$$

Enter it into your calculator and then edit it as indicated.

STEP	CODE	PROGRAM
00	43	(
01	81	R/S
02	24	$\sqrt{x}$
03	75	+
04	75	+
05	01	1
06	44	)
07	02	2
08	85	=
09	81	R/S

a. Change step 02 to become [x^2].

b. Delete step 04.

c. Insert [÷] between the right parenthesis [)] and the digit [2].

d. Now switch to the run mode and verify that the program works correctly with the initialization CLR RST R/S enter 3 R/S. The program should output

$$\frac{(3^2 + 1)}{2} = 5.$$

3. Listed here is a program that should compute

$$\frac{a - 5}{b + 5}.$$

STEP	CODE	PROGRAM
00	81	R/S
01	65	−
02	05	5
03	45	÷
04	81	R/S
05	75	+
06	05	5
07	85	=
08	81	R/S

Initialize with CLR RST R/S enter a R/S enter b R/S.

a. Check this program in the run mode to see that it fails to give

$$\frac{5 - 5}{5 + 5} = 0 \qquad \text{for } a = 5 \text{ and } b = 5.$$

b. Edit the program.

c. Check to see that your program does now correctly compute

$$\frac{a - 5}{b + 5}.$$

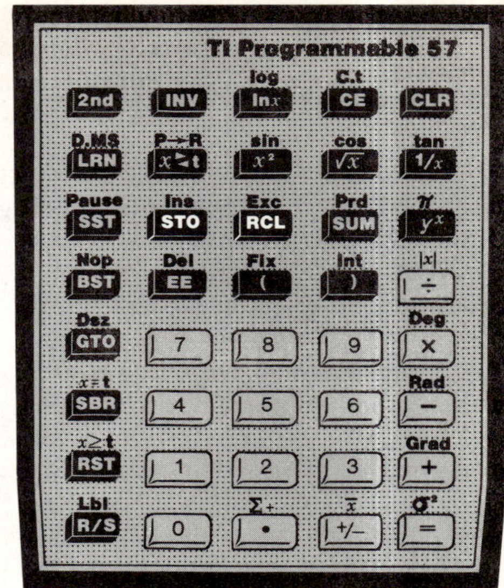

4

Using Memory to Extend Programming Capability

Section 1: Storing and Recalling Quantities

Suppose you arrange a number of pennies in a triangular pattern like one of the following:

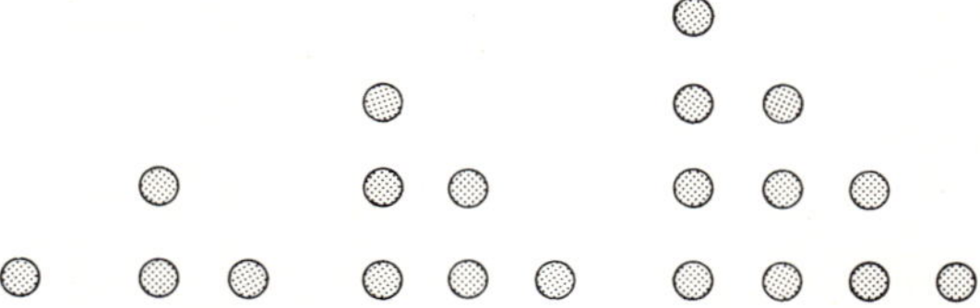

In order to make the same triangular pattern with eight pennies on a side, how many pennies are needed? For reference purposes, let t_n be the total number of pennies needed.

By putting two identical triangular patterns with 8 pennies on a side together, you could form an 8×9 array as shown in Figure 4–1.

Figure 4–1

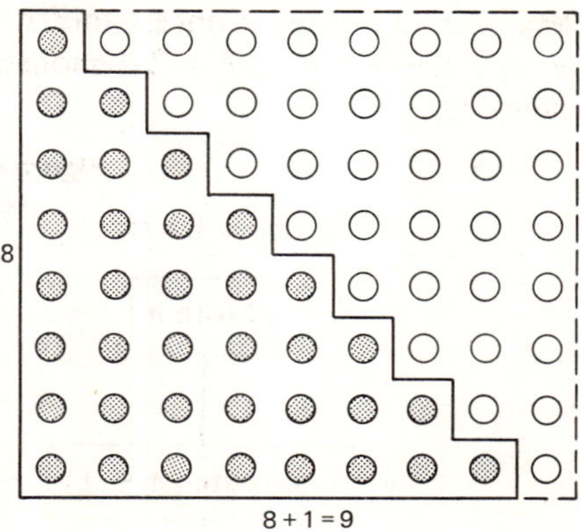

Therefore,

$$t_8 = \frac{(8 + 1) \times 8}{2} = 36$$

In general, to make such a triangle with n pennies on a side,

$$t_n = \frac{(n + 1)n}{2}$$

Now suppose you want to compute the value of t_n for $n = 222$. An obvious approach is to enter n in your calculator twice, once when computing $(n + 1)$ and a second time when multiplying by n. A very useful feature of your calculator, however, enables you to perform the calculation entering n only once. This feature is called *memory*.

Your calculator has 8 memory registers, referred to as R_0, R_1, R_2, . . . , R_7, for storing up to 8 numbers. A number in the display is stored in a register, say R_2, when you press the key sequence [STO] [2]. This stored value may be recalled for use when you press [RCL] [2]. In general, you store a number in register R_m by pressing [STO] m and you recall a number in R_m by pressing [RCL] m (where m is any digit from 0 to 7).

Using this memory feature, here is how you could calculate t_{222} in your calculator's run mode:

$$t_{222} = \frac{(222 + 1) \times (222)}{2} = 24753$$

222 [STO] [1] [+] [1] [=] [×] [RCL] [1] [÷] [2] [=]

Whenever a number or the result of a computation is used more than once, it is often helpful to store the quantity with the [STO] m instruction and recall it when needed with the [RCL] m instruction.

Consider the penny-arranging problem from Section 1. Suppose you want to program your calculator to compute the value of t_n for any n. Rather than enter n twice (once to compute $n + 1$ and a second time to multiply by n), you can enter n once, store it in a memory register, and recall it whenever needed. Figure 4–2 demonstrates a program to illustrate this use of memory.

Figure 4–2

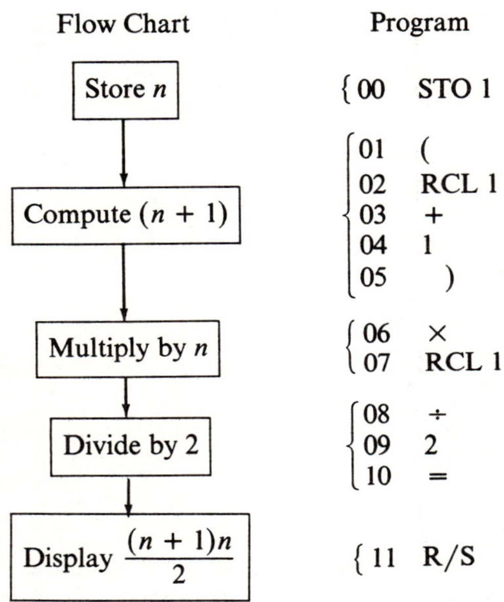

Initialize this program with [RST] enter 6 [R/S]. You should obtain $t_6 = 21$. Notice how the input value of 6 is stored at step 00 and recalled (step 02 and step 07) when needed. As a general programming technique, if an input value is to be used more than once in a program, store that value at the beginning of the program and recall it whenever needed.

There are actually a number of reasons for using memory when writing programs. One reason is to store input data that needs to be used several times during the program. Another is to store intermediate results that may be needed more than once. Yet another is to store output information for reference purposes. Examples illustrating each of these uses of memory follow.

Example 1: Storing Input Data

The program in Figure 4–3 is designed to compute the sales tax and the final price of an item sold in a state with a 5 percent sales tax. Notice how both the input price is stored at the beginning of the program and thereafter recalled when necessary. If you start with a sale of \$8.40, the sales tax is \$0.42 and the total cost \$8.82.

Figure 4–3

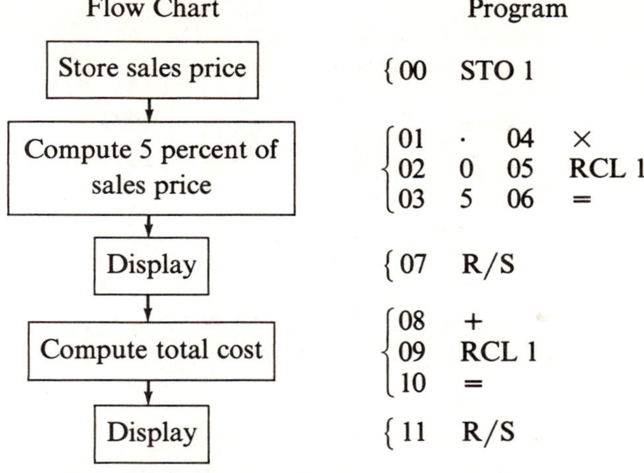

Memory usage: R_1 = sales price
Initialize: RST enter sales price R/S (see sales tax now) R/S (see total cost now)

Example 2: Storing Input and Intermediate Results

Heron's formula for the area of a triangle given the triangle's three side lengths is $A = \sqrt{s(s - a)(s - b)(s - c)}$ where the three side lengths are a, b, and c, and the number s is the semiperimeter,

$$s = \frac{a + b + c}{2}$$

Notice in Figure 4–4 that a, b, and c should be stored at the beginning of the program so that they can be recalled for later use when the area is computed by Heron's formula. Furthermore, since the semiperimeter, s, is used four times when computing the area, A, it is wise to compute s early in the program and store it for recall when needed.

Figure 4–4

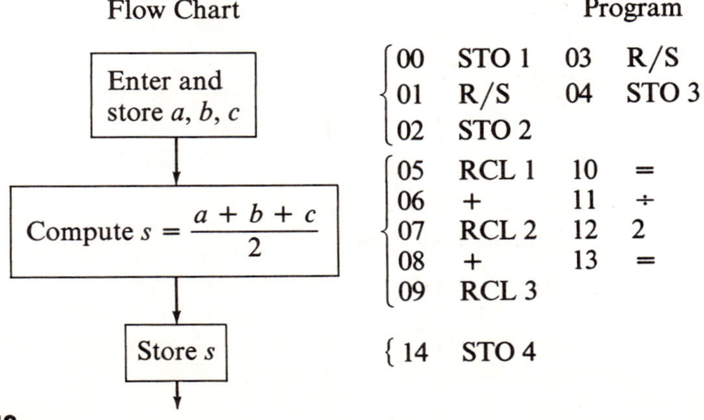

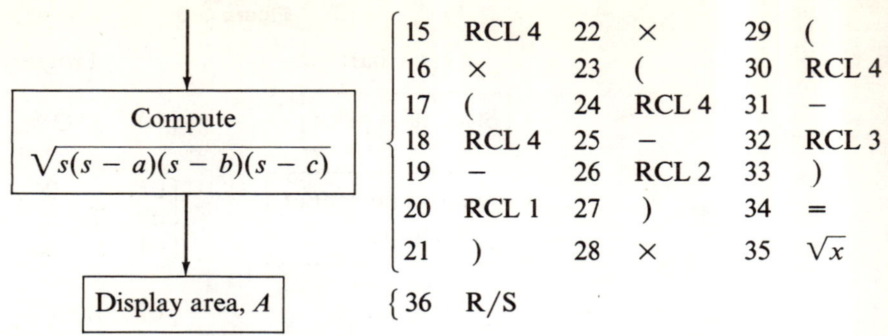

Memory usage: $R_1 = a$, $R_2 = b$, $R_3 = c$, $R_4 = s$
Initialize: [CLR] [RST] enter a [R/S] enter b [R/S] enter c [R/S].

Try this program for $a = 13$, $b = 14$, $c = 15$. When the program halts you will see the area, $A = 84$. The semiperimeter, $s = 21$, can then be seen by pressing [RCL] [4].

Example 3: Storing Input Data, Intermediate Results, and Output Information

The fraction 8/5 can also be written as 1 + 3/5. In general any fraction, n/d can be written in the form $q + r/d$, where q is the quotient and r is the remainder upon dividing n by d. The program in Figure 4–5 computes q and r, given any n and d. Furthermore, the results of the computation are stored and can be recalled for reference purposes.

Figure 4–5

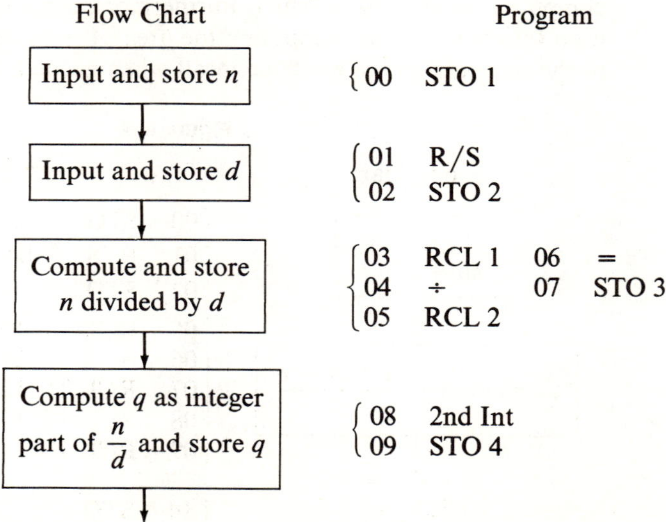

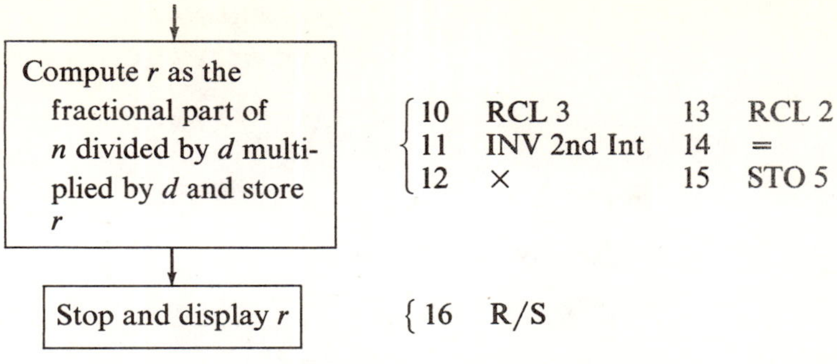

Memory usage: $R_1 = n$, $R_2 = d$, $R_3 = \frac{n}{d}$, $R_4 = q$, $R_5 = r$

Initialize: [CLR] [RST] enter n [R/S] enter d [R/S].

Try this program for $8/5 = 1 + 3/5$. In this case $n = 8$ and $d = 5$. When the program halts, you should see $r = 3$ in the display. You can now find the value of $q = 1$ by pressing [RCL] [4].

Section 3: Problems

1. Figure 4–6 shows square lattices with 1, 2, and 3 squares on a side. If you count the number of squares of any size that appear in these lattices you will find 1, 5, and 14, respectively. In general, for a square lattice with n squares on a side, the total number of squares equals

$$\frac{n(n+1)(2n+1)}{6}$$

Write a program you can use to determine the number of squares for any n. Use the data given in this problem to check your program.

Figure 4–6

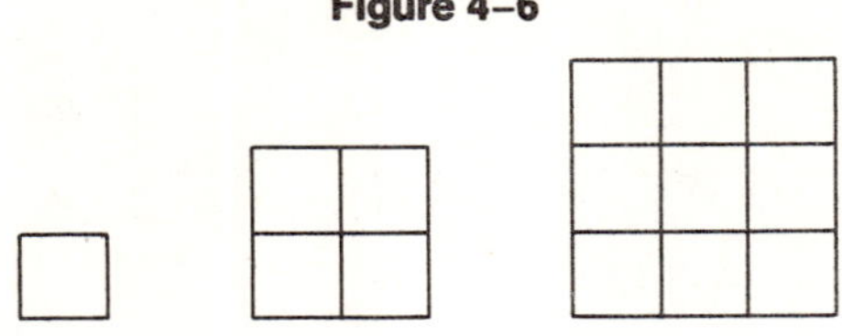

2. Program your calculator to compute

$$\left[\frac{(n+1)n}{2}\right]^2$$

This quantity yields the number of rectangles of any size that can be counted in a square lattice with n squares (see problem 1). Use your program to verify that for $n = 50$, there are 1,625,625 rectangles!

3. See Figure 4–7 for any ellipse with semi-major axis of a and semi-minor axis of b, the area, A, and (approximate) circumference, C, are

Figure 4–7

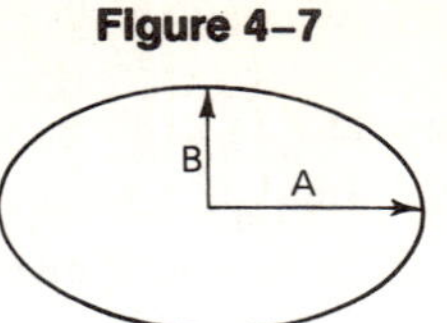

given by these formulas:

$$A = \pi ab$$

$$C = 2\pi\sqrt{\frac{a^2 + b^2}{2}} \qquad \text{(approximately)}$$

Write a single program to compute both the area and circumference of an ellipse from input values of a and b. In your program store the area in R_3 and the circumference in R_4. When all computations are completed, halt the program to display first the area, then the circumference, both rounded to two decimal places. Verify that for $a = 2$ and $b = 1$, 6.28 is the area and 9.93 is the circumference.

4. a. Use the formula

$$A = \frac{n\,l^2}{4 \tan\left(\frac{180°}{n}\right)}$$

to write a program to compute the area of a regular polygon with n sides each of length l. Verify that for $n = 4$ and $l = 3$, $A = 9$.

b. Show that the area of an equilateral triangle with each side of length 5 is 10.825318.

Figure 4–8

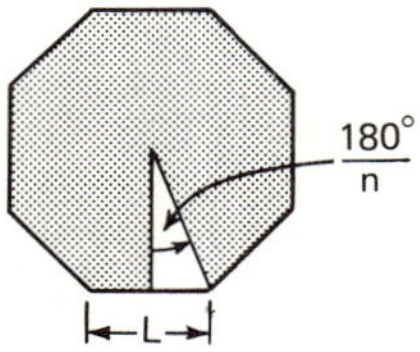

5. On what day of the week were you born? You can find the day of the week corresponding to any date from the formula:

$$R = 7 \times \boxed{\text{INV}}\ \boxed{\text{2nd}}\ \boxed{\text{Int}}\ (N/7)$$

where $$N = D + Y + \boxed{\text{2nd}}\ \boxed{\text{Int}}\left(\frac{Y-1}{4}\right) - \boxed{\text{2nd}}\ \boxed{\text{Int}}\left(\frac{Y-1}{100}\right) + \boxed{\text{2nd}}\ \boxed{\text{Int}}\left(\frac{Y-1}{400}\right)$$

where D = number of days since the beginning of the year
Y = year (Y must be after 1582 when the present Gregorian calendar system was started)
R = the resulting day of the week after rounding to the nearest integer and applying the code:

Number Code	*Day*
1	Sunday
2	Monday
3	Tuesday
4	Wednesday
5	Thursday
6	Friday
0	Saturday

a. Write a program for this formula. Check it with January 1, 1900 which was a Monday ($D = 1$, $Y = 1900$, and $R = 2$) and with July 4, 1776 ($D = 186$, $Y = 1776$, and $R = 5$).
b. On what day of the week were you born?
c. When will New Year's Day be for the year 2000?

6. Write a program to compute the quantity $\sin^2 \theta + \cos^2 \theta$ for any θ. When you input $\theta = 90$, you should get a value of 1 for $\sin^2 90 + \cos^2 90$. What happens when you input any other value of θ?
7. If n people are in a group and three of them are to be chosen to form a committee, the formula for determining the number of ways to choose those three people is as follows:

$$\frac{n(n-1)(n-2)}{6}$$

Write a program to determine the number of ways to choose the committee members when $n = 3, 4, 5, 10$, and 100. For $n = 3$, there is obviously only one way to choose the committee.

8. A sphere has a volume and a surface area of:

$$V = \frac{4}{3}\pi r^3 \qquad SA = 4\pi r^2 \qquad \text{where } r = \text{radius}$$

Write a program to find the volume and surface area of a sphere. For $r = 3$, both the volume and the surface area = 113.09734.

9. Suppose you plan to cover the outside of a jewelry box with two kinds of velvet. The box itself measures x inches by y inches by z inches. The material for the top and the four sides of the box costs 3¢ per square inch while the material for the bottom costs only 2¢ per square inch. Write a program to compute the cost of material for the covering of the box when its length, width, and height are x, y, and z respectively. Use the formula:

$$\begin{aligned} \text{Cost} &= .03(2xz + 2yz + xy) + .02(xy) \\ &= .06xz + .06yz + .03xy + .02xy \\ &= .06z(x + y) + .05xy \end{aligned}$$

For $x = 2$, $y = 3$, and $z = 4$, the cost is \$1.50.

10. If a new car dealer advertises an automobile at a delivery price of \$5,272.50, how much does this car cost the dealer and how much profit is the dealer making? Usually the dealer pays certain transportation costs (that should be listed on the sales sticker) and about 82 percent of the base price, which is the advertised price less the transportation costs. For example, if there is \$118.50 in transportation costs on a car listed at \$5,272.50, the dealer pays: (5272.50 − 118.50) × (.82) + 118.50 = 4344.78.
    a. Program your calculator to accept the input values of the delivery price and the transportation cost. Then calculate the dealer's cost.
    b. Extend your program to output not only the dealer's cost but also the dealer's profit. For a sales sticker price of \$5,272.50 and transportation costs of \$118.50, the dealer's profit is \$927.72.
    c. Adapt your program to round all calculations to the nearest cent. Do so by using the key stroke sequence [2nd] [Fix] [2] in your program.
11. Bayes' Law for probability states that

$$P(B|A) = \frac{P(A|B) \cdot P(B)}{P(A|B) \cdot P(B) + P(A|B') \cdot P(B')}$$

where $P(A)$ = probability that event A happens
$P(B)$ = probability that event B happens
$P(B')$ = probability that the complement of event B happens
$P(B|A)$ = probability that B happens given that A happens
$P(A|B)$ = probability that A happens given that B happens
$P(A|B')$ = probability that A happens given that the complement of B happens

Note that in Bayes' formula, the product $P(A|B) \cdot P(B)$ appears twice in the formula. Furthermore, use the formula $P(B') = 1 - P(B)$ for finding $P(B')$.
Write a program to compute $P(B|A)$ from the input values of $P(A|B)$, $P(A|B')$, and $P(B)$. Verify that for $P(A|B) = .7$, $P(B) = .6$, and $P(A|B') = .2$ $P(B|A) = .84$.
12. Let y be a random variable representing the number of successes on n repeated and independent binomial experiments, where the probability of success on a single experiment is p. Then the expected value $E(y)$ of y is $E(y) = n\text{p}$ and the standard deviation of y is $SD(y) = \sqrt{n\text{p}(1 - \text{p})}$. Write a program to input n and p and output $E(y)$ and $SD(y)$. If $n = 100$ and $\text{p} = .5$, then $E(y) = 50$ and $SD(y) = 5$.
13. If you shoot a projectile (assuming no air resistance and constant gravitational attraction) with an initial velocity of V_0 feet per second and at angle θ at time $t_0 = 0$, then at any later time, the x and y distances of the projectile are given by the formulas shown in Figure 4–9.

Figure 4–9

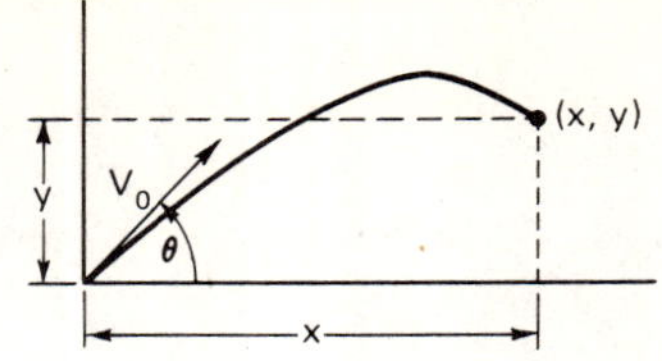

$$x = (V_0 \cos \theta)t \text{ (feet)}$$

$$y = (V_0 \sin \theta)t - 16t^2 \text{ (feet)}$$

Write a program to input the initial velocity V_0, the initial angle θ, and the time t; and then compute the x and y coordinates of the projectile. At that time verify that your program works with this test data. When $V_0 = 90$, $\theta = 45°$, $t = 2$, then $x = 127.27922$ and $y = 63.279221$, or $x = 127$ and $y = 63$ when rounded to the nearest foot.

LOOPING AND DECISION MAKING—TI 57 AND EC 4000

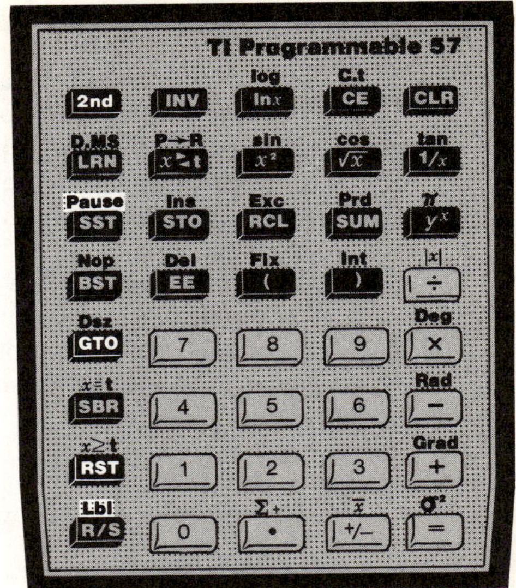

5

Getting Programs to Loop and Generate Sequences

Section 1: Having a Program to Loop and Pause

Enter the following program into your calculator:

Figure 5–1

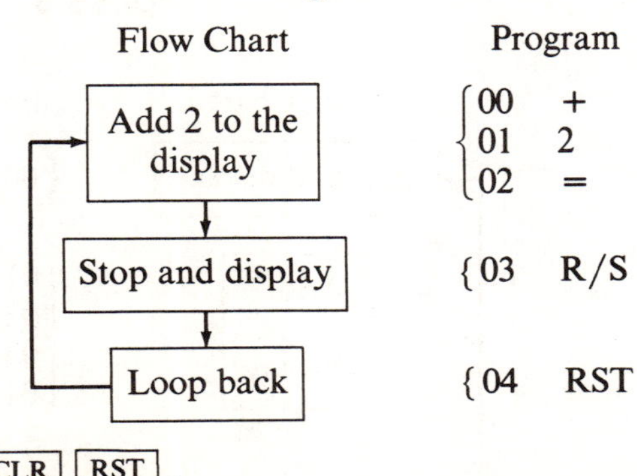

Initialize: [CLR] [RST].

Now press [R/S]. Continue pressing the [R/S] key. You should see the sequence 2, 4, 6, 8, 10, ... The purpose of the [RST] key in step 04 is to reset the program so that step 00 will be the next step executed. Pressing [RST] in the run mode or executing [RST] in the learn mode always sends the program back to step 00.

Here is another feature of your calculator that does the same looping job. It is illustrated in the program in Figure 5–2 which also generates the sequence 2, 4, 6, 8, 10, ... Read through the steps in the program. The instruction [GTO] [1] in step 05 operates quite like [RST]. Here the [GTO] [1] instruction sends the program to step 00, which has the label 1 instruction. In other words, when [GTO] [1] is encountered, the program skips (loops) to the step containing the [2nd] [Lbl] [1] instruction.

Figure 5–2

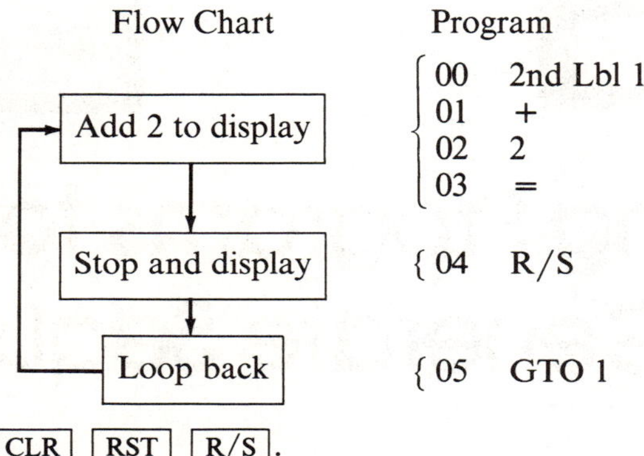

Initialize: [CLR] [RST] [R/S].

In general, [GTO] *n* must be used in conjunction with [2nd] [Lbl] *n* for any digit $n = 0, 1, 2, \ldots, 9$. Furthermore, either of the instructions may be located anywhere in the program. As such, the [GTO] *n* and [2nd] [Lbl] *n* combination can be used in a much more general way than the [RST] instruction, to skip a program ahead or loop it back to any step. Figure 5–3 contains an example: Enter and run the program shown there.

Figure 5–3

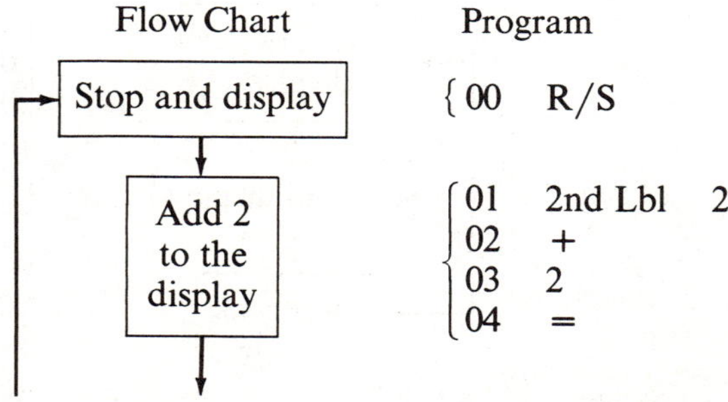

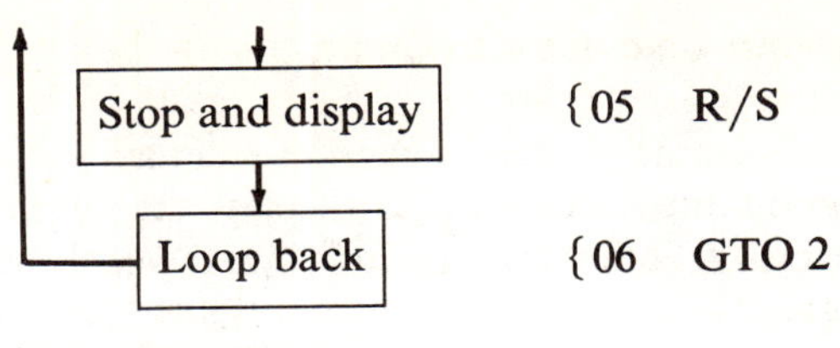

Initialize: CLR RST R/S.

When you continue pressing R/S you see the sequence 0, 2, 4, 6, 8, ... Read through the steps of the program to see where this program differs slightly from the preceding programs. This program loops back to step 01, where 2nd Lbl 2 is located, instead of looping back to step 00. Since an extra R/S is executed at the beginning of the program, the sequence 0, 2, 4, 6, 8, . . . , rather than the sequence 2, 4, 6, 8, . . . , is generated.

With all the programs previously mentioned in this section, it has been necessary to continue pressing the R/S key to see each of the terms of the sequence. You can, however, have your calculator display each of the terms automatically for you with the *pause feature*. The 2nd Pause instruction causes the program to stop running for about one second enabling you to view a quantity in the display. After one second, the program automatically continues running.

To illustrate how 2nd Pause can be used, enter the revised version of the last program, as shown in Figure 5–4.

Figure 5–4

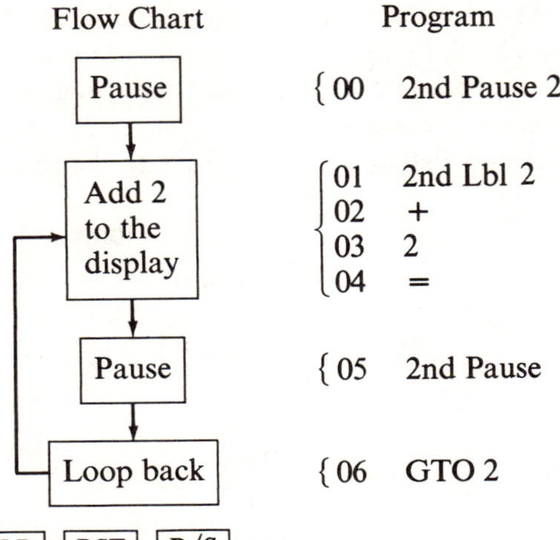

Initialize: CLR RST R/S.

You need to press R/S only once in order to generate the sequence 0, 2, 4, 6, 8, ... To stop the program, press the R/S key and hold it until the program stops.

The programs written in Section 1 actually count by twos. How would you program the calculator to display the sequence of consecutive positive integers? In other words, how would you program the calculator to count by ones?

In such a program the central idea is to calculate successive integers by adding 1 to the previous integer during each program loop. To see how this can be done, enter and run the program in Figure 5–5. In this program your calculator counts by ones displaying the consecutive integers. You can also get your calculator to count by any other number by merely programming it to add that number during each loop.

Figure 5–5

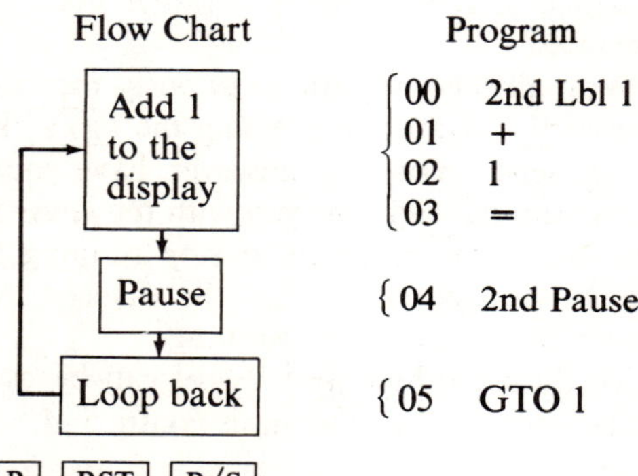

Initialize: [CLR] [RST] [R/S].

Moreover, you can get your calculator to count down, as for a space launching, by programming it to subtract 1 during each loop. If you do so, it is necessary to initialize the program differently. For example, to produce the sequence 60, 59, 58, . . . , you should begin the program with 60 in the display as illustrated with the program in Figure 5–6.

Figure 5–6

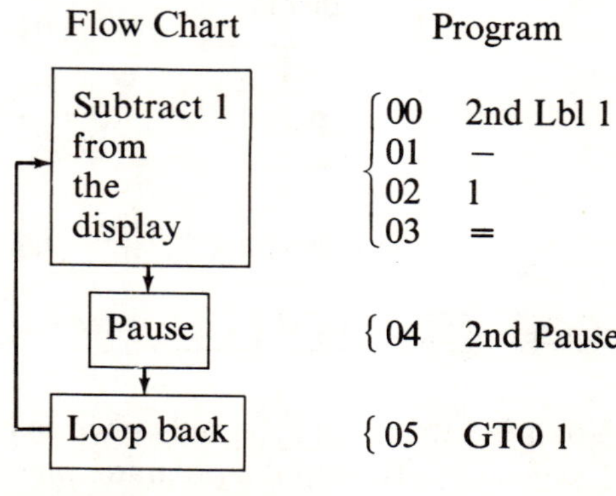

Initialize: [CLR] [RST] 60 [R/S].

Section 3: Exercises

1. What does the following program do when you enter and run it in your calculator?

00	2nd Lbl 5
01	+
02	1
03	0
04	=
05	2nd Pause
06	GTO 5

Initialize: [CLR] [RST] [R/S].

2. What sequence is produced when you change steps 02 and 03 of the program in exercise 1 to become

02	1
03	+/−

3. Write a program to get your calculator to count by fives.
4. Adapt the program from exercise 1 so that it will display the sequence 0, 10, 20, 30, 40, ...
5. Adapt the program from exercise 4 to display the sequence 7, 17, 27, 37, 47, ...
6. Write a program to get your calculator to display the sequence 1,000, 900, 800, 700, ...

Section 4: Sample Programs for Generating Sequences Recursively

Suppose you want your calculator to display the sequence: 3, 8, 13, 18, 23, 28, 33, ... This sequence can be generated by starting with the number 3, adding 5 to get 8, adding 5 to get 13, and so on. Each term is formed by adding 5 to the previous term.

When each term of a sequence is formed by performing arithmetic operations on the previous term (or terms) of the sequence, the sequence is said to be generated *recursively*, or *by recursion*. Recursively generated sequences are particularly easy to program because the repetitious operation of forming each term from the previous term can be done in a loop.

Run the program in Figure 5–7 and see that it generates the sequence 3, 8, 13, 18, 23, 28, 33, ... Notice that the sequence starts at 3 because 3 is placed in the display during the initialization. Notice also that each successive term of the sequence is formed by adding 5 to the previous term during each successive loop.

Figure 5–7

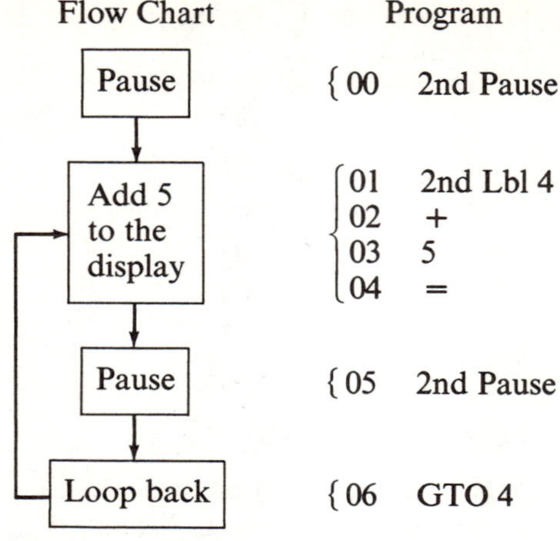

Initialize: [CLR] [RST] 3 [R/S].

Additional examples of programs that generate sequences recursively follow.

Example 1: The Sequence: 1, 2, 5, 14, 41, 122, 365, . . .

Notice that this sequence starts at 1 and that each term is then formed by multiplying the previous term by three and subtracting one: $1 \cdot 3 - 1 = 2$, $2 \cdot 3 - 1 = 5$, $5 \cdot 3 - 1 = 14$, and so on. Can you write a program of your own to generate this sequence before examining the following program? (See Figure 5–8.)

Figure 5–8

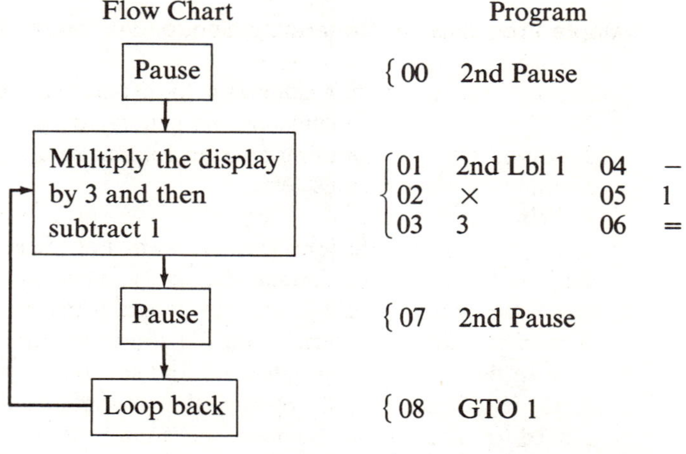

Initialize: [CLR] [RST] 1 [R/S].

Sometimes you need to store the previous term in memory when that term is needed more than once in forming the next term of the sequence.

Example 2. The Sequence 1, 2, 6, 42, 1,806, 32,634,442, ...

Notice that this sequence starts at 1. From there the terms are formed as: $1 + 1^2 = 2$, $2 + 2^2 = 6$, $6 + 6^2 = 42$, and so forth. In other words, each term is formed by adding the previous term to its square. In Figure 5–9 is a program for the sequence just discussed. Enter the program into your calculator and run it. As noted, the program illustrates an important feature. Since each previous term must be used twice when forming the new term, storing the previous term at the beginning of the loop becomes convenient. The term can then be recalled as needed.

Figure 5–9

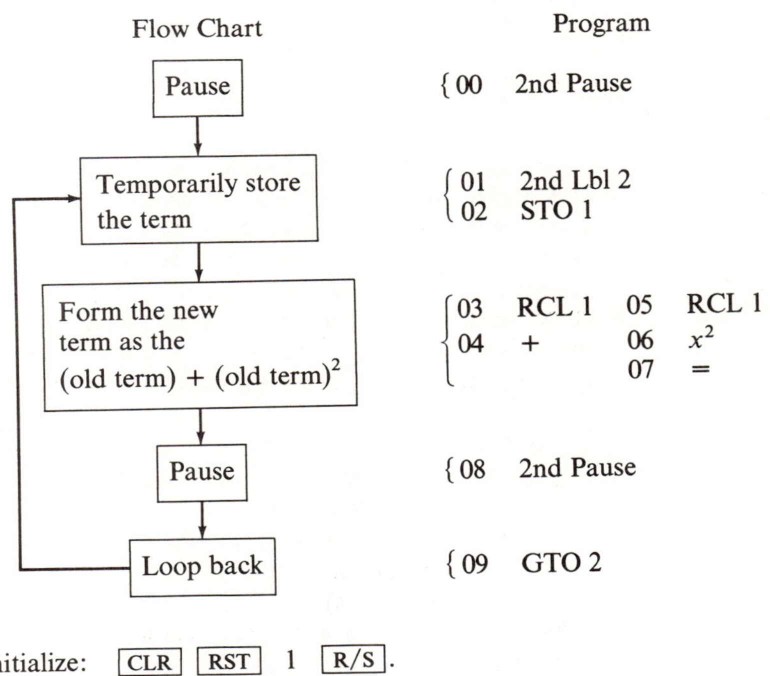

Initialize: [CLR] [RST] 1 [R/S].

You may note that step 03 is unnecessary, but it is included to make the program more readable. Delete the step and verify that the program still works. Can you explain why?

Example 3: The Sequence $1^2, 2^2, 3^2, \ldots, n^2, \ldots$

This sequence can be generated recursively with the flow chart and program in Figure 5–10.

Figure 5–10

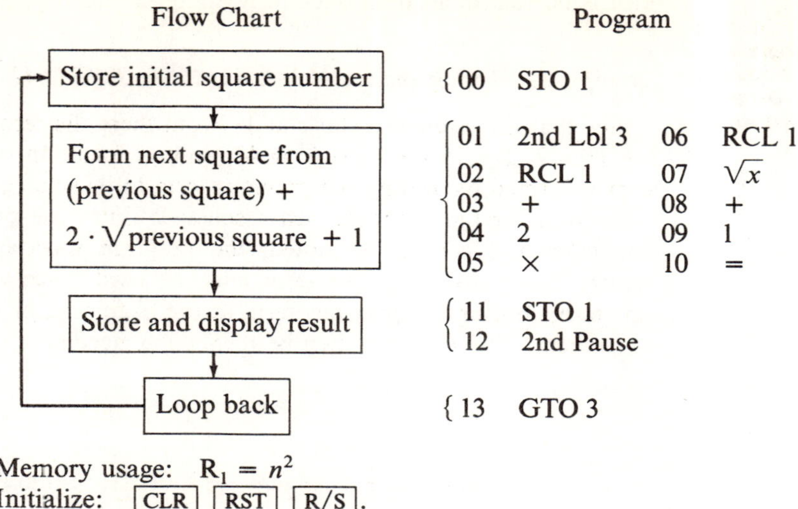

Memory usage: $R_1 = n^2$
Initialize: CLR RST R/S.

Section 5: Problems

1. In the sequence 2, 11, 20, 29, 38, . . . , each term is formed by adding 9 to the previous term. Write a program to generate this sequence.
2. Each term of the sequence 2187, 729, 243, 81, 27, . . . is formed by dividing the previous term by 3. Write a program to generate this sequence.
3. A sequence starts with 3, and each subsequent term is formed by multiplying the previous term by 2 and then adding 1.
   a. Program your calculator to generate the sequence. Verify that the sixth term is 127.
   b. Modify your program for this sequence to see which terms are generated when the first term is each of the following:
      i. The positive integer 123
      ii. The negative integer -16
      iii. The fraction $\frac{2}{3}$
      iv. The decimal .222
4. What combination of arithmetic operations produces each successive term in these sequences?
   a. 2, 4, 8, 16, 32, 64, 128, . . .
   b. 1/1, 2/3, 4/9, 8/27, 16/81, 32/243, . . .
   c. 1, 3, 7, 15, 31, 63, 127, . . .
   d. -1, -3, -7, -15, -31, -63, -127, . . .
   e. 3, 8, 23, 68, 203, 608, . . .
   f. 2, 4, 16, 256, 65536, . . .
5. Write a program to generate the sequence 15, -27, 57, -111, . . . where each term is formed by first multiplying the previous term by -2 and then adding 3.

6. Consider the sequence of odd positive integers.
   a. How do you obtain each term of the sequence from the previous term?
   b. Write a program to display this sequence.
7. Write a program to generate each of the following sequences. When you run each program to display many terms, what happens?
   a. The sequence, 2/2, 9/2, 25/4, 57/8, 121/16, . . . , has each successive term formed by first dividing the previous term by 2 and then adding 4.
   b. Start with any first term of your choice. Form each term of this sequence by first adding 2 to the previous term and then taking the square root of the result.
8. Write a program to generate either or both of the following sequences. Display many terms and see what happens. Experiment by using different first terms. Do you obtain the same results?
   a. Start with a first term of 6. Generate each subsequent term by first dividing 6 by the previous term and then adding 1.
   b. Start with a first term of 5. Generate each term by subtracting half of the previous term from 1.
9. Write a program to display the sequence formed by squaring the previous term and then subtracting the previous term. Explore what happens when you run your program for each of the following first terms.
   a. 2.1
   b. 1.9
   c. 2.0
10. Enter and run the following program to generate the sequence 3, 6, 30, 870, . . . , recursively.

00	STO 1
01	2nd Pause
02	2nd Lbl 3
03	RCL 1
04	x^2
05	−
06	RCL 1
07	=
08	2nd Pause
09	STO 1
10	GTO 2

Initialize: CLR, RST, 3, R/S

a. The program should display 3, 6, 30, 870, . . . , but does not. What does the program do?

b. What single step of the program is incorrect and needs to be changed so that the program displays the desired result? (Hint: The algebraic computations are correct.)
c. What is register R_1 used for?
d. How is each term of the sequence obtained from the previous term?
e. After the program is corrected (see part b), what sequence is generated by the initialization CLR, RST, 2, R/S?

Section 6: Sample Programs For Generating Sequences Nonrecursively

In Section 4 you saw how sequences could be generated in a program using recursion. Some sequences are more easily programmed using nonrecursive processes. Consider, for example, the sequence 1^2, 2^2, 3^2, 4^2, . . . , n^2, . . . , , presented as example 3 in Section 4. Enter and run the program in Figure 5–11, which also displays the sequence of consecutive squares.

Figure 5–11

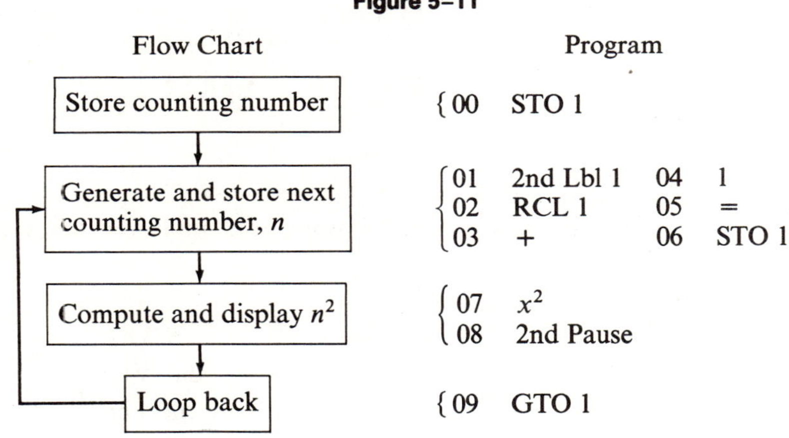

Memory usage: R_1 = counting number = n
Initialize: CLR RST R/S

Notice in the program that each term is not formed by an arithmetic operation on the preceeding term. Instead, each term is formed in a two-step process. First, each counting number from the sequence 1, 2, 3, 4, . . . , is formed by adding 1 to the previous counting number. Secondly, that counting number is squared to produce the appropriate term in the sequence 1^2, 2^2, 3^2, 4^2, ... For any sequence, each term has a corresponding counting number that indicates the position of the term in the sequence. For example, 4^2 is the fourth term in the sequence 1^2, 2^2, 3^2, 4^2, ... The counting number, representing the position of a term in a sequence, is called the *index number*, or simply the index of that term.

When each term of a sequence is formed by performing arithmetic operations on its corresponding index number, the sequence is said to be generated *nonrecursively*. Specifically, the program just presented generates the squares nonrecursively because, in general, the *n*th square is formed by squaring the corresponding index number *n*.

Figure 5–12 is another example of a program that uses a nonrecursive approach to generate a sequence. Enter and run this program to verify that it generates the sequence 1, 3, 6, 10, 15, ... Notice in the program the use of INV 2nd C.t in step 00. In general, this instruction clears everything in your machine except program instructions and decimal settings. Consequently, using the instruction at the beginning of a program effectively enters the number 0 in each memory register. This insures that the index register starts at 0.

Figure 5–12

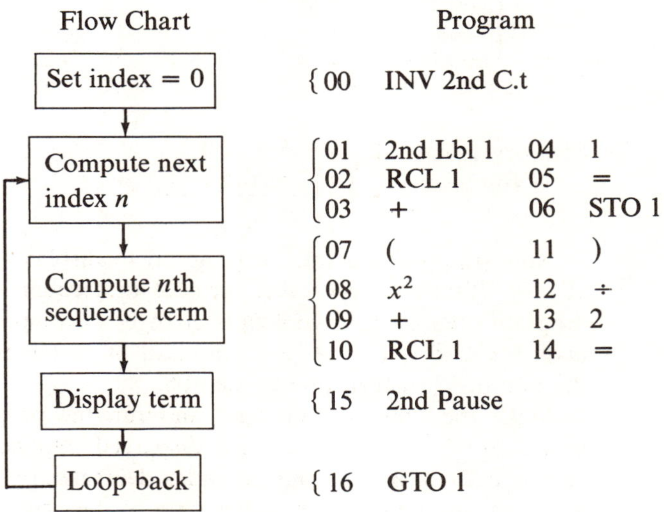

Memory usage: R_1 = index = n
Initialize: CLR RST R/S

Also notice the arithmetic operations performed on the counting index in order to generate the sequence 1, 3, 6, 10, ... If *n* is the index, then the arithmetic operations compute

$$\frac{(n^2 + n)}{2}$$

There are times in programming when you may need to be creative in setting and using the index for a nonrecursively generated sequence. The next program in Figure 5–13 is designed to generate the sequence 90, 72, 56, 42, 30, ... Enter it and verify that it does. Notice in the program that the index is set at 10, that the index decreases by 1 each time through the loop, and that each term is computed as $n(n + 1)$.

Figure 5–13

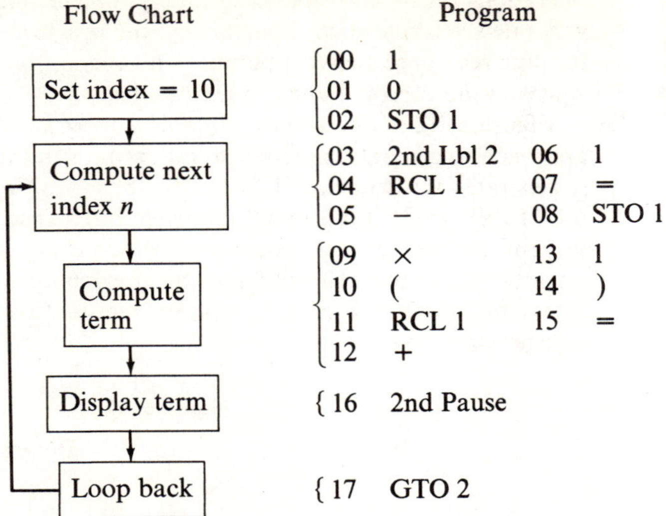

Memory usage: R_1 = index = n
Initialize: [CLR] [RST] [R/S]

Now suppose you want a program to display the sequence 90, 56, 30, 12, . . . , (that is, every other term of the sequence generated by the last program presented). Two simple changes in the program accomplishes the task. First, set the index at 11 instead of 10 (steps 00–01). Second, place the number 2 instead of 1 in step 06.

Make the suggested changes and run the program to verify that the sequence 90, 56, 30, 12, . . . , is displayed. Notice that each term is still computed by $n(n + 1)$, but the index decreases by 2 each time through the loop thus producing every other term of the original sequence.

Section 7: Problems

1. a. Write a program to display the sequence 2, 5, 10, 17, 26, 37, ... Set the index at 0 and form each term by $n^2 + 1$.
   b. Modify the program in part a by setting the index at 2. What sequence do you obtain?
2. Consider the sequence 1/2, 2, 9/2, 8, 25/2, 18, ...
   a. Write a program to display the sequence. Set the index at 0 and form each term by

$$\frac{(n + 1)^2}{2}$$

   b. Modify the program in part a to display only the integer sequence terms (that is, 2, 8, 18, . . .).

3. In order to generate each of the following sequences nonrecursively, where would you set the index and how would you compute the terms?
   a. 0, 5, 10, 15, 20, 25, ...
   b. 0, 3, 8, 15, 24, ...
   c. 8, 15, 24, 35, ...
   d. $2^1, 2^2, 2^3, 2^4, \ldots$.
4. Write a program for each of the following sequences
   a. 3, 9, 27, 81, ... Form each term as 3^n.
   b. 8, 27, 64, 125, ... Form each term as n^3.
5. Write a program to display the sequence 1, 4, 27, 256, ... With index = 1 and terms formed by n^n. How fast does this sequence grow?
6. Write a program to display the sequence with index = 1, first term = 1, and succeeding terms formed by $\sqrt[n]{n}$.
   a. Which term of the sequence is the largest?
   b. What happens as the counting number n grows very large?
7. Write a program to display the sequence with index 0, first term = − 1, and succeeding terms formed by $n^2 - 2^n$.
   a. What does this sequence tell you about the answer to the question, "Which is larger, n^2 or 2^n?"
   b. What method could you use to answer the question, "Which is larger , n^3 or 3^n?"
8. Write programs to display each sequence according to the information given. What happens in each case as n becomes very large?
   a. First index = 0, first term = 1, and terms formed by $(0.99)^n$.
   b. First index = 0, first term = 1, and terms formed by $(1.01)^n$.
   c. First index = 0, first term = 1, and terms formed by $(1.00)^n$.

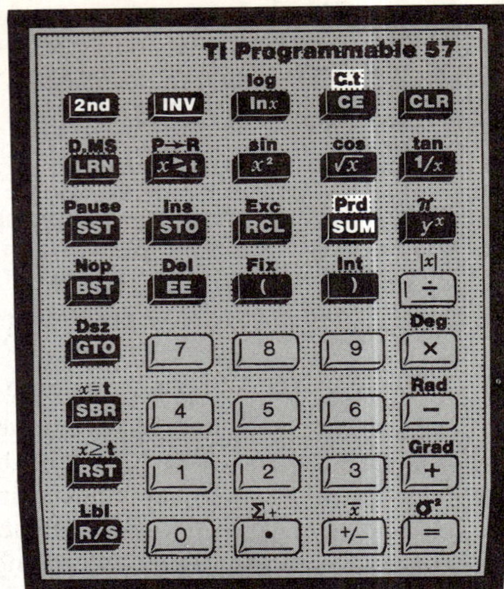

6 Using Memory Arithmetic to Compute Series

Section 1: A Series Representing the Gambler's Problem

A gambler is offered the following deal. He is to toss a coin repeatedly until the first head comes up. At that time he will receive 1, 4, 9, . . . , n^2 dollars, if the first head appears on the first, second, third, . . . , or nth toss. For example, if the first head appears on the fifth toss (that is, the preceeding four tosses are all tails), the gambler receives $25.

How much can the gambler expect to receive, on the average, each time he plays? By considering the probability decision tree shown in Figure 6–1, you can see that the probability associated with the first head coming up on the first, second, third, . . . , nth toss is 1/2, 1/4, 1/8, . . . , $1/2^n$, respectively. Therefore, the amount received if the gambler plays very many games is one dollar half of the time, 4 dollars a quarter of the time, 9 dollars an eighth of the time, . . . , n^2 dollars $1/2^n$ of the time, and so forth.

Figure 6–1

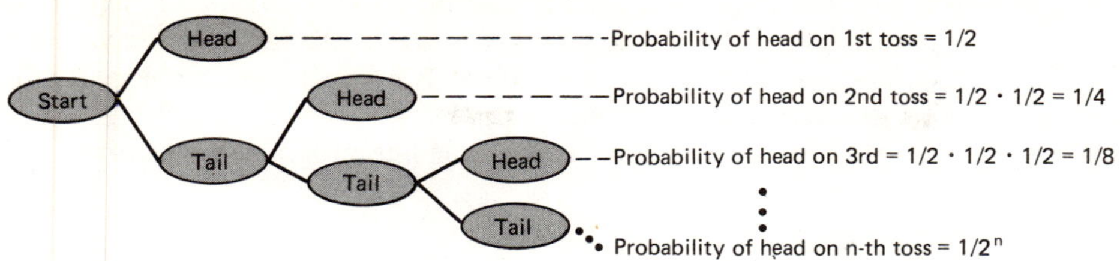

Putting this information together gives us the formula:

$$\text{Amount received} = \left(1 \cdot \tfrac{1}{2}\right) + \left(4 \cdot \tfrac{1}{4}\right) + \left(9 \cdot \tfrac{1}{8}\right) + \ldots + \left(n^2 \cdot \frac{1}{2^n}\right) + \ldots$$

which can be written as:

$$\sum_{n=1}^{\infty} \left(n^2 \cdot \frac{1}{2^n}\right).$$

The value of this series gives the average amount received assuming the gambler plays an infinite number of times. Evaluating this infinite series is rather difficult with standard mathematical techniques, but is not hard to do on your calculator. Your calculator can compute this series by first producing each term of the sequence

$$\left(1 \cdot \tfrac{1}{2}\right), \left(4 \cdot \tfrac{1}{4}\right), \left(9 \cdot \tfrac{1}{8}\right), \ldots, \left(n^2 \cdot \frac{1}{2^n}\right),$$

and then adding each term to a running total,

$$\left(1 \cdot \tfrac{1}{2}\right) + \left(4 \cdot \tfrac{1}{4}\right) + \left(9 \cdot \tfrac{1}{8}\right) + \ldots + \left(n^2 \cdot \frac{1}{2^n}\right)$$

which will eventually become very close to the value of the infinite series

$$\sum_{n=1}^{\infty} \left(n^2 \cdot \frac{1}{2^n}\right).$$

Using a feature of your calculator called memory arithmetic, your calculator can efficiently handle the simultaneous calculations of each successive term and the corresponding running total. In Section 7 of this chapter, after memory arithmetic has been introduced and after the necessary details for computing series as running totals of terms have been explained, the value of the infinite series

$$\sum_{n=1}^{\infty} \frac{n^2}{2^n},$$

representing the amount the gambler receives, will finally be calculated.

Memory arithmetic is a built-in feature of your calculator that has many applications in addition to computing series. Anytime you have a need to maintain ongoing sequences and/or running totals, memory arithmetic helps you create efficient programs.

Turn your calculator on and key in the program in Figure 6–2. What sequence is displayed?

Figure 6–2

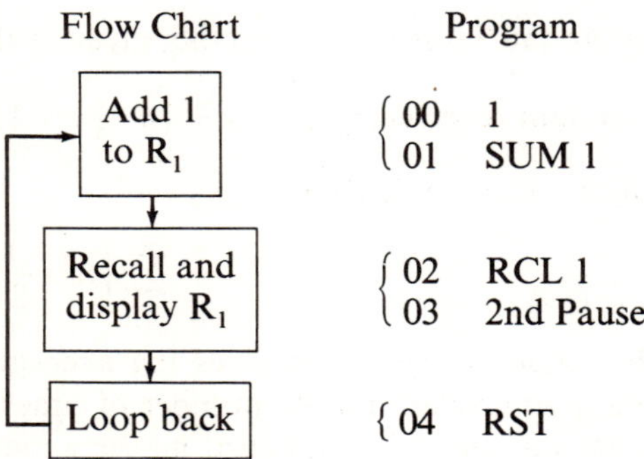

Memory usage: R_1 = sum
Initialize: [INV] [2nd] [C.t] [CLR] [RST] [R/S]

Step 01 of this program introduces a new feature of your calculator, called summing (or adding) into memory. When the key sequence [SUM] [1] is executed, the value in the display is added into memory register 1. In general the key sequence [SUM] m, where m is any one of the digits 0, 1, 2, . . . , 7, takes the value in the display and adds it into memory register R_m.

Effectively this program causes the calculator to count in memory register 1, since the number 1 is added to R_1 each time through the loop.

Your calculator can perform other memory arithmetic as well as addition. It can also subtract from memory, multiply into memory, and divide into memory. The necessary key sequences for accomplishing each of these memory arithmetic operations are described in Table 6–1. Examples of how to use these key sequences are included in the questions at the end of this section.

TABLE 6–1

Key Sequences	*Description*
SUM m	Adds display into memory R_m
INV SUM m	Subtracts display from memory R_m (and puts the result in R_m)
2nd Prd m	Multiplies display into memory R_m
INV 2nd Prd m	Divides display into memory R_m

1. In the run mode, store the value 100 in R_1. Next enter the number 4 in the display. Now key in the sequence [INV] [SUM] [1].
   a. What is the value that is now in R_1? Press [RCL] [1] to verify your answer.
   b. Now enter 6 in the display. Key in the sequence [INV] [SUM] [1]. What is the value that is now in R_1?
2. Enter the program in Figure 6–3 into your calculator.

Figure 6–3

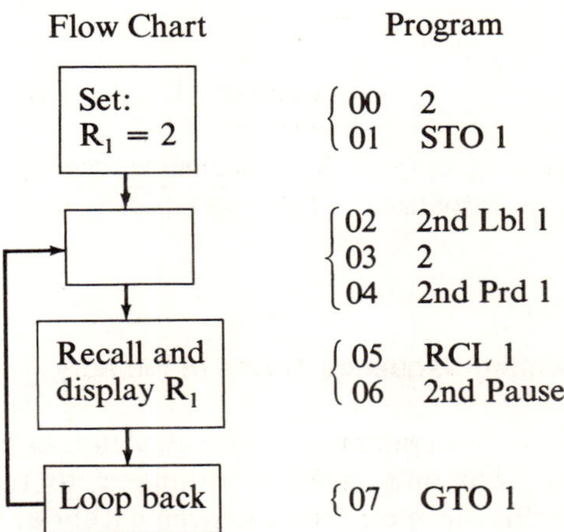

Initialize: [INV] [2nd] [C.t] [CLR] [RST] [R/S].

   a. What sequence is displayed when this program is run?
   b. What sequence of numbers is generated in memory register R_1?
   c. How is the value in R_1 changed each time through the loop?
   d. What is the effect of the key sequence [2] [2nd] [Prd] [1] in steps 03 and 04? That is, what words make sense in the blank box in the flow chart?
3. Examine the flow chart and program in Figure 6–4.
   a. What sequence is generated in memory register 1?
   b. What is the effect of the key sequence [10] [INV] [2nd] [Prd] [1] in steps 04–06; that is, what goes in the corresponding flow chart?
   c. What is the effect of the key sequence [9] [INV] [2nd] [log] [STO] [1] in steps 00–02?
   d. Notice the use of [2nd] [PAUSE] successively in steps 08 and 09. This enables the calculator to pause longer than a second.
4. What program generates the sequence 100, 96, 92, 88, 84, 80, 76, . . . in memory register R_1?

Figure 6–4

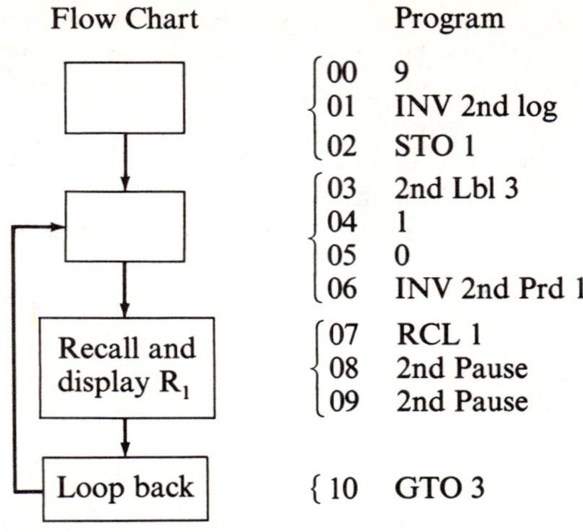

Memory usage: R_1 = sequence term
Initialize: [INV] [2nd] [C.t] [CLR] [RST] [R/S]

Section 4: Generating Sequence Terms in Memory

When programming your calculator to generate the terms of a sequence, you will find memory arithmetic to be a very efficient tool. Memory arithmetic is especially convenient for any sequence term that is computed recursively using [+] [−] [×] or [÷]. Such a term can be computed directly in memory, leaving the x-register (display) free for other calculations. Also, when each term is computed nonrecursively as a function of a counting index, n, memory arithmetic enables you to generate n directly in memory leaving the x-register (display) available for the computation of the corresponding term.

To demonstrate how memory arithmetic can be used to generate sequence terms, consider the sequence 1, 1/2, 1/4, 1/8, . . . $1/2^n$, . . . , which in decimal form looks like 1, .5, .25, .125, .0625, ... The terms of this sequence can be generated either recursively or nonrecursively; program showing both styles are found in the following examples.

Example 1: A Program to Generate 1, 1/2, 1/4, 1/8, . . . ,$1/2^n$, . . . , Recursively

Since each term, other than the first, is half of the previous term, repeatedly dividing 2 into each previous term produces each next term as the program in Figure 6–5 shows.

Note that the key strokes [.] [5] [2nd] [Prd] [1] accomplish the same purpose as steps 05 and 06 in the following program.

Figure 6–5

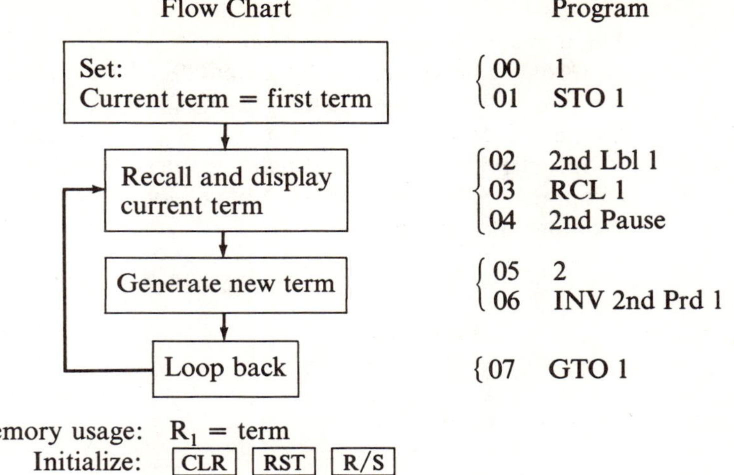

Memory usage: R_1 = term
Initialize: CLR RST R/S

Example 2: A Program to Generate 1, 1/2, 1/4, 1/8, . . . $1/2^n$, . . . , Nonrecursively

The program in Figure 6–6 generates the counting index in R_6 and calculates each corresponding term nonrecursively in the x-register.

Figure 6–6

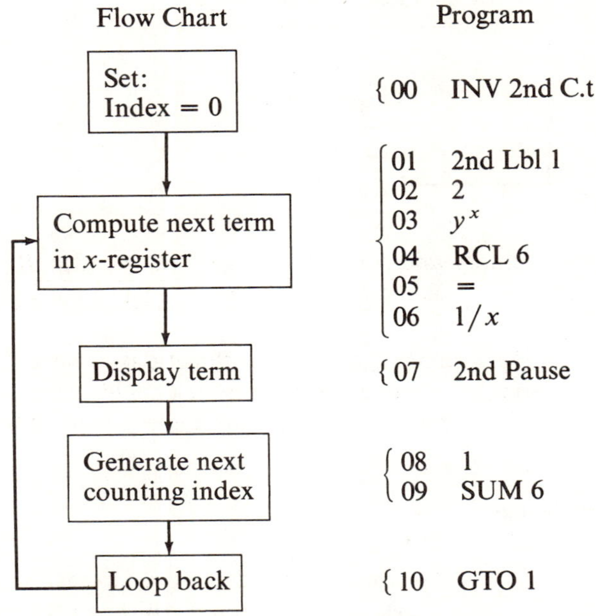

Memory and x-register usage: R_6 = index, x-register = current term
Initialize: CLR RST R/S

Example 3: A Program to Generate the Sequence 1/2, 4/4, 9/8, 16/16, . . . $n^2/2^n$.

The terms of the sequence written as .5, 1, 1.125, 1, .78125, .5625, . . . can be formed nonrecursively by generating the counting index n in R_6 and computing the corresponding term $n^2/2^n$ in the x-register. A more efficient way, however, is first to generate n in R_6, then to generate the denominator 2^n recursively in R_5, and finally to piece together the information and compute $n^2/2^n$ in the display. Notice how the program in Figure 6–7 uses the more efficient way.

Figure 6–7

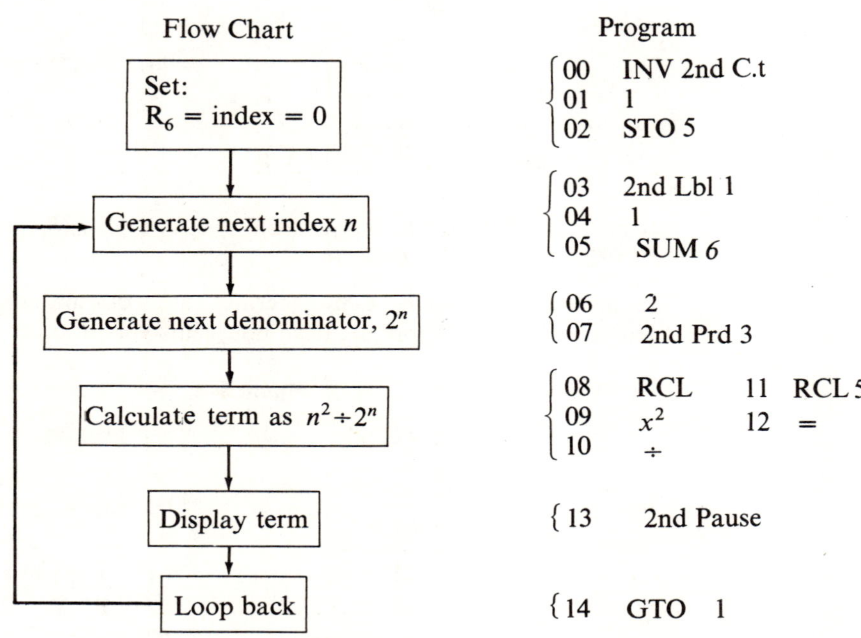

Memory and x-register usage: R_6 = index, $R_5 = 2^n$, x—reg $= n^2/2^n$
Initialize: [CLR] [RST] [R/S]

In summary, memory arithmetic is a powerful tool when generating the terms of a sequence, because it enables various calculations to be carried on in memory leaving the x-register (display) free for other calculations.

Section 5: Exercises

1. In the second and third exercises in this section, what is the purpose of [INV] [2nd] [C.t] as step 00 in the programs?
2. Consider the problem of recursively generating the terms of the sequence 1/3, 1/9, 1/27 . . . , $1/3^n$, . . . in memory R_4.

a. With what value would you initialize R_4?
b. What key strokes would you repeatedly use to obtain each successive term?

3. Suppose you wish to produce the terms of the sequence

$$\frac{3}{-2}, \frac{5}{-5}, \frac{7}{-8}, \ldots, \frac{1+2n}{1-3n}$$

by generating the sequence of numerators 3, 5, 7, 9, . . . , $1 + 2n$ recursively in R_2, generating the sequence of denominators recursively in R_3, and forming each fraction in the display.
a. What repeated key strokes will generate each successive numerator in R_2?
b. What key strokes will generate each successive denominator in R_3?
c. What key strokes will then form each fraction in the x-register (display)?

4. The function $\frac{1}{2}n(n + 1) + 1$ represents the maximum number of pieces that you can obtain when slicing a pancake with n slices. What are the steps of a program that generates the index in R_3 and the sequence 2, 4, 7, 11, 16, . . . , $[\frac{1}{2}n(n + 1) + 1]$, . . . in the x-register (display)?

Section 6: Computing Series as Running Totals

Since series are sums of terms, series can be efficiently computed with memory arithmetic. After each term is calculated, it can be summed into a memory register containing the running total of all the previous terms. In this way, a series can be computed as a running total of its terms. Memory arithmetic is useful both for generating the terms for the series and for computing the running total.

For example, consider the series $1/2 + 1/4 + 1/8 + \ldots + 1/2^n$. It may appear obvious that the series should total 1, but can you actually get your calculator to calculate that value? Figure 6–8 shows a sample program. Run this program and see how many times it pauses before the running total reaches the limiting value of 1.

Figure 6–8

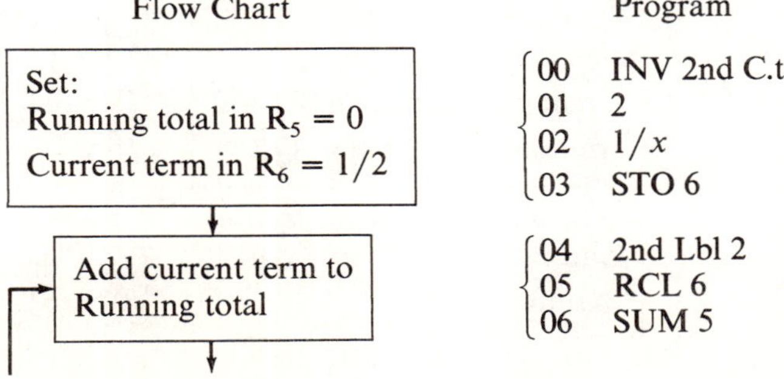

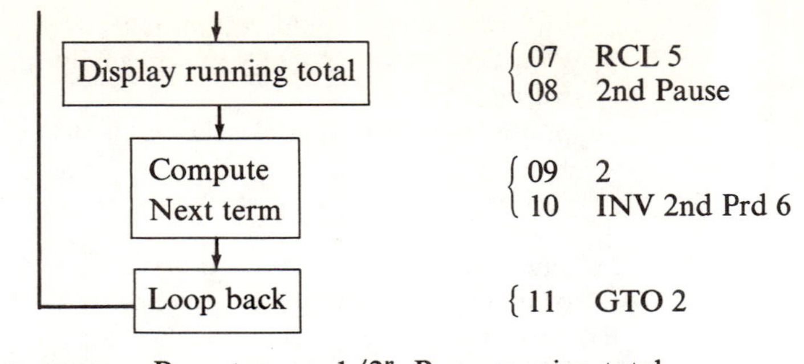

Memory usage: R_6 = term = $1/2^n$, R_5 = running total
Initialize: CLR RST R/S

As more and more terms are added, the running total comes closer and closer to the limiting value of the infinite series. Because your calculator only computes with 11 digit numbers, the running total for a convergent infinite series will actually reach a limiting value after a finite number of terms have been totaled.

Section 7: Solving the Gambler's Problem

Now you are prepared to solve the gambler's problem posed in section 1 of this chapter. Recall that the question was, "How much can the gambler expect to receive, on the average, each time he plays?" In other words, what is the value of $1/2 + 4/4 + 9/8 + 16/16 + \ldots + n^2/2^n + \ldots$ or more simply

$$\sum_{n=1}^{\infty} \frac{n^2}{2^n}?$$

You might try writing a program to evaluate this series before reading further.

Figure 6–9

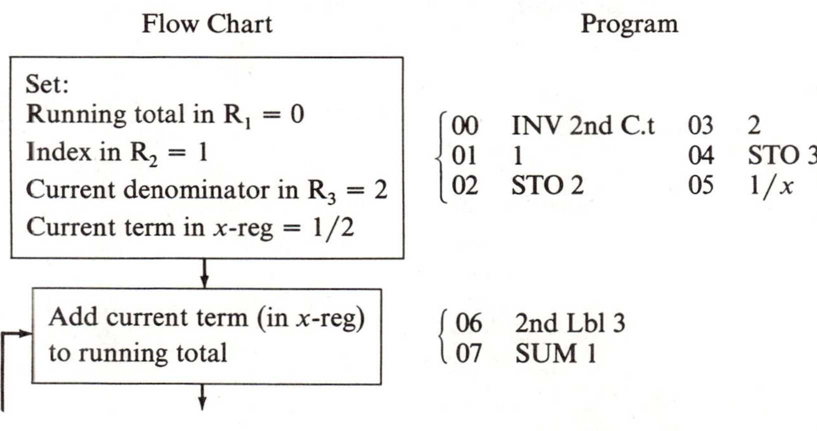

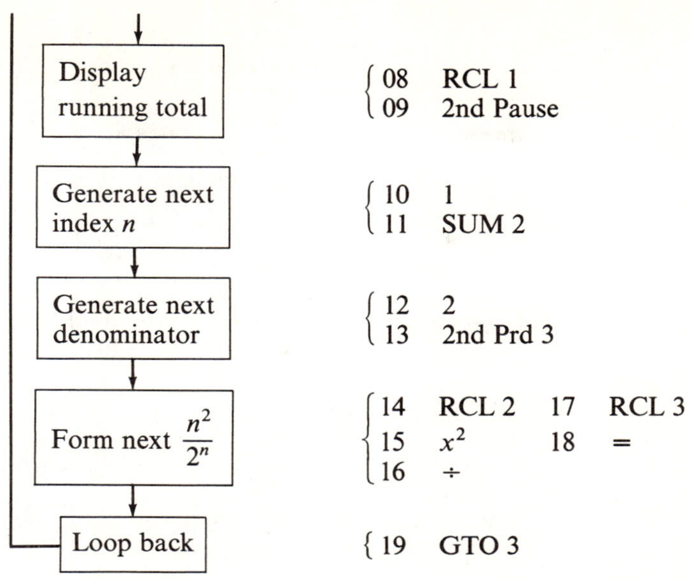

Memory and x-register usage: R_1 = running total, R_2 = index n, R_3 = denominator 2^n, x-register = term $n^2/2^n$

Initialize: CLR RST R/S

Run the program shown in Figure 6–9 to verify that the average amount received is \$6. Consequently, if the gambler has to pay \$10 each time he plays, he should expect to lose \$4 per time on the average.

Section 8: Problems

In solving these problems you may find the general flow chart in Figure 6–10 useful for organizing a program to evaluate a series.

Figure 6–10

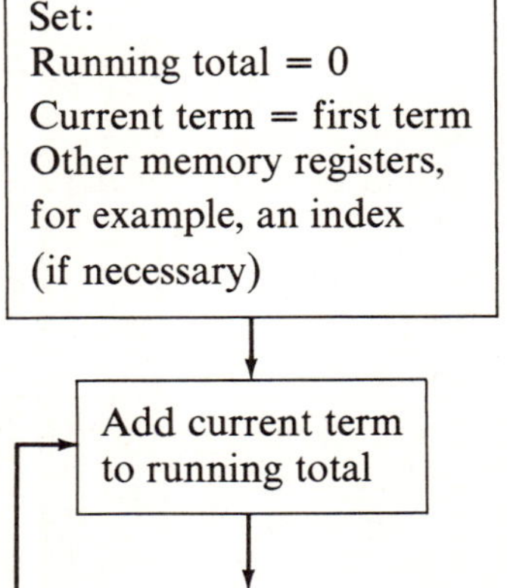

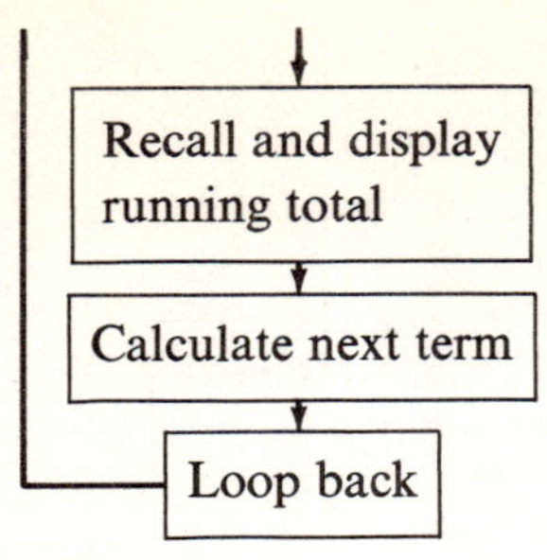

1. Consider the series

$$1 + \frac{1}{3} + \frac{1}{9} + \frac{1}{27} + \ldots + \frac{1}{3^n} + \ldots = \sum_{n=0}^{\infty} \frac{1}{3^n}$$

which has the first four partial sums of 1.0000000, 1.3333333, 1.4444444, and 1.4814815.

   a. Write a program to evaluate the series.
   b. What is the limiting value?

2. In sections 1 and 7 the gambler's problem was introduced and solved. The amount received was calculated from the series

$$\sum_{n=1}^{\infty} \frac{n^2}{2^n}.$$

Suppose instead of receiving n^2 dollars when the first head turns up (on the nth toss), the gambler receives n^3 dollars. The average amount received changes to $\Sigma_{n=1}^{\infty} n^3/2^n$.

   a. Write a program to determine this new amount. The first four partial sums being .5, 2.5, 5.875, 9.875.
   b. How much is the average amount received?
   c. Suppose the gambler has to pay $10 each time to play. What would the gambler's expected profit (or loss) be now?
   d. If the gambler receives only n dollars when the first head turned up (on the nth toss), what would his expected profit be?

3. Consider the series

$$\frac{2+3}{6} + \frac{2^2+3^2}{6^2} + \ldots + \frac{2^n+3^n}{6^n} + \ldots = \sum_{n=1}^{\infty} \frac{2^n+3^n}{6^n}$$

which has the first four partial sums of .8333333, 1.1944444, 1.3564815, and 1.4313272.

   a. Write a program to evaluate the series.
   b. What is the limiting value of the series?

4. Of the sequence of triangular numbers 1, 3, 6, 10, 15, . . . , each term can be formed by adding the preceding term and the index (or sequence position) of the new term. Thus, the 5th term can be formed as 10 + 5 = 15, the 6th term as 15 + 6 = 21, and so on. Let t_n be the nth term of the sequence, let t_{n-1} be the term preceding the nth term,

and let n be the index of the nth term. Then $t_n = t_{n-1} + n$, where $t_1 = 1$.

a. Write a program to generate the series

$$\sum_{n=1}^{\infty} \frac{6t_n + 1}{t_n^3}$$

The first three terms of the series are 7, 7.7037037, and 7.875.

b. What is the limiting value of the series in part a?

5. Given the information in problem 4,

a. Write a program to generate the series

$$\sum_{n=1}^{\infty} \frac{20t_n^2 + 10t_n + 1}{t_n^5}$$

The first term is 31.

b. What is the limiting value of the series in 5a?

6. Look at Figure 6–11. A ball is dropped from a point 5 meters above a flat surface. Each time the ball hits the ground after falling a certain distance it rebounds to a height 80 percent of that distance. Find the total distance the ball travels from the series $5 + 2(.80)^1 5 + 2(.80)^2 5 + 2(.80)^3 5 + \ldots$.

Figure 6–11

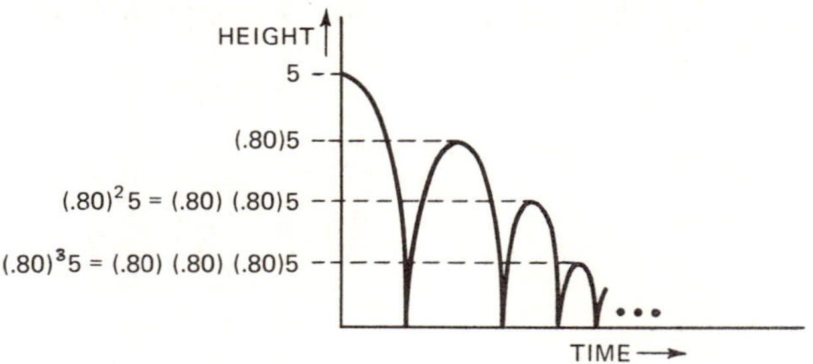

7. The Riemann zeta function is defined by

$$\zeta(s) = \sum_{n=1}^{\infty} \frac{1}{n^s} \qquad \text{for each } s > 1.$$

a. Write a program that allows you to input a value of s (where $s > 4$) and then compute $\zeta(s)$. Check your program by evaluating $\zeta(10)$; the answer should be 1.0009946, which is $\pi^{10}/93{,}555$.

b. Find $\zeta(8)$ and $\zeta(6)$. These values should correspond to $\pi^8/9450$ and $\pi^6/945$ respectively.

c. Why has the restriction that $s > 4$ been included in this problem?

8. The series

$$1 - \frac{1}{2^6} + \frac{1}{3^6} - \frac{1}{4^6} + \ldots + (-1)^{n+1} \cdot \frac{1}{n^6} + \ldots$$

should equal $(31/32)\cdot(\pi^6/945)$. However, the series causes some programming problems since it has alternating signs. Your calculator's y^x function does not allow you to compute any power of a negative number. In particular, you cannot use the y^x function to compute $(-1)^{n+1}$.

How then can you evaluate a series with alternating signs? An answer is to use a memory location, say R_3, for the appropriate sign, $(+1$ or $-1)$, which can then be multiplied onto the appropriate term. Initialize R_3 with an appropriate sign $(+1$ or $-1)$, and then repeat the key strokes [1], [+/−] [2nd] [Prd] [3] in order to alternately change the sign.

Evaluate the series by this method. After computing the term $1/n^6$, in the display, multiply it by the $+1$ or -1 from R_3 and then sum the result into the running total.

Verify that the first three terms are 1, .984375, and .9857467.

9. What is the value of the series

$$2\sqrt{3}\left(\frac{1}{1\cdot 3^0}-\frac{1}{3\cdot 3^1}+\frac{1}{5\cdot 3^2}-\frac{1}{7\cdot 3^3}+\frac{1}{9\cdot 3^4}-\cdots\right)?$$

The first three terms are 3.4641016, 3.0792014, and 3.1561815.

10. Write a program to show that

$$\frac{\pi}{4}=\sin x+\frac{\sin 3x}{3}+\frac{\sin 5x}{5}+\ldots+\frac{\sin(2n-1)x}{2(n-1)}+\ldots,$$

for any value of $0° < x < 180°$ or $0 < x < \pi$ radians. For $x = 45°$, the first three terms are 0.7071068, 0.942809, and 0.8013877.

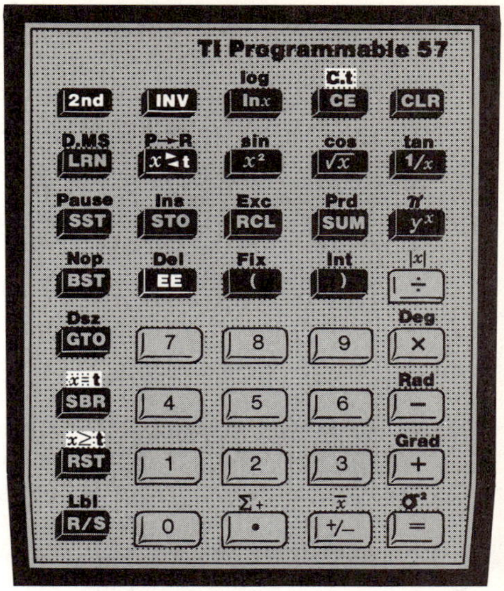

7

Programming Your Calculator to Make Decisions

Section 1: Learning About the Test Registers

Turn your calculator off, then on. Press the sequence of keys: [9] [$x \gtrless t$]*. You should see 0 in the display. The number 9 has been placed in memory register R_7, referred to as the test or t-register of your calculator. Now press [1]. It appears in the display (referred to as the x-register). Now press [$x \gtrless t$] again. What happens? The value 1 in the x-register is exchanged with the value 9 in the t-register. Continue pressing the [$x \gtrless t$] key. Each time the values in the x- and t-registers are exchanged.

The t- and x-registers can be used in a special way. Numbers in the t- and x-registers can be compared in a program. Together with other features, such as decision tests and branching, your calculator can make a variety of decisions within programs.

*The symbol $x \gtrless t$ represents the "x exchange t" key on the calculator.

The t-register contains 0 unless another number is placed there with the [$x \gtrless t$] key or [STO] [7] sequence. In order to clear the t-register either place 0 in the t-register or use the key sequence [2nd] [C.t], which will do just that without changing the x-register.

Section 2: A First Program that Makes a Decision

Enter the program from Figure 7–1 into your calculator.

Figure 7–1

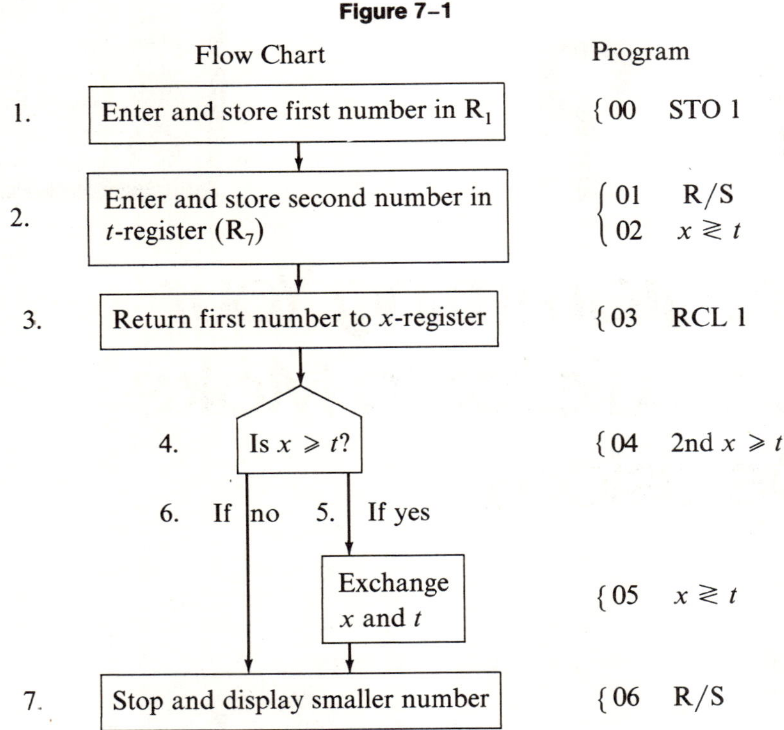

Memory usage: R_1 = first number entered, R_7 = t-register = 0
Initialize: [RST] enter first number [R/S] enter second number [R/S]

Notice that a new shape has been introduced to surround the decision-making step in the flow chart. This shape always indicates that the flow of the program goes (branches) in either of two directions depending on the decision the calculator makes in that step.

Now run the program. Let 100 be the first number and 500 the second. You should see "100" in the display.

What do you see in the display if you press [RST] enter 85 [R/S] enter 2 [R/S]? What result do you obtain for each of the following pairs of numbers?

a. 36, 360
b. 900, 20
c. 8, 3
d. 65, 1
e. 0, 1065

What decision is your program making?

In each case the two numbers you entered are being compared and the smallest is placed in the *x*-register and displayed when the program stops. To understand what is happening in this program, walk through it step by step.

Notice that the number before each of the following paragraphs corresponds to the same number on the flow chart. This correspondence indicates which of the parts of the program is discussed in each paragraph.

1. The first number entered is stored in R_1 (step 00) and the calculator stops (step 01), so that the second number can be entered.
2. When you restart the calculator by pressing [R/S] the program encounters the [$x \gtrless t$] instruction (step 02) which places the second number in the *t*-register, R_7.
3. Next, the first number stored in R_1 is recalled (step 03) and placed in the *x*-register.
4. Next, the [2nd] [$x \geqslant t$] (step 04) instruction causes the calculator to decide whether the value in the *x*-register (display) is greater than or equal to the value in the *t*-register. Effectively, the calculator answers the question, "Is the *x*-register value greater than or equal to the *t*-register value?" with yes or no. Depending upon the answer, the calculator goes (branches) either to the next program memory location or to the one after that and continues execution from there.
5. If the answer is yes (the *x*-register value is greater than or equal to the *t*-register value), then the calculator goes to the next program step immediately following the [2nd] [$x \geqslant t$] instruction. In this program, a yes decision causes the calculator to exchange the values in the *x*- and *t*-registers (step 05).
6. If the answer is no (the *x*-register value is not greater than or equal to the *t*-register value), then the calculator skips the step immediately after [2nd] [$x \geqslant t$] and goes to the next instruction. In this program, an answer of no causes the calculator to go to step 06.
7. Whatever decision is made in step 04, in this program the calculator eventually comes to the [R/S] instruction in step 06. When the calculator stops, the number displayed in the *x*-register is the smaller of the two numbers originally entered.

Section 3: Using Comparison Tests to Make Decisions

In the last section your calculator made a decision by comparing two numbers, one in the *t*-register and the other in the *x*-register. In fact the only way your calculator can make a decision is by comparing the value in the x-register to the value in the t-register. There are in total four specific comparison tests that your calculator can make:

KEY SEQUENCE	COMPARISON TEST
[2nd] [$x = t$]	Is $x = t$?
[2nd] [$x \geqslant t$]	Is $x \geqslant t$?
[INV] [2nd] [$x = t$]	Is $x \neq t$?
[INV] [2nd] [$x \geqslant t$]	Is $x < t$?

To illustrate the use of these comparison tests in getting your calculator to make decisions, consider the following examples. Importantly, remember that if the answer to a comparison question is yes, the calculator executes the next step. If the answer is no, the calculator skips the next step and executes the next step after that.

Example 1: For a specific value x, is $x^2 - 2x - 3 = 0$?

First put 0 into the t-register, as in Figure 7–2. Next have your program compute the value of $x^2 - 2x - 3$ for a specific x. Then with the comparison test, 2nd $x = t$, your program will be able to decide whether $x^2 - 2x - 3 = 0$ or not.

You can see how this is accomplished in the following program, which is designed to display x if $x^2 - 2x - 3 = 0$, or will display $\pi = 3.1415927$ otherwise.

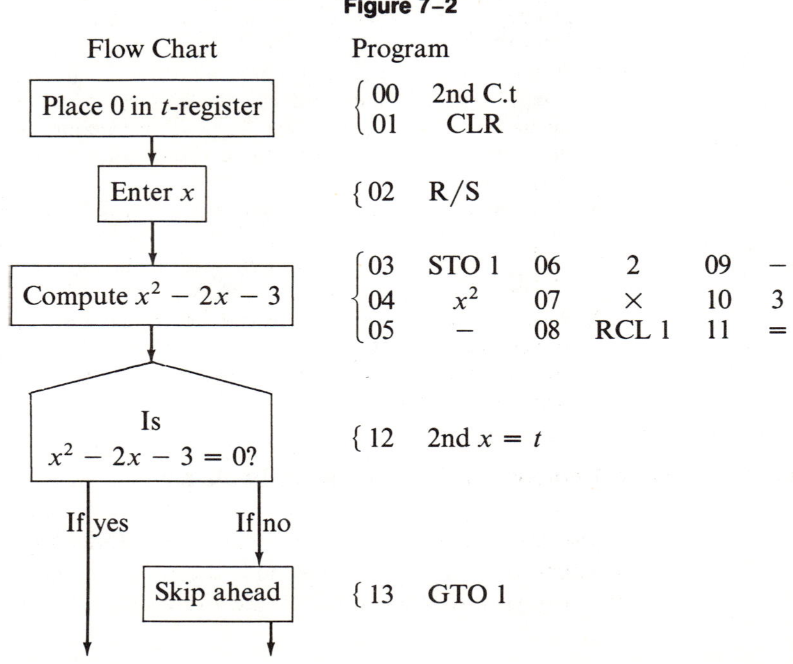

Figure 7–2

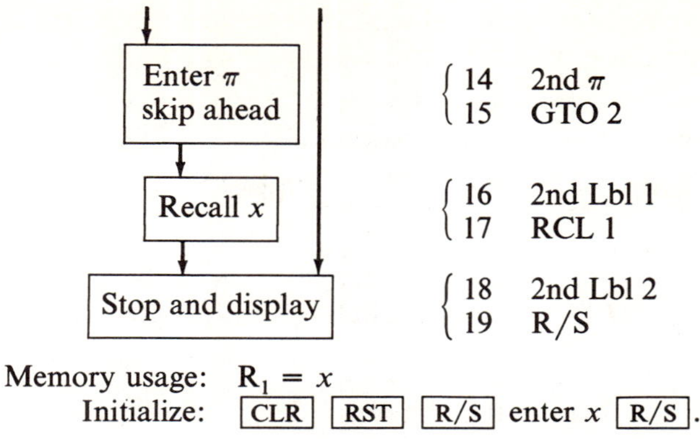

Memory usage: $R_1 = x$
Initialize: [CLR] [RST] [R/S] enter x [R/S].

Example 2

Suppose you are working for a bank that offers home mortgages at $8\frac{1}{4}$ percent if a customer places 30 percent or more of the cost of the house as a down payment. Otherwise the mortgage rate is $8\frac{1}{2}$ percent.

How can you program your calculator to answer the question, "For a given house cost and customer's down payment, is the down payment greater than or equal to 30 percent of the house cost?" First compute 30 percent of the house cost and place it in the t-register. Next place the customer's down payment in the x-register. Finally, with the comparison test [2nd] [$x \geqslant t$] your program will be able to decide whether the down payment is greater than or equal to 30 percent of the house cost.

You can see how this comparison test is used in the program in Figure 7–3. If the down payment is 30 percent or more of the house cost, the program stops and displays "8.25" representing the fact that the $8\frac{1}{4}$ percent mortgage rate applies. Otherwise the program stops and displays "8.5." Verify that for a house costing $50,000 with a customer putting $10,000 down, the program shows "8.5" in the display.

Figure 7–3

Flow Chart	Program
Enter and find 30 percent of house cost	00 . 03 × 01 3 04 R/S 02 0 05 =
Place in t-register	06 STO 7
Enter customer's down payment	07 R/S

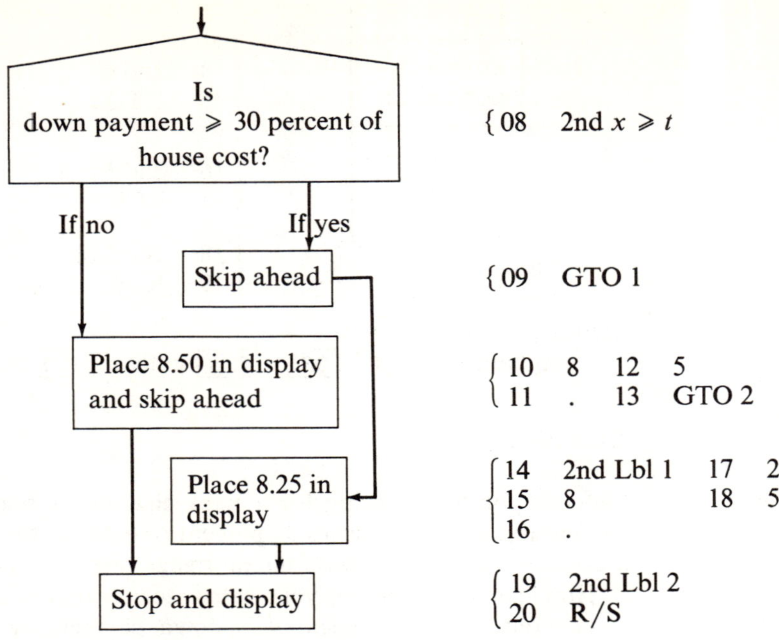

Memory usage: R_7 = t-register = 30 percent of house cost
Initialize: [RST] [CLR] [R/S] enter house cost [R/S] enter customer's down payment [R/S].

Section 4: Problems

1. A certain bank has "now" accounts in which the balance at the end of a month earns interest at the monthly rate of $\frac{1}{2}$ percent as long as the balance is $200 or more. Otherwise the balance earns no interest. Write a program to accept a monthly balance as input, and decide whether that amount is greater than or equal to $200. If it is, add $\frac{1}{2}$ percent of that amount and display the new balance. If it is not, merely display the balance. Test your program by entering a balance of $500. You should obtain $502.50 in the display.
2. Postal rates (effective May 29, 1978) for first and second class are:

Class	*Rate*	
1	15¢ for first ounce plus 13¢	for each additional ounce or fraction thereof.
2	10¢ for first 2 ounces plus 6¢	for each additional ounce or fraction thereof.

In other words, if z is the weight in ounces rounded up to the nearest integer equal or greater than the actual weight, the rates are:

Class	*Rate*	
1	$.15 + .13(z - 1)$	for z being 1 or larger
2	$.10 + .06(z - 2)$	for z being 2 or larger

Write a program to compute the correct postal rate from two input numbers: the rounded-up weight, z, and the number 1 or 2 indicating the class. Use this data to verify that your program works: For $z = 5$, the class 1 postal rate is 67¢, and the class 2 postal rate is 28¢.

3. Faced with a set of numbers how do you choose the smallest? One process is to systematically examine each number in the set. First examine the first number and choose it as the smallest number examined so far. Next examine the second number; if it is smaller than the first, choose the second number instead of the first as the smallest so far. Continue examining each successive number, choosing it if it is smaller than the previously chosen smallest number. After examining all the numbers, the smallest of all of them will have been chosen.

   Write a program to find the smallest of a set of numbers by the above process. Initially store the first number in R_1. After that, accept each next number as input, decide whether the new number is smaller than the previous smallest number saved in R_1, and replace the contents of R_1 with the new number if appropriate. At the end, recall the contents from R_1 to display the smallest number.
4. A point (x_0, y_0) is on a line if the coordinates x_0 and y_0 satisfy the equation of the line. For example, the point (7, 32) is on $y = 5x - 3$ since $32 = (5 \cdot 7) - 3$. Write a program to decide whether a point is on the line $y = 5x - 3$ or not. In case the point is on the line, display the number 1, otherwise display 0. These points are on the line: (3, 12), (5, 22), $(-3, -18)$. These points are not on the line: $(-2, 5)$, (6, 20), $(-2, 3)$.
5. Write a program to decide whether a number is between 14.5 and 25.5 or not. If it is, display the number. If not, display 0.
6. The United Parcel Service has a maximum package size requirement that the length plus girth may not exceed 108 inches. If the length, width, and height of a rectangular box are l, w, and h, the girth, which is the distance around the box, is $(2w + 2h)$. (See Figure 7–4.) Write a program to accept input values for l, w, and h (in inches), calculate the length plus girth, and compare it with 108. If the size of a package is too large, display 0; if its size is acceptable, display 1. To check your program, for $l = 20$, $w = 14$, and $h = 20$, a one should appear in the display; and for $l = 30$, $w = 14$, and $h = 30$, a zero should appear in the display. (Hint: Deciding whether $l + 2w + 2h > 108$ is equivalent to deciding whether 108 is not $\geqslant l + 2w + 2h$.)

Figure 7–4

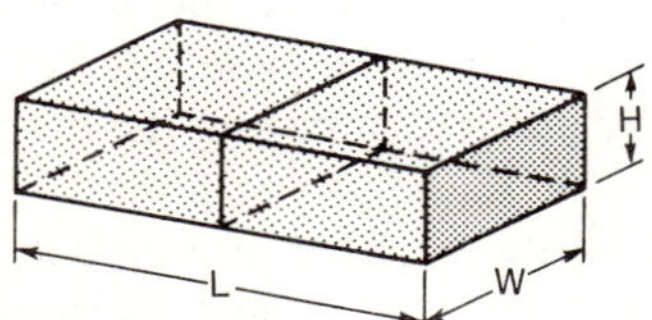

7. Not only does United Parcel Service have a maximum size for packages, they also have a maximum weight of 50 pounds. Write a program to accept input values for length, width, and weight, and decide whether the package can or cannot be sent by U.P.S.
8. A quadratic equation $ax^2 + bx + c = 0$ has the roots

$$x_1, x_2 = \frac{-b \pm \sqrt{d}}{2a}$$

where $d = b^2 - 4ac$. When $d \geqslant 0$, the roots are real and are

$$x_1 = \frac{-b + \sqrt{d}}{2a}, \qquad \frac{-b - \sqrt{d}}{2a}.$$

When $d < 0$, the roots are complex and are

$$x_1 = u + vi, \quad x_2 = u - vi \qquad \text{where } i = \sqrt{-1}$$

and $u = -b/2a, \quad v = \sqrt{-d}\,/2a.$

Write a program to allow for the input numbers a, b, and c; then compute d and test for real or complex roots. If the roots are real, display x_1 and x_2; and if the roots are complex, display u and v.

Test your program with

i. for $x^2 - 2x - 8 = 0, \quad d = 36; \quad x_1, x_2 = 4, -2$
ii. for $9x^2 - 3x - 2 = 0, \quad d = 81; \quad x_1, x_2 = +2/3, -1/3$
iii. for $x^2 + 2x + 3 = 0, \quad d = 8; \quad x_1, x_2 = -1 \pm \sqrt{2}\,i$

Section 5: Making Decisions Involving Whole Numbers

As you have seen, the four comparison tests [2nd] [$x = t$], [2nd] [$x \geqslant t$], [INV] [2nd] [$x = t$], and [INV] [2nd] [$x \geqslant t$] can be used to make decisions in a program. Often it is obvious which comparison test will make a particular decision. Sometimes, however, it is not obvious. This usually happens when the corresponding comparison test for a decision requires some special knowledge about your calculator, mathematics, or both. Consider, for instance, how you would test to see whether a number is a whole number.

Every number has an integer part and a fractional part. For example, 3.157 has an integer part of 3 and a fractional part of .157, while 7 has an integer part of 7 and a fractional part of 0. Notice that a number is a whole number when its fractional part is 0 or when it is the same as its integer part. Using the [2nd] [Int] and [INV] [2nd] [Int] instructions on your calculator, you can find the integer and fractional parts of a number, respectively. Therefore, you can test to see whether a number is a whole number by either comparing its integer part to itself or its fractional part to zero.

Determining whether a number is or is not whole can be useful in making a variety of other decisions. For example, deciding whether a number, n, is divisible by four (or d) can be accomplished by testing whether the quotient $n/4$ (or n/d) is a whole number or not. Similarly, deciding whether a number is a perfect square (or a perfect kth power) can be accomplished by testing whether the square root (or kth root) is a whole number or not.

For your interest, here are two programs illustrating the ideas just presented. The first decides whether a number, n, is divisible by four, by comparing the fractional part of the quotient $n/4$ to zero. The second program decides whether a number is a perfect square by taking the square root of the number and then comparing the square root to its integer part.

Program 1

This program generates the sequence of counting numbers 1, 2, 3, 4, . . . , pauses to show those terms that are not divisible by 4, and stops to display those terms that are. (See Figure 7–5.)

Figure 7–5

Flow Chart	Program
Place 0 in t-register	00 CLR 01 $x \gtrless t$
Compute the next integer, n, and store in R_1	02 2nd Lbl 1 03 + 04 1 05 = 06 STO 1
Divide n by 4	07 ÷ 08 4 09 =
Keep fractional part of $\frac{n}{4}$ dropping the integer part	10 INV 2nd Int
Is n evenly divisible by r i.e., is $\frac{n}{4}$ a whole number?	11 2nd $x = t$ 12 GTO 2
If yes / If no	
Recall n and pause	13 RCL 1 14 2nd Pause

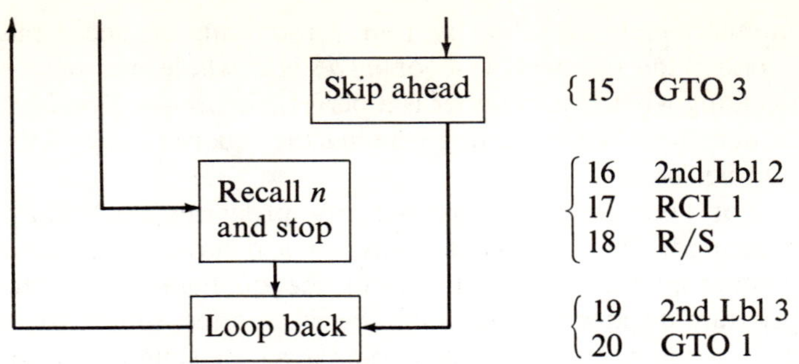

Memory usage: $R_1 = n$, $R_7 = t$-register $= 0$
Initialize: [RST] [CLR] [R/S]

Comment: When the calculator stops to display an integer evenly divisible by 4, press [R/S] to restart the program.

Program 2

The program in Figure 7–6 generates the sequence of counting numbers 1, 2, 3, 4, . . . , pauses to show those terms that are not perfect squares, and stops to display those terms that are.

Figure 7–6

Flow Chart	Program
Compute the next integer n, and store in R_1	00 + 01 1 02 = 03 STO 1
Compute $\sqrt{n}$ and store in R_2	04 $\sqrt{x}$ 05 STO 2
Keep integer part of $\sqrt{n}$ dropping fractional part	06 2nd Int
Place integer part in t-register	07 $x \gtrless t$
Bring $\sqrt{n}$ into x-register	08 RCL 2

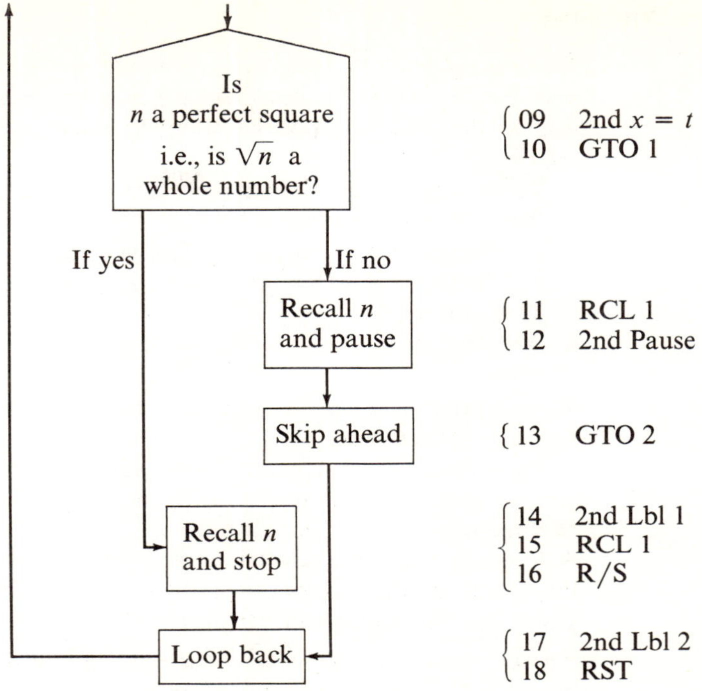

Memory usage: $R_1 = n$, $R_2 = \sqrt{n}$, $R_7 = t$-register = integer part of $\sqrt{n}$
Initialize: RST CLR R/S

Comment: When the calculator stops to display an integer that is a perfect square, press R/S to restart the program.

When testing to see whether a number is a whole number, you may sometimes obtain unexpected results, due to the way in which your calculator is engineered to make various computations. For example, if you compute the cube root of 125, in spite of the fact that the display shows 5., the actual value computed internally by the calculator differs from 5. in the tenth or eleventh decimal places. (See the owner's manual of your calculator for details.) So, in a program that tests whether the cube root of 125 is a whole number, the calculator will conclude that it is not whole! If your calculator computes a value involving only + − × ÷ or x^2 you need not worry about obtaining unexpected results of this type. However, you should expect them with other functions, especially with y^x and INV y^x.

For your interest, a sequence of three key strokes avoids this difficulty. The sequence EE INV EE changes the (internally stored) value of the number in the x-register to the value that the display shows. Include this sequence in a program after computing a value and before performing any test.

Section 6: Problems

1. Write a program to accept any year between 1901 and 2099 as input and decide whether or not that year is a leap year. If it is a leap year, display the year as a positive number; if not, display it as a negative number.
2. a. Write a program to decide whether a positive number is both less than 100 and a perfect cube. If it is, have your calculator display the number, otherwise, display 0. Test your program for 4, 100, and 125 which should give 0 in the display, and then for 27 which should give 27 in the display.
   b. What happens when you test your program for a negative number? Why?
3. Write a program to decide whether a number is between -100 and 100 and is a perfect cube.
4. Write a program to generate the sequence of multiples of three. Have your program pause to display each multiple and stop for each multiple of three that is a perfect square.
5. A Pythagorean triple is a triple of integers (a, b, c) that represent the lengths of the three sides of a right triangle. Necessarily, $c^2 = a^2 + b^2$. Find all Pythagorean triples of the form a, $a + 1$, and $c = \sqrt{a^2 + (a + 1)^2} = \sqrt{2a^2 + 2a + 1}$, where a, $a + 1$, and c are all integers. Have your program begin with $a = 1$, increment a by 1 each time through the loop, and stop to display c when c is integral. Hint: (3, 4, 5) is the first triple of this type. There are four solutions with c less than 1,000. Can you find them all? (See Figure 7–7.)
6. The triangular numbers T_n can be defined recursively $T_n = T_{n-1} + n$ with $T_1 = 1$. For which n is T_n a perfect square? For $n < 2{,}000$, there are exactly 5 solutions. Can you find them all?
7. Many problems of a puzzle nature involve dividing numbers by other numbers and can be solved directly with the use of your calculator. Find the smallest positive whole number having a remainder of 5 when divided by 6 and a remainder of 8 when divided by 11. (Hint: You are looking for a number n so that $n = 6k + 5$ and $n = 11l + 8$. Write a program to let $l = 1, 2, 3, \ldots,$ compute n, solve for k, and test whether k is an integer. Have the program stop at the first instance when k is integral and then display n).

Figure 7–7

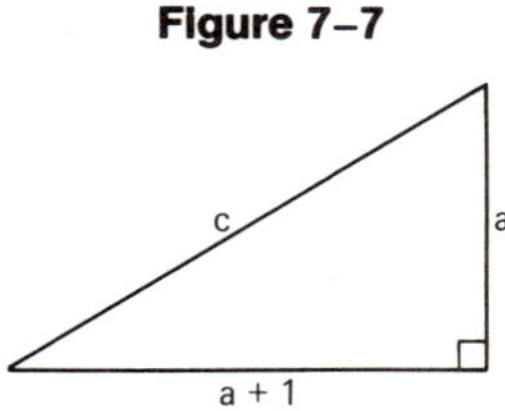

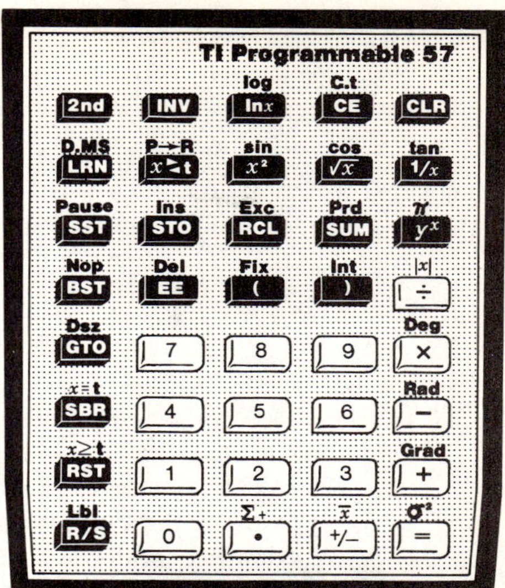

Programming Finite Loops

Section 1: Having Your Calculator End Loops

A square-based pyramid is formed using cannonballs with a single cannonball on top and a square number on each layer as shown in Figure 8–1. How many cannonballs are there in 10 layers? How many layers can be made from 10,000 cannonballs? Rephrased in mathematical language these questions become:

1. How large is

$$\sum_{k=1}^{10} k^2 = 1^2 + 2^2 + 3^2 + \ldots + 10^2?$$

2. What is the largest value of n so that

$$\sum_{k=1}^{n} k^2 = 1^2 + 2^2 + \ldots + n^2 \leqslant 10{,}000?$$

Figure 8–1

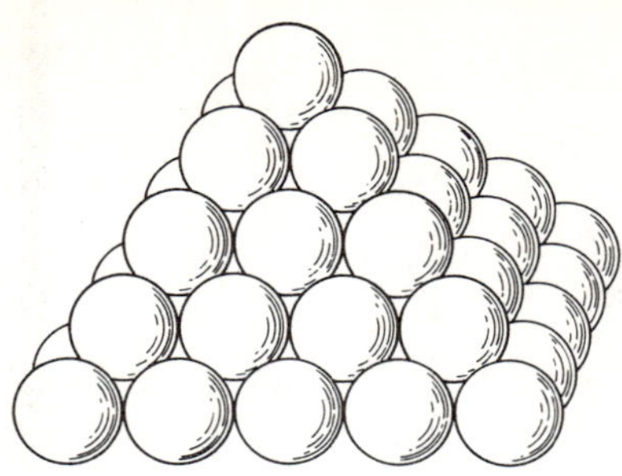

You could answer each of these questions by setting up an infinite loop to calculate $1^2 + 2^2 + 3^2 + \ldots$ as a running total. During each loop the calculator computes the next integer k, adds k^2 to the running total, and displays the current running total. Then you can answer question 1 by counting the loops and stopping the calculator after the 10th loop. Similarly, you can answer the second question by counting the loops and stopping the calculator just as the total goes over 10,000. (In this case you will have counted one loop too many, that is, $n + 1$ loops, so you must subtract one from the number of loops counted to get n, the answer.)

Nonetheless, your calculator can do the watching, counting, and the decision-making for you. By including within the loop a comparison test to check whether it is time to end the loop, you can convert an infinite loop into a finite one.

For the first cannonball question, have the program loop to compute the running total $1^2 + 2^2 + 3^2 + \ldots$. Include in the loop a comparison test to decide when the number of times through the loop has reached 10. At that time, have the program stop to display the current running total, the answer to the first question. You will find a flow chart and program to do the Cannonball Problem in the next section.

For the second question, use the same type of loop as in the previous program. Include in this loop a comparison test to determine when the running total becomes at least 10,000. At this time the number of completed loops minus 1 answers the question.

All loops you program are infinite loops unless you include in the loop a comparison test to decide when to terminate it. Sections 2 and 3 of this chapter present examples and problems for which the terminating condition is simply, "Has the number of completed loops reached a predetermined number yet?" Sections 4 and 5 go on to present examples and problems of other conditions for terminating a loop.

Section 2: Calculating Finite Sums or Products

How can you set up a finite loop to calculate a finite sum, such as $1^2 + 2^2 + 3^2 + \ldots + n^2$, or a finite product like $n! = (n)(n - 1)(n - 2) \ldots (2)(1)$?

Example 1: The Cannonball Problem

As mentioned in the previous section, the calculation of the sum $1^2 + 2^2 + 3^2 + \ldots + 10^2$ in the Cannonball Problem can be set up as a loop designed to compute a running total. To make the loop finite, include within the loop a comparison test to see whether the loop has been processed 10 times yet or not. How would you set up a finite loop to compute $1^2 + 2^2 + 3^2 + \ldots + n^2$ where n may be different each time you run the program, but will be known at the start of the program each time you run it? You may want to try to program this on your own before reading further.

Figure 8–2 contains a flow chart and corresponding program to enter the value of n and then compute $1^2 + 2^2 + 3^2 + \ldots + n^2$ for the Cannonball Problem. Run this program for $n = 10$ to verify that the number of cannonballs in 10 layers is 385. Then modify your program to show that for $n = 30$, the number of cannonballs is just less than 10,000.

Figure 8–2

Flow Chart	Program
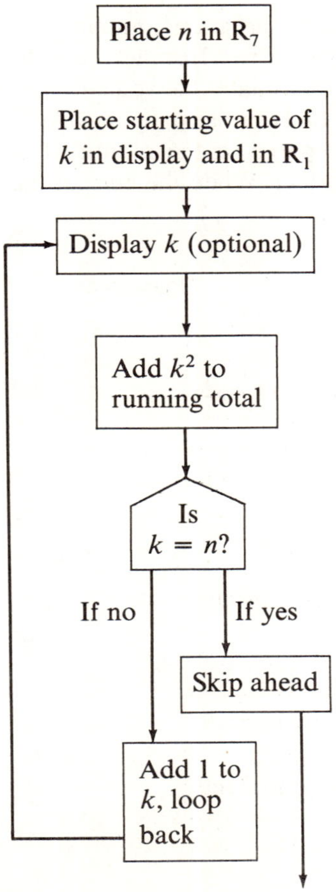 Place n in R_7	00 STO 7
Place starting value of k in display and in R_1	01 1 02 STO 1
Display k (optional)	03 2nd Lbl 1 04 2nd Pause
Add k^2 to running total	05 x^2 06 SUM 2 07 RCL 2 08 2nd Pause 09 RCL 1
Is $k = n$? (If no → Add 1 to k, loop back; If yes → Skip ahead)	10 2nd $x = t$
Skip ahead	11 GTO 2
Add 1 to k, loop back	12 1 13 SUM 1 14 RCL 1 15 GTO 1

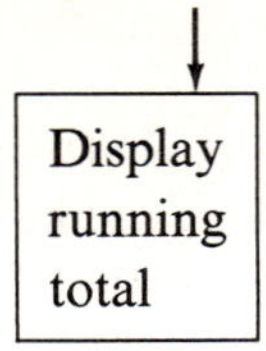

Flow chart	Program
Display running total	16 2nd Lbl 2 17 RCL 2 18 R/S

Memory usage: $R_1 = k$ $R_2 =$ sum $R_7 = n = t$-register
Initialization: [INV] [2nd] [C.t] [RST] enter n [R/S]

Comments:

1. Notice the pauses in steps 04 and 08 which show k and the running total as the program proceeds. If either of these pauses are not desired, delete step 04 or delete steps 07 and 08.
2. For $n = 10$, there are 385 cannonballs.
3. For $n = 30$ the number of cannonballs is $< 10{,}000$ and for $n = 31$ the number is $> 10{,}000$.

Example 2: Computing n!

This next flow chart and program compute $n!$ from an entered value of n. The computation is performed from left to right according to $n! = (n)(n - 1)(n - 2) \ldots (3)(2)(1)$. Initially the value of n is used as the current factor, and the current factor is reduced by 1 each time through the loop. The current factor is compared to the number 1 after multiplying the factor onto the running product. When the current factor becomes 1 the product is complete.

Figure 8–3

Flow Chart	Program
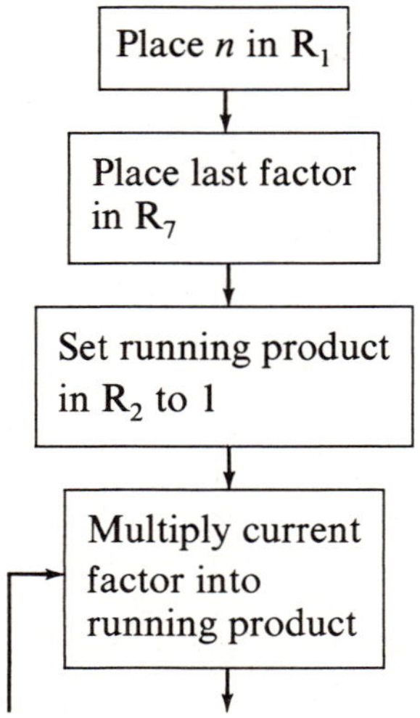 Place n in R_1	00 STO 1
Place last factor in R_7	01 1 02 STO 7
Set running product in R_2 to 1	03 1 04 STO 2
Multiply current factor into running product	05 2nd Lbl 1 06 RCL 1 07 2nd Prd 2

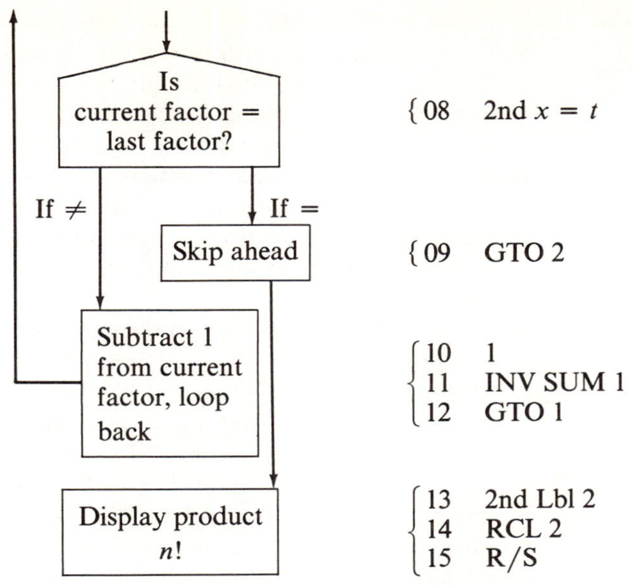

Memory usage: R_7 = end factor = 1, $R_1 = n$, R_2 = running product

Initialize: INV 2nd C.t RST enter n R/S

Comments: Here are 11 steps of another program using the same initialization which calculate $n!$

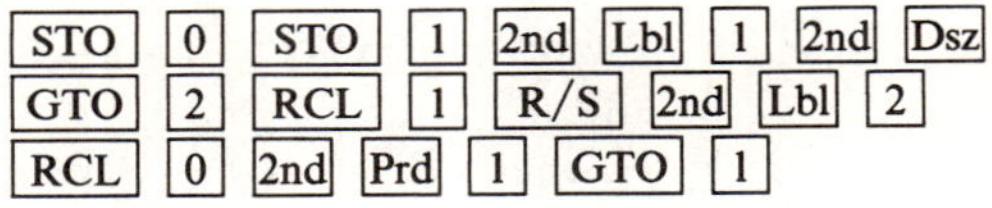

Notice the use of your calculator's 2nd Dsz features which automatically decrements R_0 by one each time through the loop.

Section 3: Problems

1. How many cannonballs are there in a triangular-based pyramid with 1 cannonball on the top, 3 on the second layer, 6 on the third layer, $k(k+1)/2$ balls on the kth layer, and n layers all together? When $n = 1, 2, 3, 4$, the correct numbers are 1, $1 + 3 = 4$, $1 + 3 + 6 = 10$, and $1 + 3 + 6 + 10 = 20$. How many cannonballs are there in 10 layers? In 20 layers? In 50 layers?
2. Find

$$\sum_{k=1}^{n} [3k(k-1)+1]$$

for values of n equal to 2, 3, 4, and 5. Do you recognize the sequence that is generated?

3. The Fibonacci numbers are the numbers in the sequence $f(0) = 0$, $f(1) = 1$, $f(2) = f(1) + f(0) = 1 + 0 = 1$, and $f(k) = f(k-1) + f(k-2)$ for all $k > 1$. Write a program to compute a running total of Fibonacci numbers, display each number as it is calculated, and then display the sum of the first ten Fibonacci numbers.
4. Permutations are finite products. Specifically, $P_y^n = n(n-1)(n-2) \ldots (n-y+1)$. The permutation P_y^n is similar to $n!$ but differs in the fact that the last factor is $(n-y+1)$ instead of 1.
   a. Write a program to allow inputs of y and n and then compute the permutation P_y^n.
   b. How many ways could you choose a committee of a president, vice-president, secretary, and treasurer from a group of 10 people? This number is symbolized by P_4^{10}. What is its value?
   c. How many ways could 5 out of a group of 12 people seat themselves in five chairs placed in a row? In other words, what is P_5^{12}?
5. When y objects are chosen from a collection of n objects, but the order of choosing the objects is irrelevant, the number of choices is called the number of combinations of y chosen from n, symbolized by C_y^n—specifically, $C_y^n = P_y^n / y!$ But the computation can be more efficiently performed as a product of fractions:

$$C_y^n = \frac{n}{y} \cdot \frac{n-1}{y-1} \cdot \frac{n-2}{y-2} \cdots \frac{n-y+2}{2} \cdot \frac{n-y+1}{1}$$

   a. Program your calculator to compute C_y^n with given input values of y and n.
   b. How many ways can you choose 4 people out of 10 when order is unimportant?
   c. If you have a collection of 10 different coins, how many different subcollections of 6 coins could you choose?
6. The efficient formula for calculating a value of e, the base of the natural logarithms is:

$$e = 1 + \frac{1}{1!} + \frac{1}{2!} + \frac{1}{3!} + \frac{1}{4!} + \cdots .$$

   Find the sum of the first 20 terms of this series.

Section 4: Ending a Loop When a Condition is Met

With the use of the comparison tests, you can set up a program loop that ends when any of a number of different types of conditions is met. An exhaustive list of such conditions is impractical since they depend upon the context of an individual problem and on the particular approach you use to solve the problem. Instead, two characteristic examples are given in this section.

Example 1: Finding the Maximum of a Finite Number of Possibilities—the Volume of the Box Problem

If a piece of paper 22 cm. by 28 cm. is marked off into centimeter squares, has an x-cm. square cut off each corner, and is then folded into an open box (see Figure 8–4), what value of x yields the box with the maximum volume?

Figure 8–4

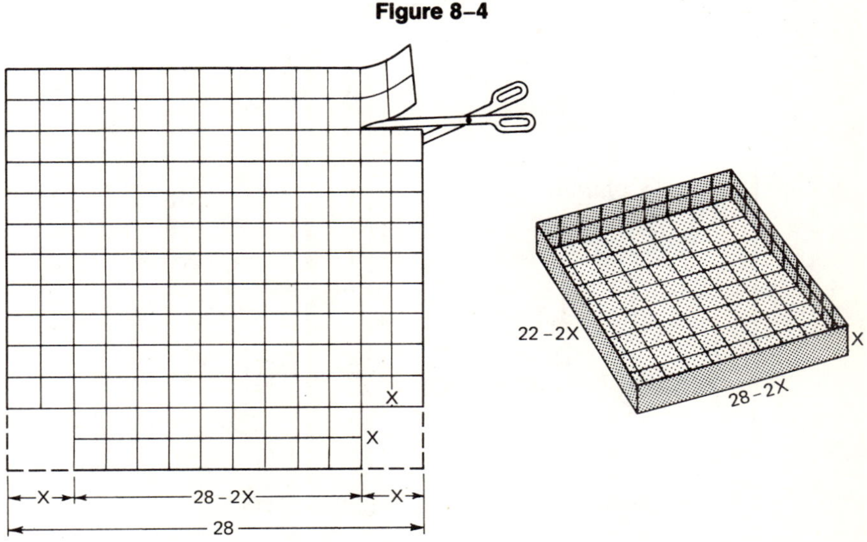

The volume is given by $V(x) = (22 - 2x)(28 - 2x)(x)$, and x may take on the (whole) values 1, 2, . . . , 10. Notice that if $x = 11$, the box has no width since 11 is half of 22. Consequently, x cannot exceed 10.

A program to find the x value corresponding to the maximum volume can test each possible value of x, saving x if $V(x)$ is larger than the volume for any previous x value. The looping in the program ends when all values of x have been tested. Therefore, this program is similar to those described in sections 2 and 3 in the sense that the program stops after the loop has been processed a predetermined number of times (ten in this case). Figure 8–5 (page 104) contains a flow chart and program to solve this problem.

Example 2: Finding a First Value When a Condition is Met—the Stacking Problem

Suppose you have a large collection of n congruent unit length objects, such as bricks, books, or cards. If you stack them so that the one on top extends as far to the right of the bottom one as possible (see Figure 8–6, page 105), can the top one overhang more than one unit length to the right? If so, how many objects are necessary to achieve this condition?

Figure 8–5

Flow Chart | Program

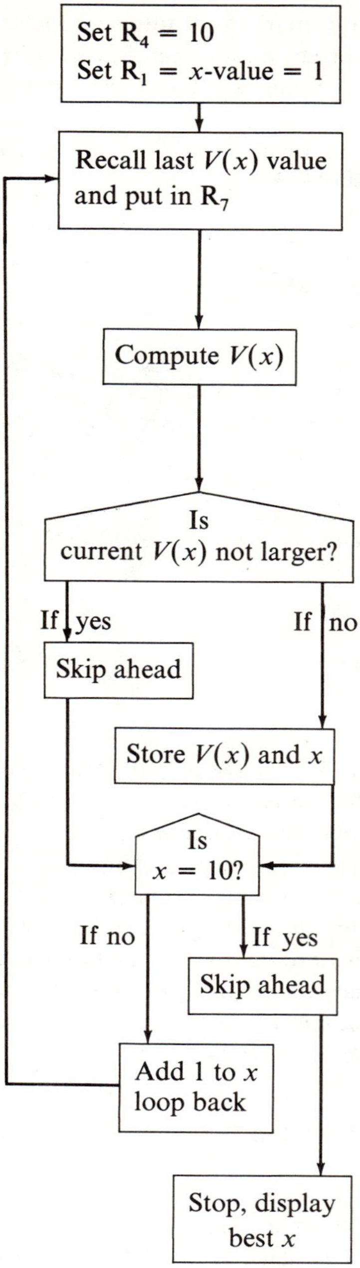

Flow Chart	Program
Set R_4 = 10 Set R_1 = x-value = 1	00 1 02 STO 4 04 STO 1 01 0 03 1
Recall last $V(x)$ value and put in R_7	05 2nd Lbl 1 06 RCL 2 07 STO 7
Compute $V(x)$	08 (15) 22 × 09 2 16 × 23 RCL 1 10 2 17 (24) 11 – 18 2 25 × 12 2 19 8 26 RCL 1 13 × 20 – 27 = 14 RCL 1 21 2
Is current $V(x)$ not larger?	28 INV 2nd $x \geqslant t$
If yes: Skip ahead	29 GTO 2
If no: Store $V(x)$ and x	30 STO 2 31 RCL 1 32 STO 3
Is x = 10?	33 2nd Lbl 2 35 STO 7 37 2nd $x = t$ 34 RCL 4 36 RCL 1
If yes: Skip ahead	38 GTO 3
If no: Add 1 to x loop back	39 1 40 SUM 1 41 GTO 1
Stop, display best x	42 2nd Lbl 3 43 RCL 3 44 R/S

Memory usage: R_7 = t-reg., R_4 = 10, R_1 = x, R_2 = best $V(x)$, R_3 = best x

Initialize: [INV] [2nd] [C.t] [RST] [R/S].

Comments:

1. The best x is $x = 4$. To see the best $V(x)$ press [RCL] [2].
2. If you use R_6 to store 10 instead of R_4, this program fails because during the calculation of $V(x)$, R_6 is used for temporary storage of intermediate calculation values. When there are more than 3 pending operations, your calculator may change the values in R_5 and R_6.

Considering physics, the maximum overhang length occurs if the center of mass of the top object is balanced over the right edge of the next object down. If the center of mass is to the right of that point, the object will fall; if the center of mass is to the left, the overhang is not maximal. Similarly, the center of mass of the top two objects needs to balance on top of the right edge of the third. In general, the center of mass of the top $n - 1$ objects needs to balance on top of the right edge of the nth object. This describes a way to actually build such a stack from the top down and mathematically leads to the overhang length of

$$\sum_{k=1}^{n} \frac{1}{2k}$$

for n objects stacked for the maximal overhang length.

Now the mathematical question becomes: For what first value of n (if any) does

$$\sum_{k=1}^{n} \frac{1}{2k} > 1?$$

A flow chart and program for the stacking problem are found in Figure 8–7 (page 106). The program loops for each consecutive value of k, starting at $k = 1$, computes $\frac{1}{2k}$ and adds $\frac{1}{2k}$ to a running total. The looping ends when the running total first exceeds the value 1. Then, the current value of k, representing the desired number of objects, is displayed.

Figure 8–6

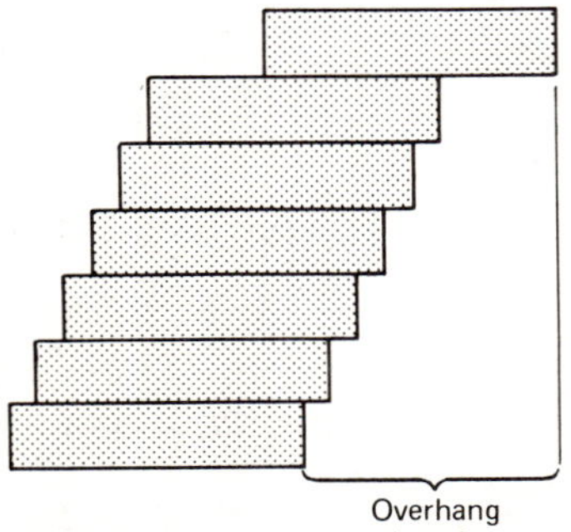

Overhang length

Figure 8–7

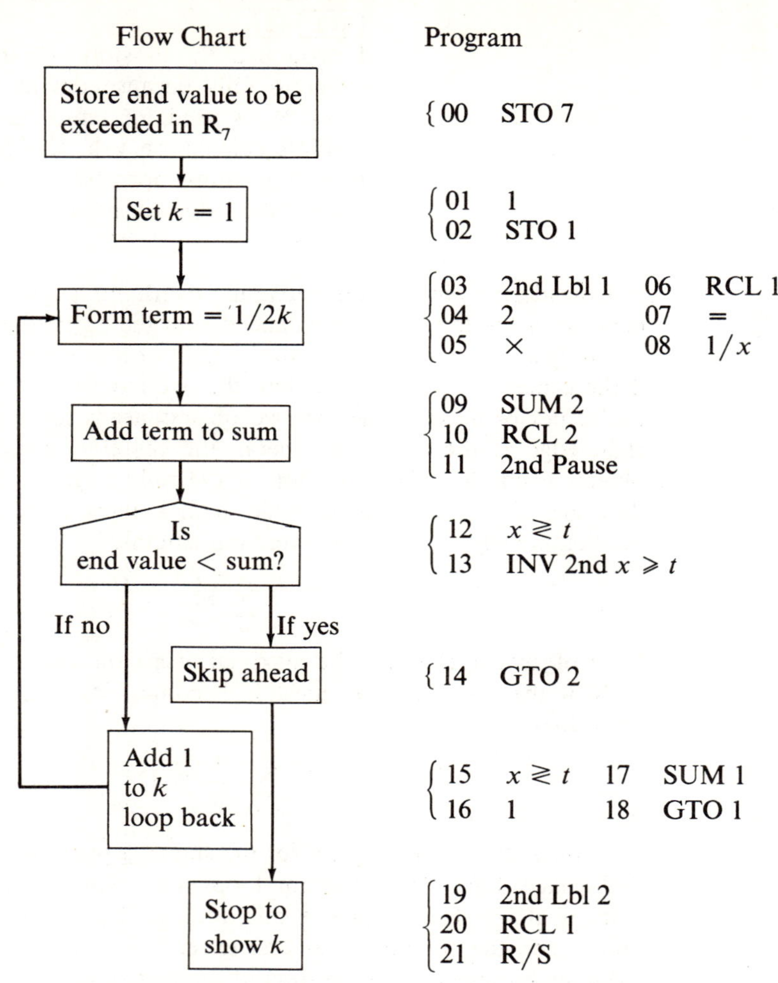

Memory usage: R_7 = end value to be exceeded, $R_1 = k$, R_2 = sum

Initialization: [INV] [2nd] [C.t] [RST] enter 1 [R/S]

Comment: This program gives an n of 4. To find n for a sum greater than 2, use the initialization [INV] [2nd] [C.t] [RST] enter 2 [R/S] to obtain 31.

According to this program only 4 objects are necessary so that

$$\sum_{k=1}^{n} \frac{1}{2k} > 1.$$

It is possible to find an n so that

$$\sum_{k=1}^{n} \frac{1}{2k} > 2.$$

Change the initialization in the program to [INV] [2nd] [C.t] [RST] [CLR] enter 2 [R/S] and see if you obtain 31.

Section 5: More Problems

1. Write a program to generate the values $\sqrt[1]{1}$, $\sqrt[2]{2}$, $\sqrt[3]{3}$, $\sqrt[4]{4}$, . . . , $\sqrt[30]{30}$, that is, the values $\sqrt[n]{n}$ for n going from 1 to 30. Have your program find and display the maximum of these values.
2. a. Write a program to compute the fourth root of n = 1, 2, 3, 4, . . . , and to stop and display the first one exceeding π.
   b. How would you change the program to allow for any number rather than just π to be used for the test value?
3. Suppose you paint k faces of a cube red and the other $6 - k$ faces blue. Then, when the paint has dried, you toss the cube three times hoping to obtain red on the top face twice and blue once in any order. How many faces should you paint red and how many blue so that what you wish to obtain has the maximum possible probability? (Hint: k = 0, 1, 2, 3, 4, 5, or 6.)
4. What is the largest number of levels you can build in a square-based pyramid made from 10,000 cannonballs? (See Section 1 if you need to.)
5. At a local school benefit dance, students paid $4 a couple and others paid $5 a couple to attend. In total, $77 was collected. Phrased mathematically, this last sentence becomes: for positive integers x and y, $4x + 5y = 77$.
   a. Find all four integer pairs (x, y) that solve the equation $4x + 5y = 77$.
   b. If the number of students and the number of other people who came to the dance were as close together as possible, how many of each came?
6. Jack's beanstalk was most unusual. Someone said that on the first day it grew to a short height and then grew according to the following pattern. On the second day it increased its height by $\frac{1}{2}$, on the third day by $\frac{1}{3}$, and on the fourth day by $\frac{1}{4}$, and so on. How long did it take for Jack's beanstalk to reach 100 times its height on the first day? (Caution: The answer is *not* given by the first n for which $\Sigma_{k=1}^{n} 1/n \geqslant 100$.)
7. At a special fund-raising banquet, 100 senators, congresspersons, and lobbyests showed up. Senators paid $75 each; congresspersons paid $99; and lobbyests, $40 each. If $7,869 was collected, how many of each came to the banquet? Hint: If S, C, and L represent the respective numbers of senators, congresspersons, and lobbyests, then

$$S + C + L = 100 \text{ people}$$

$$\$75S + \$99C + \$40L = \$7{,}869$$

Since there are at most 100 senators from 50 states, set up a loop with S as an index, letting S go from 1 to 100. By solving the two equations algebraically for C and L, you obtain

$$C = \frac{(3{,}869 - 35S)}{59}$$

$$S = \frac{(2{,}031 - 24S)}{59}$$

In the program, compute C and L from these formulas and test to see whether each is an integer. Stop to display any integer triple solution for S, C, and L.

EVALUATING FUNCTIONS–
HP 33E

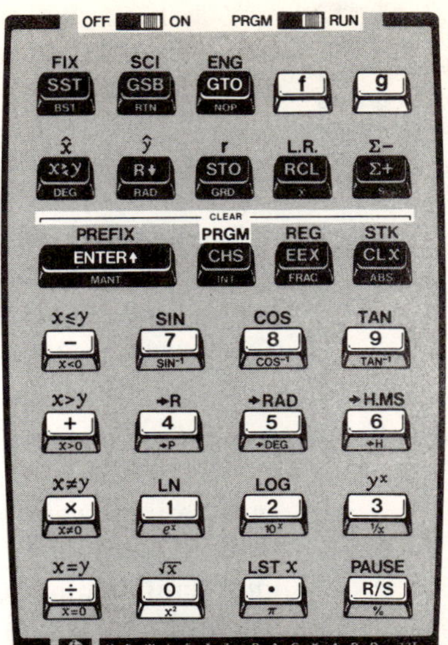

9

Writing Your First Programs to Compute Answers

Section 1: Calculating $2(n+1)^2$ in the Run Mode

Turn your calculator on and make sure that the PRGM-RUN switch (located to the right of the ON-OFF switch) is set to RUN. Press this sequence of key strokes:

Step	*Key Stroke(s)*	*Display Shows*
00	4	4.
01	↑	4.0000
02	1	1.
03	+	5.0000
04	g x^2	25.0000
05	2	2.
06	×	50.0000

You have just computed the value of $2(4 + 1)^2$ on your calculator. Using a similar sequence of key strokes, compute the value of $2(9 + 1)^2$ to obtain 200.

You have been using your calculator in what is called the *run mode*. In this mode the calculator's primary purpose is to perform basic arithmetic operations.

Suppose you want to compute $2(7 + 1)^2$, $2(11 + 1)^2$, $2(16 + 1)^2$, and $2(25 + 1)^2$. You can do so in the run mode by using a sequence of key strokes almost identical to that described in steps 00 to 06. The only difference for each computation is the first number entered.

Section 2: Programming $2(n + 1)^2$ in the Learn or Program Mode

In situations when you find it necessary to use a particular sequence of key strokes repeatedly, you can avoid a great deal of work by using an important feature of your calculator called the *program mode*. In this mode, the calculator is able to "memorize" sequences of key strokes, called a program. This program can then be executed (or run) in the run mode of the calculator. You switch your calculator from one mode to the other with the PRGM-RUN switch.

In Section 1 you considered the computation of $2(n + 1)^2$ where n could be any number. Using this computation, you will now program your calculator to memorize the appropriate sequence of key strokes to perform the calculation.

First, turn your calculator off, then on. Now switch the calculator to the program mode. You should see "00" in the display.[1] Now press this sequence of key strokes:

STEPS	KEY STROKE(S)	DISPLAY SHOWS
01	↑	01- 31
02	1	02- 1
03	+	03- 51
04	g x^2	04- 15 0
05	2	05- 2
06	×	06- 61

Now switch the calculator back to the run mode where the program can be executed. To initialize (start) the program, press f PRGM. Then enter any value for n, say 3, and press R/S. The quantity "32.0000" should appear in the display. To run the program to compute $2(n + 1)^2$ for other values of n, merely enter the desired value of n and press R/S each time. Doing so for $n = 7$, 11, 16, and 25, the display should show "128.0000, 288.0000, 578.0000, and 1352.0000," respectively.

[1]When the calculator is memorizing a key stroke, you see a different display from when the calculator is performing the instruction represented by the key stroke. See your owner's manual for details.

Actually, your calculator is executing more for the program than just the six steps you entered. There is a step preceeding step 01, called step 00, that always contains the [R/S] key stroke. Every one of the program steps after those you entered contain the key sequence instruction [GTO] [00], an instruction that sends the calculator back to step 00 of the program. That means that your program is really as follows:

STEP	PROGRAM
00	(R/S)
01	↑
02	1
03	+
04	$g \quad x^2$
05	2
06	×
07	GTO 00
08	GTO 00
09	GTO 00

The [R/S] instruction at the beginning of your program allows you to enter a data number, n. Steps 01 through 06 then compute $2(n + 1)^2$. Finally, the [GTO] [00] instruction in step 07 sends your calculator back to step 00 at which time the program halts, displays the result of the calculation $2(n + 1)^2$, and awaits the entry of a new data number.

Remember that your calculator has exactly two modes of operation, the program mode and the run mode. In the program mode the calculator can only memorize a sequence of key strokes. In the run mode the calculator can either perform any key stroke sequence that is pressed or execute a memorized key stroke sequence.

Furthermore, any program always begins with [R/S] in step 00 and, unless otherwise designed, ends with [GTO] [00].

Section 3: Using $2(n + 1)^2$ to Solve a Problem

You may wonder why you would ever want to program your calculator to compute $2(n + 1)^2$. There might be any number of reasons. This particular computation was selected because it happened to provide the "answer" to an interesting question suggested by the American flag.

Have you ever noticed how the 50 stars are arranged on the present-day American flag? There are 4 short rows of 5 stars in each row and 5 longer rows of 6 stars each. (See Figure 9–1.)

Similar patterns of stars can be formed with 8, 16, and 32 stars. See Figures 9–2, 9–3, and 9–4, respectively. Notice that the 8-star pattern uses 1 short row of 2 stars and 2 longer rows of 3 stars; the 18-star pattern uses 2 short rows of 3 stars and 3 longer rows of 4 stars; the 32-star pattern

Figure 9–1

Figure 9–2

Figure 9–3

Figure 9–4

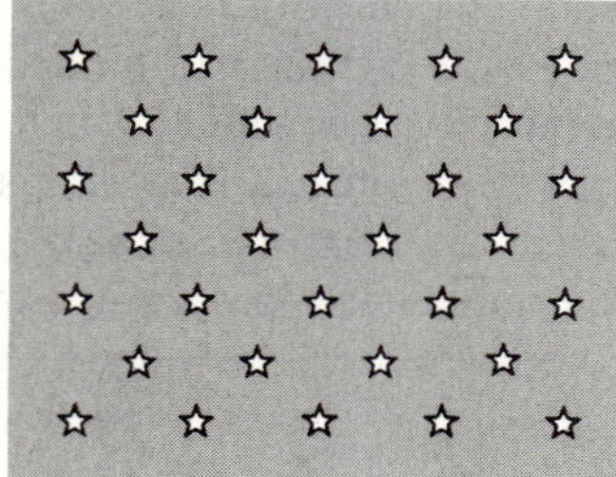

has 3 short rows of 4 stars and 4 longer rows of 5 stars. What other numbers of states would have to be in the United States for this specific type of star pattern to be used on the flag?

There would have to be n short rows of $(n + 1)$ stars and $(n + 1)$ longer rows of $(n + 2)$ stars. So in total there would be $n(n + 1) + (n + 1)(n + 2) = 2(n + 1)^2$ stars. Since each star represents one state, there would have to be $2(n + 1)^2$ states in the United States for the same type of star pattern to be used.

Using the program in Section 2 for computing $2(n + 1)^2$ you can find all the numbers of states for which the stars could be arranged in the same type of pattern as the 50 star-pattern.

Section 4: Exercises in Analyzing the Program for $2(n + 1)^2$

1. In the example in Section 2, the program was [R/S] [↑] enter 1 [+] [g] [x^2] enter 2 [×] [GTO] [00].
   a. What was the purpose of the first [R/S] encountered in the program?
   b. What was the purpose of the up arrow [↑]?
   c. When the [GTO] [00] instruction is encountered, the program is sent back to the first [R/S]. What does the [R/S] instruction do now?
2. Program your calculator to compute $2n^2 + 1$ for any value of n.

Section 5: Making Flow Charts

The program to compute $2(n + 1)^2$ is summarized by the two diagrams in Figure 9–5 called flow charts. One, the *general flow chart*, presents an overview of what the program is designed to do. The other, the *detailed flow chart*, presents step-by-step instructions (based on the general flow chart) for writing the actual program.

Figure 9–5

General Flow Chart	Detailed Flow Chart	Program
Enter n ↓	{put n in x-register	{(R/S)
Add 1 ↓	{lift n to y-register put 1 in x-register add 1 to n	{↑ {1 {+
Square ↓	{square $(n + 1)$	{g x^2
Multiply by 2 ↓	{put 2 in x-register multiply $(n + 1)^2$ by 2	{2 {×
Stop and display	{go to step 00 in order to stop and display	{GTO 00

By comparing the flow charts to the program, you can see that each rectangle in either flow chart corresponds to one or more key strokes in the program. The vertical arrows in the general flow chart indicate the order in which instructions are to be carried out.

Making flow charts can help you organize your thoughts when writing programs. The general flow chart should consist of a few instructions to make it clear at a glance what a program is designed to accomplish. The detailed flow chart should show how to do each instruction in the general flow chart. The detailed flow chart should make writing the actual program easy. You may find it helpful to make one or both of the flow charts before writing a program. As you become better at writing programs, you may find less of a need for the detailed flow chart.

As another example of the use of flow charts, consider writing a program to compute the area of a triangle according to the formula:

$$A = \frac{b \cdot h}{2}$$

where b is the base length and h is the height of the triangle. (See Figure 9–6.)

Figure 9–6

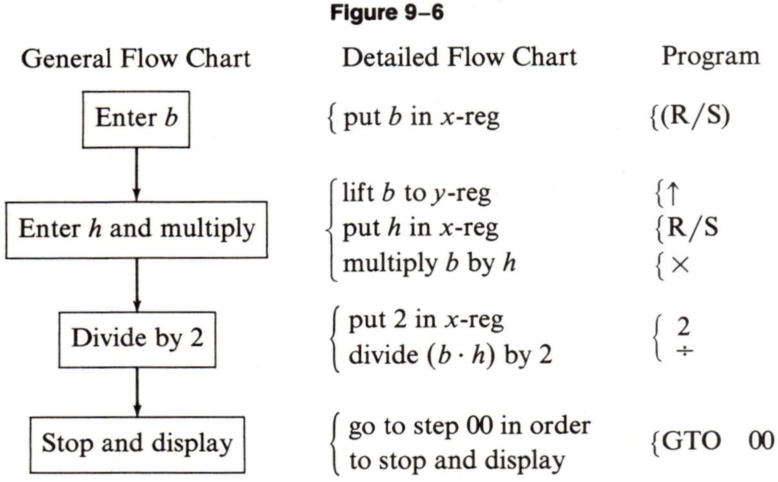

Section 6: Exercises Using Flow Charts When Writing Programs

Here are a few helpful hints that you may need to know in order to proceed with the problems in this section.

Before entering any program, you should clear (or erase) any program previously in the calculator. Clearing can be done in a number of ways. The most obvious way is to turn the calculator off, then back on. However, if your calculator is in the program mode, you can press the key sequence [*f*] [PRGM] and accomplish the same purpose.

If you find that you have entered a step of your program incorrectly, you can correct the error in a variety of ways. For now, you should simply clear your calculator and re-enter the program. Ways to edit a program without erasing it are described in Chapter 11, Section 4.

1. In some states there is a special tax on food served in restaurants. If the tax is 8 percent and the cost of a dinner is $5.00, then $5.40 is the cost of the dinner plus tax. The general flow chart in Figure 9–7 describes a

Figure 9–7

General Flow Chart

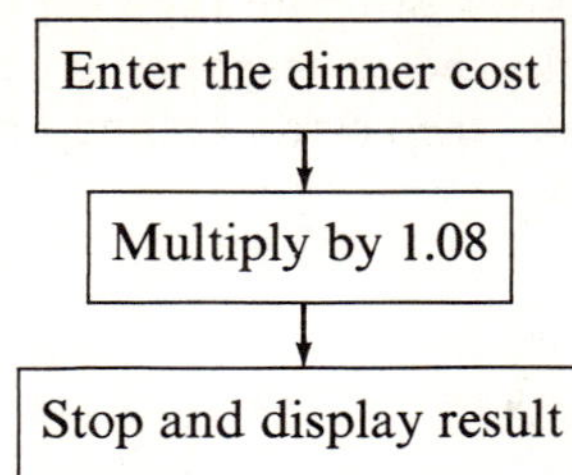

program that computes the total cost of a dinner (including tax) with the formula: Total cost of the dinner = 1.08 · Dinner cost.

a. Make a detailed flow chart for this program.

b. Write the corresponding program from the detailed flow chart.

2. Make a detailed flow chart for a program that will convert measurements in feet to meters according to the formula,

$$\text{Number of meters} = \frac{\text{Number of feet}}{3.28}$$

3. In order to convert temperatures from Fahrenheit, F, to Celsius (centigrade), C, you may use the formula,

$$C = \frac{F - 32}{1.8}.$$

A detailed flow chart for a program to make the conversions is given in Figure 9–8.

a. Complete the corresponding general flow chart in that figure.

b. Write the corresponding program.

Figure 9–8

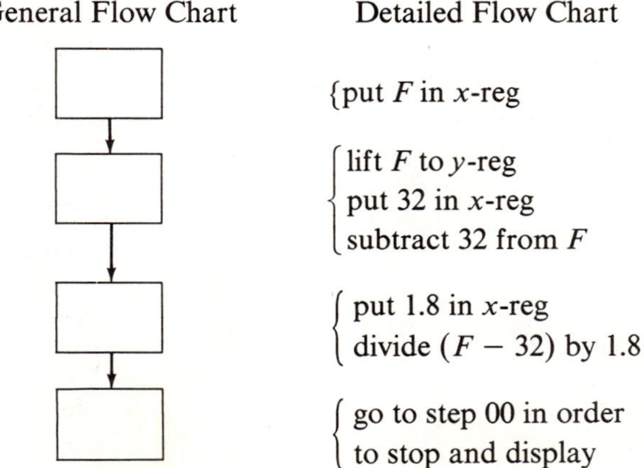

4. The average of two numbers is found by adding the two numbers together and then dividing by two. The general flow chart in Figure 9–9 describes a program for averaging two numbers.
   a. Make the corresponding detailed flow chart.
   b. Write the corresponding program.

Figure 9–9

General Flow Chart

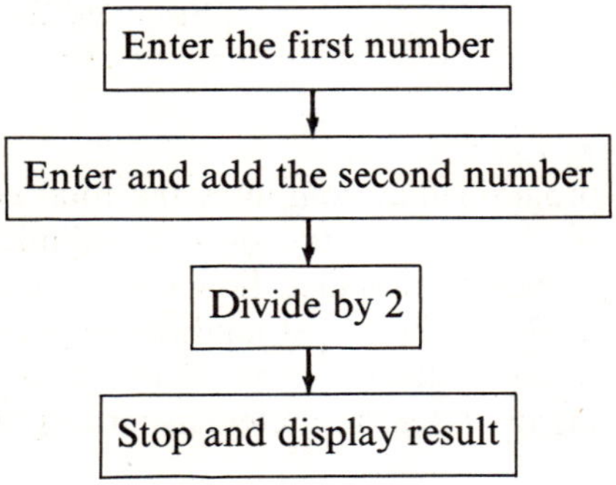

Enter the first number

Enter and add the second number

Divide by 2

Stop and display result

5. You can find the volume of a box (Figure 9–10) by multiplying together the length, width and height of the box. Make flow charts for a program that will calculate the volume of a box. Now write the program.

Figure 9–10

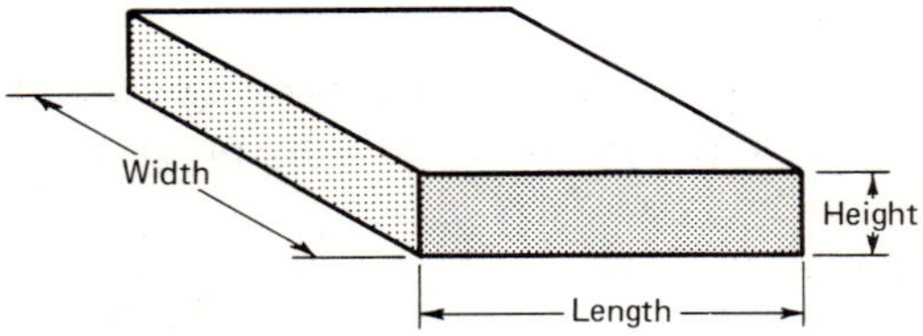

Width

Height

Length

6. Consider the flow chart in Figure 9–11.
   a. Write a program to correspond to the flow chart.
   b. When you run this program, what is always displayed, regardless of the value of *n*?

Figure 9–11

Flow Chart

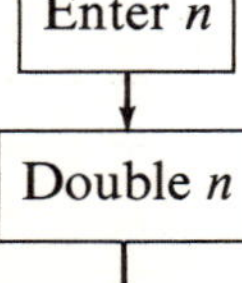

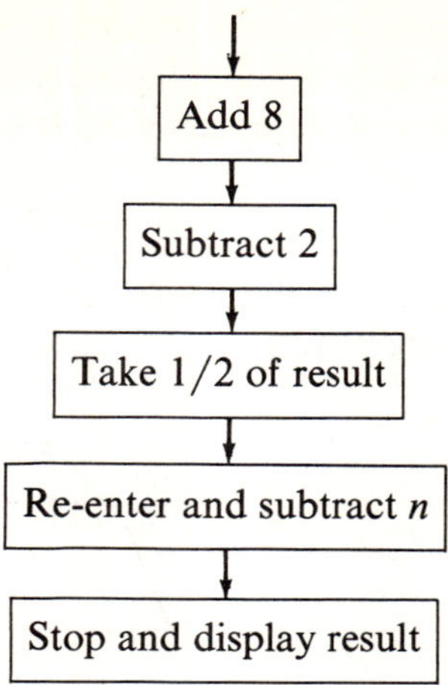

Section 7: Problems

For the following exercises you may find it helpful to use flow charts.

1. Write a program to convert miles to kilometers using the formula,

$$\text{Number of kilometers} = \frac{\text{Number of miles}}{.62}.$$

   How many kilometers is 5 miles, 8 miles, 31 miles, 500 miles, and 3,000 miles?
2. Write a program to compute the weekly salaries of someone who works part-time for $2.85 per hour and works 12 hours, 18 hours, 14 hours, and 22 hours. Use the formula, Salary = Number of hours · Hourly wage.
3. Following two formulas work for converting Celsius to Farenheit temperatures and vice versa:
   a. $C = (F + 40) \cdot \frac{5}{9} - 40$
   b. $F = (C + 40) \cdot \frac{9}{5} - 40$
   Write a program for each conversion.
4. A company is selling cardboard in rectangular sheets at 3¢ a square unit. Write a program to compute the cost of any rectangular sheet using the formula, Cost in dollars = $.03 \cdot (l \cdot w)$, where l and w are the length and width of any rectangle. For $l = 10$ and $w = 8$, the cost is $2.40.
5. A dog owner wants to build a fence around a rectangular piece of land that measures l by w meters. Her choice of fencing costs $5.89 per meter. Write a program to determine the cost of the fencing with the formula, Cost = $5.89 \cdot (2l + 2w)$. For $l = 5$ and $w = 4$, the cost is $106.02.

6. a. Write a program to average 3 numbers, *a*, *b*, and *c*.
   b. How would you adapt this program to average 4 numbers?
7. The area, *A*, of a trapezoid is given by,

$$A = h \cdot \frac{b_1 + b_2}{2},$$

   where *h* is the height and b_1 and b_2 are the two base lengths. (See Figure 9–12.)

Figure 9–12

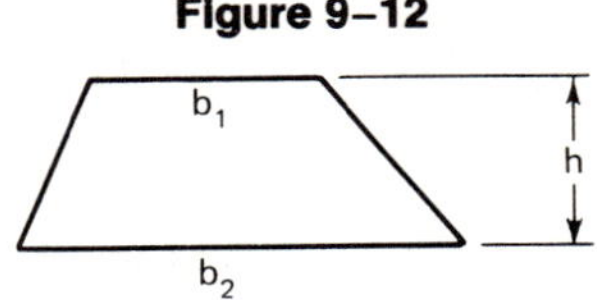

   Write a program for computing the area of a trapezoid. For $b_1 = 8$, $b_2 = 10$, and $h = 3$, $A = 27$.
8. When \$*n* is invested in a bank at 6 percent interest, the value after 1 year will be, \$$n(1 + .06)$.
   a. Write a program to compute this value for any invested number of dollars, *n*.
   b. What will be in the bank at the end of one year if you start with \$100?
   c. Run your program again and find out what will be in the bank at the end of the second year.
   d. What will be in the bank at the end of 5 years if you start with \$100?
9. A rectangle has area, $A = l \cdot w$.
   a. Write a program to compute the width of a rectangle, *w*, with length, *l*, and an area, *A*, 360.
   b. What are the widths of the rectangles when *l* is 5, 8, 10, and 15?
   c. Use your program to find the values of *l* and *w* when the area of the rectangle is 360 and the length is two more than the width.

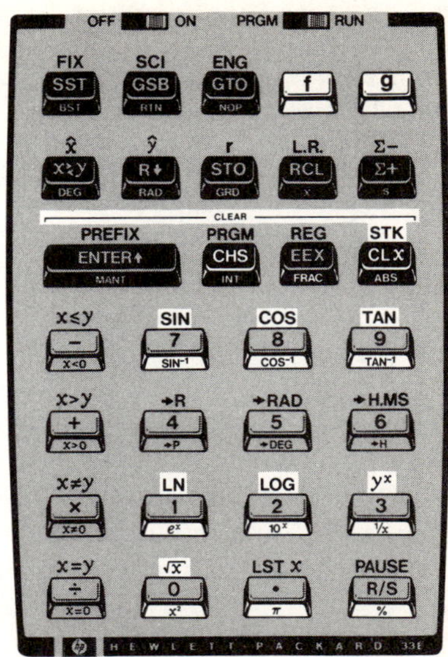

Using Preprogrammed Functions in Writing Programs

Section 1: An Investment Problem Introducing the Function y^x

Pieter Minuit, a Dutch colonist, bought Manhatten Island from the Indians in 1626 for a few trinkets, thought to be worth about $24. If instead, Pieter Minuit had invested $24 in a bank at 5 percent interest per year, what would he have earned after 1 year? After 2 years? By the end of 1638 when he moved to Delaware? Or by 1641 when he died? For that matter, how much would be in his account now assuming nothing had ever been removed?

Clearly, after one year Minuit would have earned $\$24 \times .05 = \$1.20$ interest. Thus, his account would have had a total of $25.20. At the end of the second year he would have earned $\$25.20 \times .05$ in interest. Using your calculator, compute this value and determine the total amount in the bank account. Do the calculations in the run mode.

To answer the rest of the questions, a well known finance formula for computing compound interest is helpful. The formula is $t = p \times (1 + i)^n$, where p is the original amount invested, i is the yearly interest rate expressed as a decimal, and t is the total at the end of n years. Specifically, in the Minuit problem, the total becomes $\$24(1 + .05)^n$ or, simply, $\$24(1.05)^n$.

When Minuit moved to Delaware in 1638, twelve years had passed. So the total in the bank would have been the value of $\$24(1.05)^{12}$ or, \$43.10 to the nearest penny.

The goal here is to develop a program to compute $\$24(1.05)^n$ for any n. Before doing so, you need to know how to compute $\$24(1.05)^n$ for specific values of n. This requires the use of the preprogrammed (built-in) function key on your calculator, identified by the symbol, [y^x].

Turn your calculator on and press the following sequence of keys in the run mode: [1] [·] [0] [5] [↑] [1] [2] [f] [y^x] [2] [4] [×]. Your display should show "43.1006" representing 43.10055182. Rounded to the nearest hundredth, $\$24(1.05)^{12}$ represents \$43.10.

Essentially the same sequence of key strokes can be used to compute $\$24(1.05)^n$ for any value of n. Switch your calculator to the program mode. Press [f] [PRGM] to clear out any old program in your calculator. Then enter steps 01 through 10 of the following program and try it out. You do not need to enter [R/S] in step 00 nor [GTO] [00] in step 11 because those instructions are already in your calculator. The program is shown in Figure 10–1. To test the program, use 20 for n, and "63.6791" should appear in the display.

Figure 10–1

Flow Chart	Step	Program
Start	{00	(R/S)
Enter 1.05	01	1
	02	.
	03	0
	04	5
Calculate $(1.05)^n$	05	↑
	06	R/S
	07	f y^x
Multiply $24(1.05)^n$	08	2
	09	4
	10	×
Loop back to stop and display result	{11	GTO 00

Initialize: (switch back to run mode), [f] [PRGM] [CLX] [R/S] enter n [R/S]

Notice that step 06 is the key stroke [R/S], which stops the program so you can enter the value of n. Steps 00 and 11 are already in the calculator for the purpose of stopping the program to display the result of the computation $24(1.05)^n$.

Using this program you can answer each of the questions raised at the beginning of the section concerning the \$24 investment since each of the questions is answered by essentially the same keystroke sequence. Running the program is easier than entering the key stroke sequence over and over again. Furthermore, the program is easily adaptable for solving similar investment problems requiring the formula $p \times (1 + i)^n$.

Section 2: Exercises Relating to the Investment Problem

1. Enter the program shown in Figure 10–1 of the previous section and check to see if the totals in the bank after one year and after twelve years agree with information in the section. Such checking is a good technique to insure that you have entered a program correctly.
2. How much money would have been in the bank when Minuit died at the end of 1641, fifteen years after he bought the island?
3. How much money would have been there at the end of 1664 ($n = 38$) when Peter Stuyvesant surrendered Manhattan to the British?
4. How much would be in the bank after 300 years?
5. Write a program to compute the value of \$100 invested at 6 percent for any number of years, n.

Section 3: Single and Double Variable Preprogrammed Functions

Your calculator comes equipped with many preprogrammed functions, most of which are accessed with one or two key punches. You have already used some of these functions, such as [g] [x^2] [f] [y^x] [+] [×] and the like. These functions can be classified into two types—single variable functions and double variable functions. There is an important difference in how your calculator uses each type of function.

All single variable functions are computed immediately with the quantity in the x-register, that is, the quantity in the display. While all double variable functions are also computed immediately, they operate on two quantities, one in the x-register and the other in the y-register.

TABLE 10–1 Single Variable Functions

Key Stroke(s)	*Description of the Function*
[CHS]	changes the sign of value in display
[g] [ABS]	computes the absolute value of quantity in display
[g] [1/x]	computes the reciprocal of x (in display)
[g] [π]	inserts $\pi = 3.141592654$ in display

TABLE 10–1 (Continued)

Key Stroke(s)	*Description of the Function*
[f] [√x]	takes square root of x (in display)
[g] [x^2]	squares value in display
[f] [SIN] [f] [COS] [f] [TAN]	computes trigonometric functions of angle in display
[g] [SIN^{-1}] [g] [COS^{-1}] [g] [TAN^{-1}]	computes the inverse trigonometric functions
[f] [LOG]	takes the base 10 logarithm of the display
[g] [10^x]	raises 10 to the x power
[f] [ln]	takes the natural logarithm of x
[g] [e^x]	raises $e = 2.718281828$ to the x power
[g] [INT]	deletes fractional part of number in display keeping integer part
[g] [FRAC]	deletes integer part of number in display keeping the fractional part

TABLE 10–2 Double Variable Functions

Key Stroke(s)	*Description of the Function*
[+]	adds
[−]	subtracts
[×]	multiplies
[÷]	divides
[f] [y^x]	raises the y-register value to the x-register power[a]
[g] [%]	finds the display value percent of the quantity in the y-register

[a] $\sqrt[x]{y}$ or xth root of y can be calculated with the key sequence [g] [1/x] followed by [f] [y^x].

Section 4: Exercises in Analyzing Programs

1. One of the following programs correctly computes the product of 3 and 4 when initialization sequence [f] [STK], [f] [PRGM], enter 3, [R/S] is punched.

PROGRAM 1		PROGRAM 2	
00	(R/S)	00	(R/S)
01	4	01	↑
02	×	02	4
03	GTO 00	03	×
		04	GTO 00

a. Which program correctly computes $3 \cdot 4 = 12$?

b. What does the other program compute? Why?

2. Which of the following programs correctly computes $\sqrt{1+n}$?

PROGRAM 1		PROGRAM 2		PROGRAM 3	
00	(R/S)	00	(R/S)	00	(R/S)
01	1	01	1	01	1
02	↑	02	↑	02	↑
03	R/S	03	R/S	03	R/S
04	f $\sqrt{x}$	04	+	04	f $\sqrt{x}$
05	+	05	f $\sqrt{x}$	05	GTO 00
06	GTO 00	06	GTO 00		

Each initializes with [f] [PRGM], [R/S] enter n, [R/S]. When $n = 24$, $\sqrt{1+n} = 5$.

3. What is the algebraic expression that each of the following key sequences evaluates? Hint: Each sequence evaluates a different expression (computation).

SEQUENCE 1	SEQUENCE 2	SEQUENCE 3
1	1	1
↑	↑	↑
enter n	enter n	g 10^x
+	g 10^x	enter n
g 10^x	+	+

4. The following program is designed to compute y^x when values for x and y are entered.

STEP	PROGRAM
00	(R/S)
01	↑
02	R/S
03	f y^x
04	GTO 00

In order to compute $3^5 = 243$, which of the following initialization sequences works?

a. [f] [PRGM], enter 3, [R/S] enter 5, [R/S].

b. [f] [PRGM] enter 5, [R/S] enter 3, [R/S].

In this section examples of programs illustrate how various preprogrammed functions may be used. With each program there are general and detailed flow charts. As you will see, they are useful for reading and understanding programs that are already written.

Example 1: Finding the Hypotenuse of a Right Triangle

The hypotenuse, c, of a right triangle is related to the two legs, a and b, by the formula, $c = \sqrt{a^2 + b^2}$. (See Figure 10–2.) If you are programming your calculator to compute c, you could proceed as shown in Figure 10–3. Now, make sure your calculator is switched to the RUN mode before you press [f] [PRGM]. In the RUN mode, [f] [PRGM] resets your calculator to step 00, whereas in the program mode, it erases your program! Thus, initialize the program with [f] [PRGM] enter 3 [R/S] enter 4 and press [R/S]. You should obtain 5.0000. For $a = 5$, $b = 12$, do you get $c =$ 13.0000?

Figure 10–2

Figure 10–3

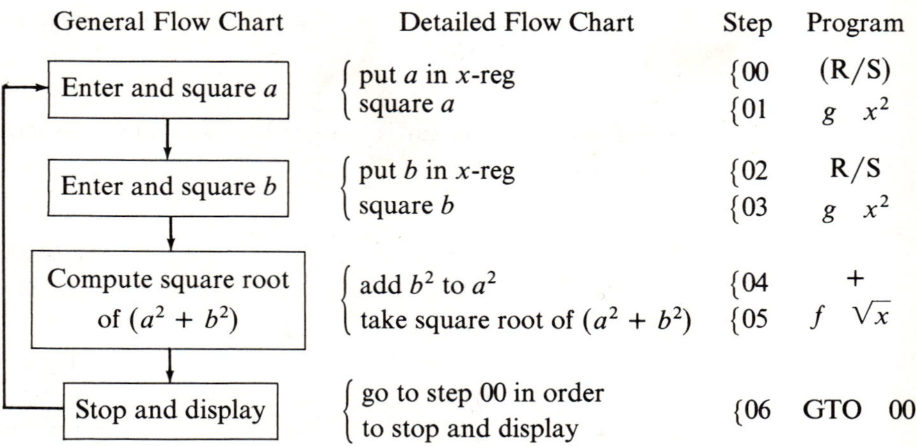

Example 2: A Ladder Problem Using Trigonometry

Suppose you have a 4-meter long ladder and rest it against a wall so that the bottom of the ladder is d meters out from the wall, as shown in Figure 10–4. What angle does the ladder make with the ground?

Figure 10–4

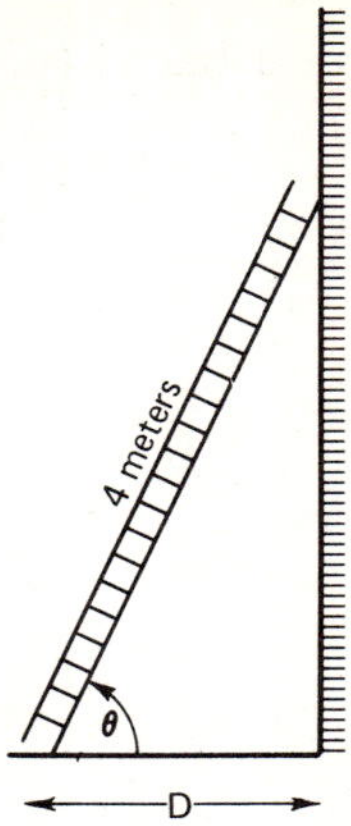

In order to solve this problem, label the unknown angle as θ and use the fact that the cosine of θ is $d/4$, that is, $\cos\theta = d/4$. Since θ is to be found, you can solve for θ algebraically and program your calculator with the resulting formula:

$$\theta = \cos^{-1}\left(\frac{d}{4}\right).$$

The flow chart and program are shown in Figure 10–5. Initialize this program by pressing [f] [PRGM] in the RUN mode. Then enter the value of d and press [R/S].

Figure 10–5

Flow Chart

Step	Program
00	(R/S)
01	↑
02	4
03	÷
04	g COS^{-1}
05	GTO 00

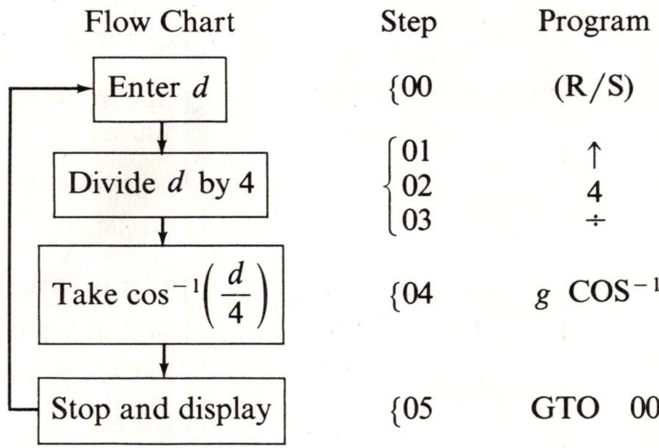

If you wish to verify that this program works, use the data below:

d IN METERS	θ IN DEGREES
0	90.0000
1	75.5225
1.5	67.9757
2	60.0000

Example 3: The Volume of a Barrel

The volume of a barrel (with congruent top and bottom) is given by the formula:

$$V = (r^2 + 2s^2) \cdot \frac{\pi h}{3}$$

Figure 10–6

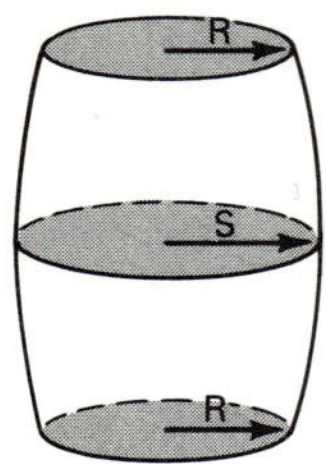

Initialize the program shown in Figure 10–7 with [f] [PRGM]. Then enter r press [R/S] enter s press [R/S] enter h [R/S]. Verify that a rain barrel with $r = 21$ cm., $s = 30$ cm., and $h = 90$ cm. has a volume of 211209.2741 cubic centimeters (about 211 liters).

Figure 10–7

General Flow Chart	Detailed Flow Chart	Step	Program
Enter r and s and compute $r^2 + 2s^2$	put r in x-reg	00	(R/S)
	square r	01	g x^2
	put 2 in x-reg	02	2
	put s in x-reg	03	↑
		04	R/S
	square s	05	g x^2
	multiply 2 by s^2	06	×
	add $2s^2$ to r^2	07	+
Enter h and compute $\frac{\pi h}{3}$	put π in x-reg	08	g π
	put h in x-reg	09	R/S
	multiply π by h	10	×
	divide $\pi \cdot h$ by 3	11	3
		12	÷
Multiply $r^2 + 2s^2$ by $\frac{\pi h}{3}$	multiply	13	×
Stop and display	go to step 00 in order to stop and display	14	GTO 00

1. Program your calculator to find the arithmetic mean of three numbers, a, b, and c. Use the formula,

$$\text{Arithmetic mean} = \frac{a + b + c}{3}.$$

The mean for 10, 20, and 30 is 20.

2. Suppose the point P lies on the diameter of a semicircle and divides that diameter into two segments of length a and b, respectively. (See Figure 10–8.) Then the height from P to the circumference of the circle is the geometric mean of a and b. The geometric mean $= \sqrt{a \cdot b}$. Program your calculator to compute the geometric mean. When $a = 63$ and $b = 7$, the geometric mean is 21.

Figure 10–8

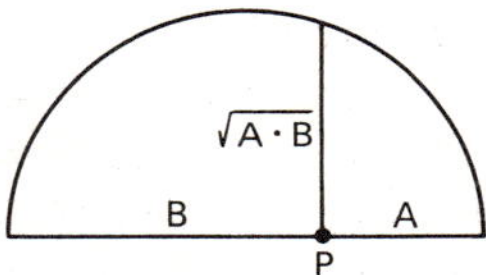

3. The geometric mean of three numbers is $\sqrt[3]{a \cdot b \cdot c}$. Write a program to compute this. For $a = 11$, $b = 22$ and $c = 44$, the geometric mean is 22.

4. The two resistors hooked up in parallel in Figure 10–9 produce a combined resistance in ohms given by the formula:

$$\frac{1}{\frac{1}{R_1} + \frac{1}{R_2}}.$$

Program your calculator to find this combined resistance. When $R_1 = 36$ ohms and $R_2 = 45$ ohms, you should obtain $R = 20$.

Figure 10–9

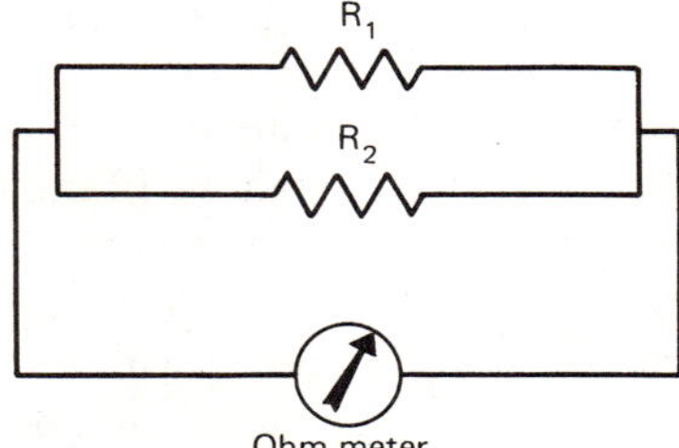

5. Your calculator has the trigonometric functions sine, cosine, and tangent but not their reciprocal functions, cosecant, secant and cotangent, respectively.

a. Program your calculator to compute one or more of the following:

$$\text{cosec}\,(\theta) = \frac{1}{\sin(\theta)} \qquad \text{for } \theta = 30°,\ \text{cosec}\,(\theta) = 2.0000$$

$$\sec\,(\theta) = \frac{1}{\cos(\theta)} \qquad \text{for } \theta = 30°,\ \sec\,(\theta) = 1.1547$$

$$\text{cotan}\,(\theta) = \frac{1}{\tan(\theta)} \qquad \text{for } \theta = 30°,\ \text{cotan}\,(\theta) = 1.7321$$

b. An alternate method of calculating cotan (θ) is by: cotan (θ) = tan(90° $-$ θ). Program your calculator for this formula. If θ = 20, then the cotan(θ) = 2.7475.

6. An ancient puzzle, shown in Figure 10–10, called the Towers of Hanoi puzzle, has n discs of increasing size and three pillars. The object is to move the entire tower of discs from one pillar to another in the fewest possible moves given these two conditions:
   a. move only one disc at a time,
   b. never place a larger disc on top of a smaller one.

   It is known that the fewest possible number of moves is $2^n - 1$. Program your calculator to compute this number for any number, n, of discs. For n = 10, $2^n - 1$ = 1023.0000.

Figure 10–10

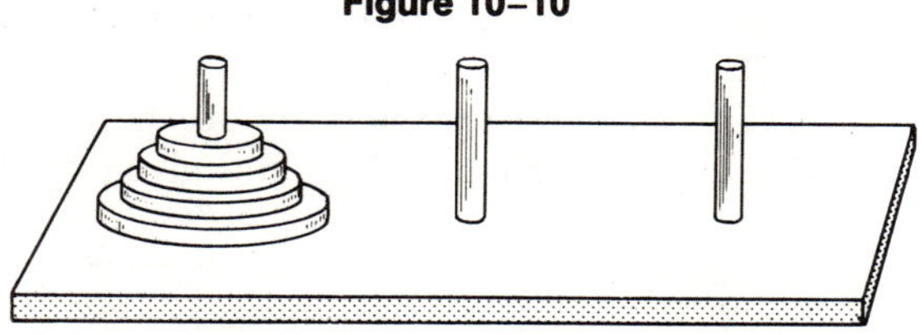

7. At the time of the printing of this book, the first class postal rate was 15¢ for the first ounce. At the rate of 15¢ per ounce, the cost of sending a letter that weighs n ounces (where n is less than 32) can be computed from the formula:

$$\text{Charge} = .15[32 + \text{INT}(n - 32)] \text{ dollars}$$

   Program your calculator to determine the postal charges for various letters. A letter weighing 12 ounces would cost \$1.80 in postage.

8. If you want to find the number of years between two dates, you can take their difference. However, if the first date is smaller than the second, the difference will be negative. Using the absolute value function, you can make this difference positive regardless of what it was. In other words, the number of years between two dates equals the absolute value of their difference. Write a program to compute the number of years between two dates. For example, between 1930 and 1810 there were 120 years.

9. How many digits does a whole number have? You can count this number easily by eye when you look at any particular integer, n. For example, 3,269 has four digits. You can also have your calculator determine the number of digits by the formula: Number of digits = 1 + Integer part of the log of n. Program this formula and try it out for various values of n.
10. Suppose you blow a volume of 1,000 cubic centimeters (1 liter) of air into a spherically shaped balloon. (See Figure 10–11.) What will the radius of the balloon be? From the formula for the volume of a sphere,

$$V = \frac{4}{3}\pi r^3,$$

you can algebraically solve for the radius, r. It is $\sqrt[3]{3V/4\pi}$. Program this formula and compute r. When $V = 100$, $r = 2.8794$.

Figure 10–11

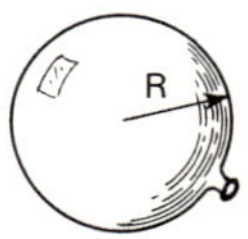

11. The formula for finding the volume of a barrel used in this section is a special case of a more general formula known as the prismoidal formula. It is

$$V = (T + 4M + B) \cdot \frac{h}{6}$$

where T, M, and B are the areas of the top, middle and bottom cross sections of the object while h is its height. This formula works for any sphere, cylinder, cone, pyramid, or prism, as well as for many other solids including a barrel, a donut, and a bead. Write a program to find the volume for each of the following solids using the prismoidal formula. (See Figure 10–12.)
    a. Rectangular prism—for $a = 2$, $b = 3$, and $c = 4$, the volume is 24.0000.
    b. Circular cone—for $r = 2$ and $h = 6$, the volume is 25.13
    c. Frustum of a square pyramid—for $a = 3$, $b = 5$, and $c = 6$, the volume is 98.0000.

Figure 10–12a

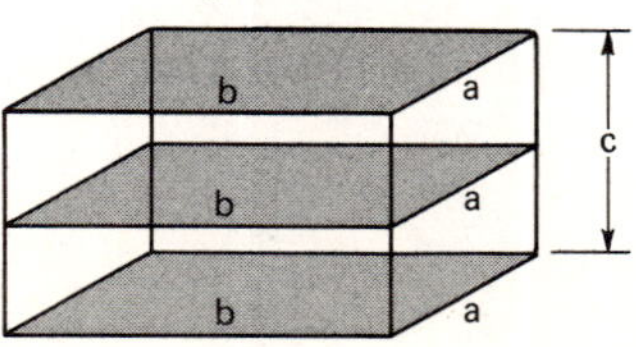

Figure 10–12b

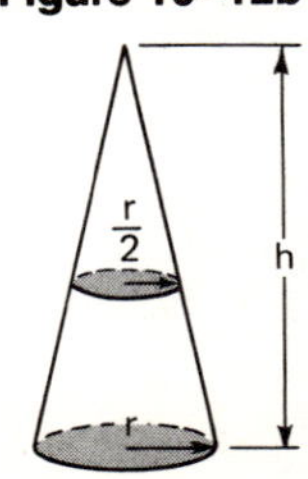

Figure 10–12c

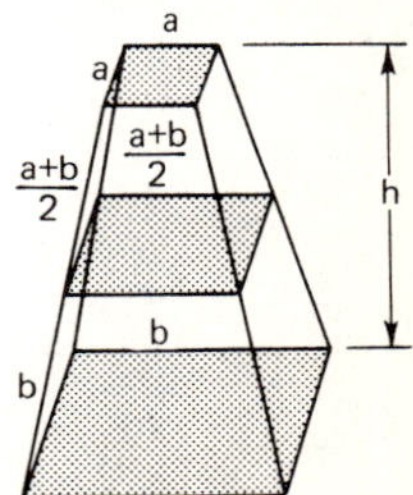

12. When a baseball is thrown from the ground (assuming no air resistance and a constant gravitational attraction throughout flight) with an initial velocity of V_0 ft./sec. and an angle θ, it will land back on the ground at a distance d from its starting position where

$$d = V_0^2 \sin(2\theta) \text{ feet.}$$

   a. Write a program to compute d.
   b. Verify that for $V_0 = 90$ ft./sec. and $\theta = 60$, $d = 219.2$ feet to the nearest tenth of a foot.
   c. For what angle, θ, will a baseball thrown at 90 ft./sec. go the farthest? How many feet will it travel?

Figure 10–13

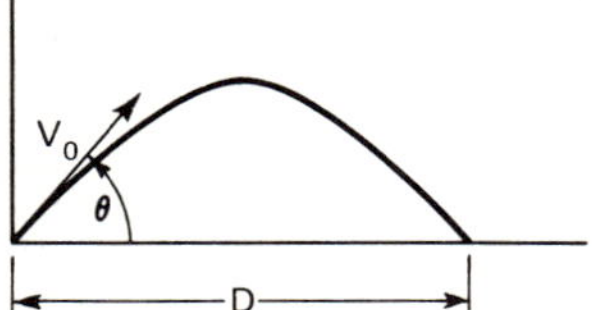

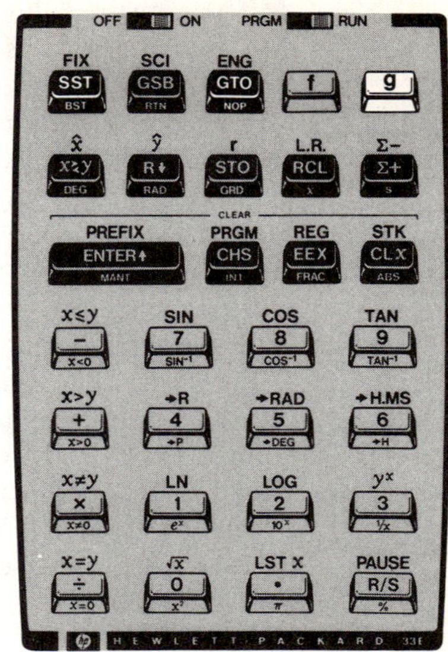

Checking and Editing Programs

Section 1: Detecting Incorrect Programs

Here is a program to compute $(n + 1)/2$. Enter the program and press [CLX] [f] [PRGM] enter 99 [R/S].

STEP	PROGRAM
00	(R/S)
01	↑
02	1
03	↑
04	2
05	÷
06	+
07	GTO 00

If you entered the program as written, you should see "99.5000" in the display. An error has been made. In this case the error is in the set-up of the arithmetic operations. As it stands, the program first divides 1 by 2 and then adds $\frac{1}{2}$ to n giving $n + \frac{1}{2}$. Instead, the program should first add 1 to n and then divide $(n + 1)$ by 2 giving $(n + 1)/2$.

After you enter any program, you should always check it to see whether it is correct. A good way to do so is to enter input data for which you know (or can easily determine) the correct output. For example, in the previous program to compute $(n + 1)/2$, the input value $n = 99$ should have given an output of $(99 + 1)/2 = 50$.

Programs can be in error in lots of ways. To name a few, a program could be written, entered, or initialized incorrectly. Usually when a program is in error, the calculator computes some result other than what you intended. For another example, consider a program to solve the following problem shown in Figure 11–1: 9 glass panels, each of side length s, fit together to form a square window of area A. Find the side length, s, of each glass panel.

Figure 11–1

Since $A = 9s^2$, solving for s algebraically gives the formula

$$s = \sqrt{\frac{A}{9}}\ .$$

The following program was designed to evaluate this formula. Enter the program and keep it in your calculator for use in this and the next section of this chapter.

STEP	PROGRAM
00	(R/S)
01	÷
02	9
03	f $\sqrt{x}$
04	GTO 00

Upon checking this program with the initialization [f] [PRGM] enter 9 [R/S] you will discover an incorrect result. The side length should be 1.0000 rather than 3.0000. Why?

In order to answer this question recall that the double variable function [÷] is performed when the key stroke [÷] is encountered. That means that the program first divides whatever was in the y-register by the number placed in the display during the initialization. Next the program enters 9 in the display in step 02 (while pushing the result of the division up to the y-register). Finally the square root of the 9 in the display is taken, giving "3.0000". Therefore, the program computes $\sqrt{9}$ rather than the desired value of $\sqrt{9/9}$.

Whenever you check your program and find that there is an error, you need to discover what the error is and then to correct it. Sections 2, 3, and 4 of this chapter discuss features of your calculator that you can use to locate and correct program errors. Section 5 provides some exercises on editing programs.

Section 2: Reading a Program

You should have the incorrect program, designed to solve the square window problem (at the end of Section 1), in your calculator. Before being able to correct the program, you have to locate the error and decide how to change it.

A good first step toward this goal is to read the program that your calculator has memorized. Switch your calculator to the program mode. The display should show "00." Now press [SST] the "single-step" instruction. This key stroke advances the calculator to the next step of the program. You should see "01-   71" in the display. Each of the two-digit numbers is a special code. The two-digit number 01 on the *left* of the hyphen names the program memory location where the program step is memorized. There are 50 such program memory locations, each identified by one of the code numbers 00 through 49. The two-digit number on the *right*, 71, is called the program instruction code and refers to the memorized program instruction [÷]. In Section 3 you will learn which program instruction codes correspond to specific key stroke instructions.

Press [SST] again. The program will advance showing step 02. You should see "02-   9." Pressing [SST] twice more, you should see "03-   14-   0" and "04-   13-   00." Altogether the program reads as follows:

STEP	CODE
00	blank
01	71
02	09
03	14 0
04	13 00

Now press [g] [BST]. You see "13- 14 01." The purpose of the [g] [BST] key is to skip backwards through the program memory and display the previous program memory location. Press [g] [BST] three times more. You should see "00."

Using the [SST] and [g] [BST] in the program mode, you can go to and display any particular program memory location you wish. In the run mode, SST and g BST also advance or step back the program. Furthermore, when SST is pressed in the run mode, the calculator executes the particular program instruction located at the program memory location.

In the run mode, however, there is another way to go to any particular program memory location, without having the calculator actually perform any of the memorized program instructions. The key sequence GTO *n, n* (where the digit pair *n, n* is one of the program memory locations 00, 01, . . . , 49) will send the program to that particular location.

Switch your calculator back into the run mode. Enter 25 and then press ↑ so that you see "25.0000" in the display. Next press GTO 03. Notice that the display does not change. This is because the calculator advances the program to step 03 but does not perform any memorized program instructions. Now switch into the program mode. You should see "03- 14- 0" verifying that the program did advance to step 03.

Again switch back to the run mode. You will again see "25.0000" in the display. Switching in and out of the program mode does not affect the display and stack registers.

Now stay in the run mode and press down SST and hold it down. You now see the program memory location "03- 14- 02" where the program is at the moment. Release the SST and you will notice that the number in the display changes to "5.0000." This is the result of the calculator actually performing the memorized instruction "14 0" which refers to the *f* $\sqrt{x}$ instruction, taking the square root of 25 and then single-stepping on to step 04 of the program.

Verify that the program advanced to step 04 by switching into the program mode. You should see "04- 13- 00."

In summary, you can go to and read program memory locations in either the program or the run modes. In the program mode, you see the memory locations in the display and can move to see another memory location with the use of SST and g BST. In the run mode you see the *x*-register in the display. With the sequence GTO *n, n* (where *n, n* is one of the pairs 00, 01, 02, . . . , 49), you can move the program to any of the program memory locations and see that location by switching into the program mode. The GTO *n, n* instruction in the run mode does not cause the calculator to perform any memorized program instructions. Furthermore, in the run mode you can use SST and g BST to advance or step back the program one memory location. When SST is pressed down (in the run mode) the present program memory location is displayed; and when it is released, the corresponding instruction is performed, and then the program advances to the next program memory location.

Section 3: Interpreting Program Instruction Codes

After entering the program from the end of Section 1 into your calculator and reading the memorized instruction codes, you discovered the following correspondence.

STEP	CODE	PROGRAM
00	blank	(R/S)
01	71	÷
02	9	9
03	14 0	$f\sqrt{x}$
04	13 00	GTO 00

Look at step 01 and its program instruction code, 71. This instruction code indicates that the corresponding key stroke is located in the seventh row (from the top) and the first column (from the left) on the face of your calculator. Since [÷] is the key on your calculator in the 7th row and 1st column, the code 71 refers to the [÷] instruction. All program instruction codes with a left-most digit other than zero are row-column codes and indicate the key located on the face of your calculator in the corresponding row and column.

Now look at step 02. The one-digit program instruction code on the right is 9 and refers to the instruction "enter the digit 9." Each of the keys with the digits [0] [1] [2] [3] . . . , [9] on them correspond to the program instruction codes 0, 1, 2, 3, . . . , 9, respectively.

In step 03, the program instruction code, "14 0," is a multiple code. Its first pair of digits, 14, refers to the key in the first row and fourth column, that is, the [f] key. Its digit, 0, refers to the digit 0 key. Together they indicate the instruction [f] [$\sqrt{x}$] since the $\sqrt{x}$ is written in yellow above the digit 0 key.

Finally in step 04 the multiple program instruction, "13 00", has yet another interpretation. The 13 refers to the key in the first row, third column i.e., [GTO]. Since [GTO] requires a two-digit program memory location to follow it, the next pair of digits is such a program memory location. Thus, "13 00", indicates the instruction [GTO] [00], which when executed sends the program back to step 00.

Whether program instructions are merged or not, each is composed of one or more of three basic code components:

a. each digit key has itself as its code
b. each other key on the face of the calculator is represented by a row-column code
c. each program memory location is coded by one of the pairs of digits from 00 to 49.

Section 4: Editing a Program

In your calculator you should still have the (incorrect) program, designed to compute $s = \sqrt{A/9}$ and described in Section 1, namely:

STEP	CODE	PROGRAM
00	blank[a]	(R/S)
01	71	÷

STEP	CODE	PROGRAM
02	9	9
03	14 0	f $\sqrt{x}$
04	13 00	GTO 00

This program fails to compute s correctly because the instructions [÷] and [9] are in the wrong order. The correct program should be:

STEP	CODE	PROGRAM
00	blank[a]	(R/S)
01	9	9
02	71	÷
03	14 0	f $\sqrt{x}$
04	13 00	GTO 00

[a]The 74 code corresponding to [R/S] is not displayed in step 00 but is displayed when [R/S] is memorized in any other location.

Comparing the listing of the incorrect program with that of the correct program, you see that steps 01 and 02 need to be exchanged. Since no special feature of your calculator allows you to insert, delete, or exchange a program step, you have to write over the steps as follows:

1. write over step 01 with a [9] and
2. write over step 02 with a [÷].

With your calculator in the program mode use [SST] and/or [g] [BST] until the display shows program memory location 01, the first location to be changed. Press [9]. You will see "02- 9" indicating that a [9] has been inserted in step 02 rather than step 01! This display demonstrates an important fact. When you see a certain program memory location and then press a new key instruction, that new instruction is memorized in the *next* location.

Now use [g] [BST] to back-step the calculator to step 00. Press [9]. Notice that you see "01- 9" showing that [9] has now been memorized in step 01 where it should be. Next by pressing [÷], you rewrite step 02 with the divide instruction and see "02- 71". Because of your editing, your calculator now has a correct program for computing $s = \sqrt{A/9}$.

Here is one other example of editing a program in the program mode, illustrating how to delete an unwanted program step. Suppose you have entered a program to compute the area of a circle according to the formula $A = \pi r^2$ and then have discovered that the program failed to work. Upon listing the program, you find that you had keyed in the multiplication operation twice accidentally (see steps 03 and 04 in the following program):

STEP	CODE	PROGRAM
00	blank	(R/S)
01	15 0	g x^2
02	15 73	g π
03	61	×
04	61	×
05	13 00	GTO 00

Enter the program in your calculator. Using [SST] and [g] [BST] check to see that you have entered the program as listed, including the doubly punched multiplication operation. Switch back to the run mode and see what the program does when it tries to compute $A = \pi \cdot 2^2$ with the initialization [f] [PRGM] enter 2 [R/S].

Now switch into the program mode. Use the single-stepping feature to display program memory location 03 so that you can delete step 04 where the second of the multiplication operations is located. Press [g] [NOP]. Do you see "04- 15 13" in the display showing that you have written over the second multiplication operation with [g] [NOP]? When a program with [g] [NOP] is executed in the run mode and the instruction [g] [NOP] is encountered, the calculator performs no operation and moves on to the next program step.

Now switch your calculator back into the run mode and check the program with the initialization [f] [PRGM] enter 2 [R/S] to see that the program now computes the correct value $A = 12.5664$.

In summary, the only way to edit a program step is to write over it. If you want to insert a program step between, say, steps 08 and 09, you need to see step 08 in the display, write over step 09 with the new instruction, and then proceed to key in all the remaining steps of the program. If you wish to delete a program step, you can write over it with [g] [NOP].

Section 5: Exercises

1. The following program was incorrectly written to compute $(n^2 + 1)/2$. Enter it into your calculator and then edit it as indicated.

STEP	CODE	PROGRAM
00	blank	(R/S)
01	14 0	f $\sqrt{x}$
02	1	1
03	0	0
04	51	+
05	71	÷
06	13 00	GTO 00

a. Change step 01 to become [g] [x^2].
b. Delete step 03.
c. Insert 2 between steps 04 and 05 by changing step 05 to [2] and then re-entering the rest of the program, namely the [÷] instruction.
d. Now switch to the run mode and verify that the program works correctly with the initialization [f] [PRGM], enter 3 [R/S]. The program should output $(3^2 + 1)/2 = 5.0000$.

2. The following program should compute the hypotenuse of a right triangle according to the formula $c = \sqrt{a^2 + b^2}$:

STEP	CODE	PROGRAM
00	blank	(R/S)
01	15 0	g x^2
02	51	+
03	74	R/S
04	15 0	g x^2
05	14 0	f $\sqrt{x}$
06	13 00	GTO 00

It is initialized with [f] [PRGM] enter a [R/S] enter b [R/S].
a. Run this program for $a = 3$ and $b = 4$. You do not get $c = 5.0000$.
b. Read this program in the program mode to make sure that you have not mis-keyed any steps.
c. The addition operation in the program is in the wrong location. It should come after b is entered and squared and before the square root is taken. Correct this error by rewriting steps 02, 03, and 04 with [R/S] [g] [x^2] and [+] respectively.
d. Now run your program again for $a = 3$ and $b = 4$. You should obtain $c = 5.0000$.

3. A program that should compute $(a - 5)/(b + 5)$ follows:

STEP	CODE	PROGRAM
00	blank	(R/S)
01	5	5
02	41	−
03	74	R/S
04	71	÷
05	5	5
06	51	+
07	13 00	GTO 00

Initialize with [*f*] [PRGM] enter a, [R/S], enter b, [R/S].

a. Check this program in the run mode to see that it fails to give $(5 - 5)/(5 + 5) = 0.0000$ for $a = 5$ and $b = 5$

b. Edit the program.

c. Check to see that your program does now correctly compute $(a - 5)/(b + 5)$.

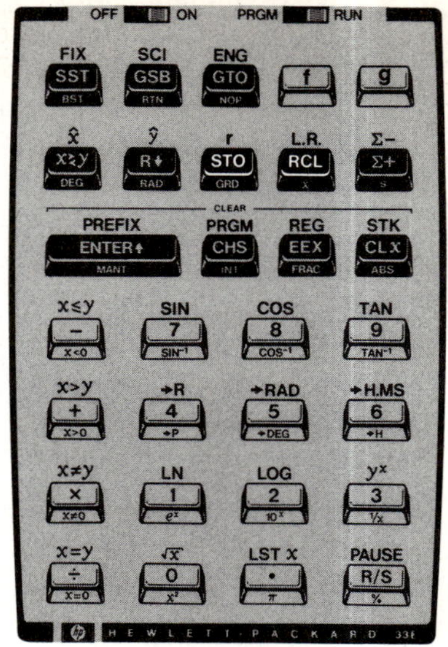

Using Memory to Extend Programming Capability

Section 1: Storing and Recalling Quantities

Suppose you arrange a number of pennies in a triangular pattern like one of the following:

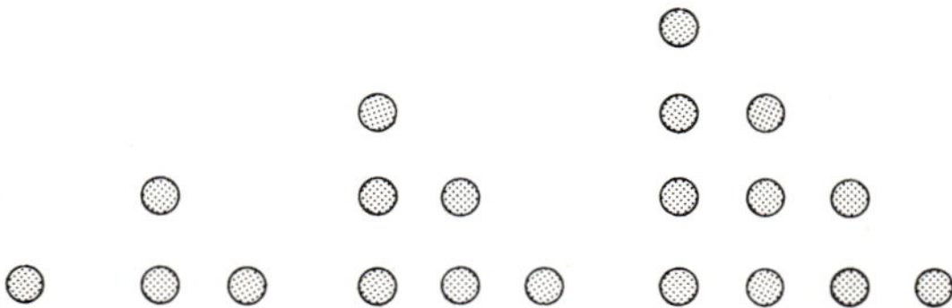

In order to make the same triangular pattern with eight pennies on a side, how many pennies are needed? For reference purposes, let t_n be the total number of pennies needed.

By putting two identical triangular patterns with 8 pennies on a side together, you could form an 8×9 array as shown in Figure 12–1.

Figure 12–1

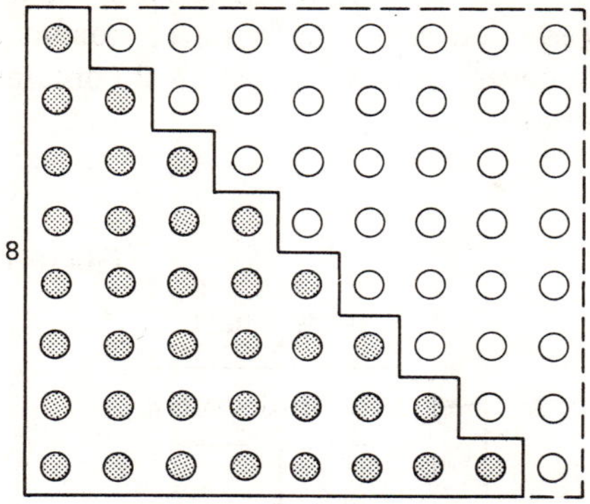

Therefore,

$$t_8 = \frac{(8 + 1) \cdot 8}{2} = 36.$$

In general, to make such a triangle with n pennies on a side,

$$t_n = \frac{(n + 1) \cdot n}{2}.$$

Now suppose you want to compute the value of t_n for $n = 222$. An obvious approach is to enter n in your calculator twice, once when computing $(n + 1)$ and a second time when multiplying by n. A very useful feature of your calculator, however, enables you to perform the calculation entering n only once. This feature is called *memory*.

Your calculator has 8 memory registers, referred to as R_0, R_1, R_2, . . . , R_7, for storing up to 8 numbers. A number in the display is stored in a register, say R_2, when you press the key sequence [STO] [2]. This stored value may be recalled for use when you press [RCL] [2]. In general, you store a number in register R_m by pressing [STO] m and you recall a number in R_m by pressing [RCL] m (where m is any digit from 0 to 7).

Using this memory feature, here is how you could calculate t_{222} in your calculator's run mode:

$$t_{222} = \frac{(222 + 1)(222)}{2} = 24{,}753$$

enter 222 [STO] [1] [1] [+] [RCL] [1] [×] [2] [÷]

Whenever a number or result of a computation is used more than once, it is often helpful to store the quentity with the [STO] m instruction and recall it when needed with the [RCL] m instruction.

Consider the penny-arranging problem from Section 1. Suppose you want to program your calculator to compute the value of t_n for any n. Rather than enter n twice (once to compute $n + 1$ and a second time to multiply by n), you can enter n once, store it in a memory register, and recall it whenever needed. Figure 12–2 contains a program to illustrate this use of memory.

Figure 12–2

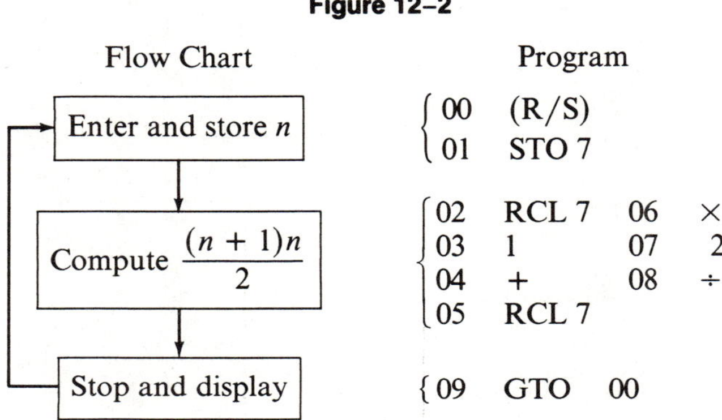

Initialize this program with [f] [PRGM] enter 6 [R/S]. You should obtain $t_6 = 21.0000$. Notice how the input value of 6 is stored at step 01 and recalled (step 02 and step 05) when needed. As a general programming technique, if an input value is to be used more than once in a program, store that value at the beginning of the program and recall it whenever needed.

There are actually a number of reasons for using memory when writing programs. One reason is to store input data that needs to be used several times during the program. Another is to store intermediate results that may be needed more than once. Yet another is to store output information for reference purposes. Examples illustrating each of these uses of memory follow.

Example 1: Storing Input Data

Figure 12–3 demonstrates a program designed to compute the sales tax and the final price of an item sold in a state with a 5 percent sales tax. Notice how the input price is stored at the beginning of the program and thereafter recalled when necessary.

If you start with a sale of \$8.40, the sales tax is 42 cents and the total cost, \$8.82.

Figure 12–3

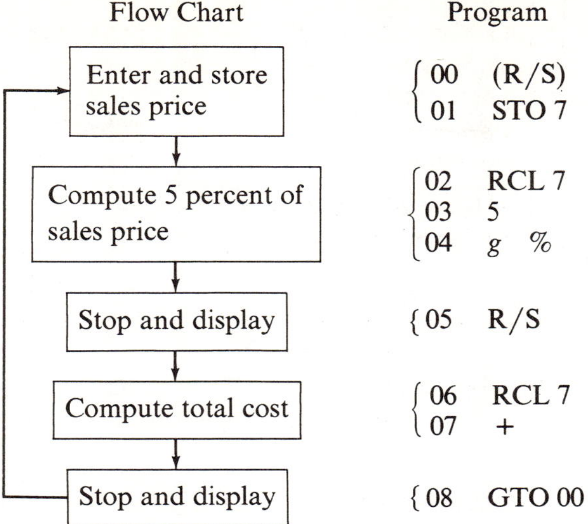

Memory usage: R_7 = sales price
Initialize: [f] [PRGM] enter sales price, [R/S] (see sales tax now), [R/S] (see total cost now)

Example 2: Storing Input and Intermediate Results

Heron's formula for the area of a triangle, given the triangle's three side lengths, is $A = \sqrt{s(s - a)(s - b)(s - c)}$ where the three side lengths are a, b, and c, and the number is the semiperimeter,

$$s = \frac{a + b + c}{2}.$$

Notice in Figure 12–4 that a, b, and c should be stored at the beginning of the program so that they can be recalled for later use when the area, A, is computed by Heron's formula. Furthermore, since the semiperimeter, s, is used four times when computing the area, A, it is wise to compute s early in the program and store it for recall when it is needed.

Figure 12–4

Flow Chart	Program
Enter and store a, b, and c	00 (R/S) 02 R/S 04 R/S 01 STO 7 03 STO 6 05 STO 5
Compute $s = \frac{a + b + c}{2}$	06 + 08 2 07 + 09 ÷

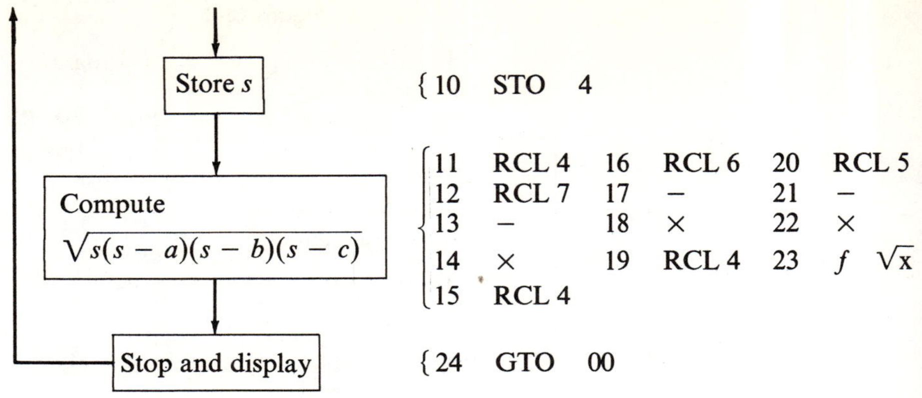

Memory usage: $R_7 = a$, $R_6 = b$, $R_5 = c$, $R_4 = s$
Initialize: [f] [PRGM] enter *a* [R/S] enter *b* [R/S] enter *c* [R/S]

Try this program for $a = 13$, $b = 14$, $c = 15$. When the program halts, you will see the area, $A = 84.0000$. You can see the semiperimeter, $s = 21.0000$, by pressing [RCL] [4].

Example 3: Storing Input Data, Intermediate Results, and Output Information

The fraction 8/5 can be written as 1 + 3/5. In general, any fraction n/d, can be written in the form $q + r/d$, where q is the quotient and r is the remainder upon dividing n by d. The program in Figure 12–5 computes q and r, given any n and d. Furthermore, the results of the computation are stored and can be recalled for reference purposes.

Figure 12–5

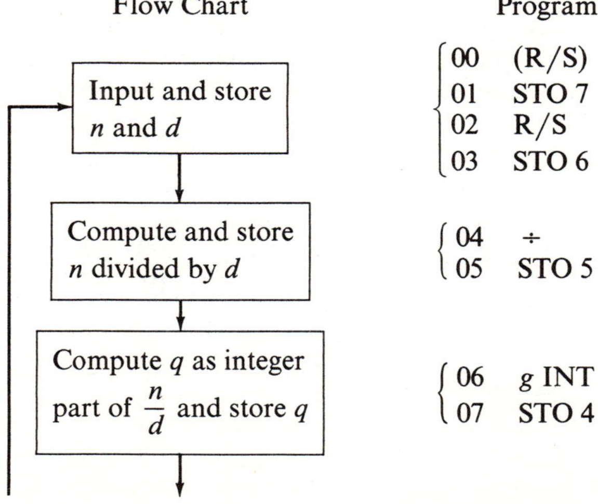

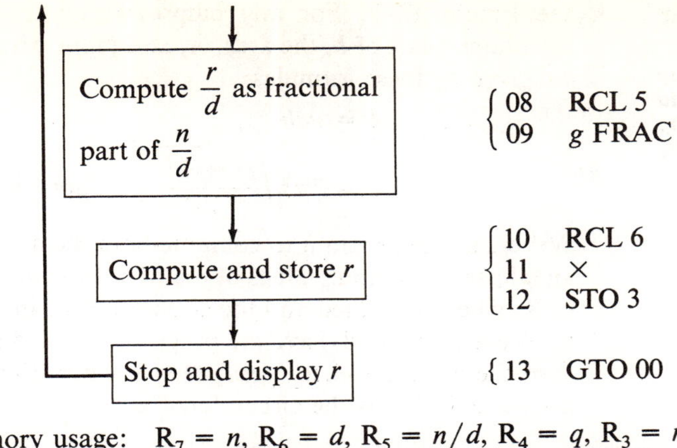

Memory usage: $R_7 = n$, $R_6 = d$, $R_5 = n/d$, $R_4 = q$, $R_3 = r$
Initialize: f PRGM enter n R/S enter d R/S

Try this program for $\frac{8}{5} = 1 + \frac{3}{5}$. In this case, $n = 8$ and $d = 5$. When the program halts, you should see $r = 3.0000$ in the diaplay. You can now find the value of $q = 1.0000$ by pressing RCL 4.

Section 3: Problems

1. Figure 12–6 shows square lattices with 1, 2, and 3 squares on a side. If you count the number of squares of any size that appear in these lattices you will find 1, 5, and 14 respectively. In general for a square lattice with n squares on a side, the total number of squares equals:

$$\frac{n(n+1)(2n+1)}{6}$$

Write a program to determine the number of squares when $n = 4$, 5, 10, and 50. Use the data given in this problem to check your program.

Figure 12–6

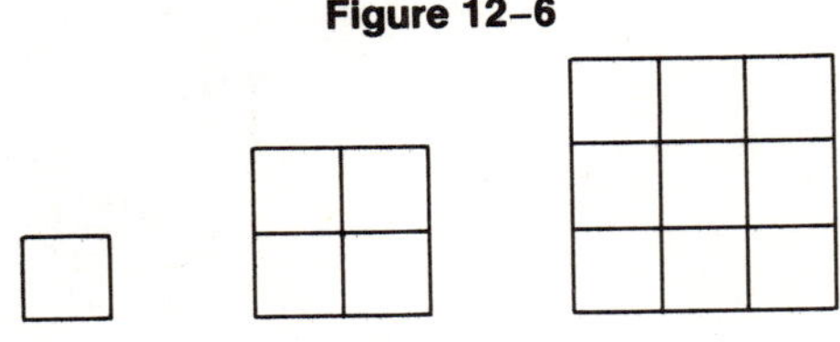

2. Program your calculator to compute

$$\left[\frac{(n+1)\cdot n}{2}\right]^2.$$

This quantity yields the number of rectangles of any size that can be counted in a square lattice with n squares (see problem 1). Use your program to verify that for $n = 50$, there are 1,625,625 rectangles!

3. See Figure 12–7. For any ellipse with semi-major axis of a and semi-minor axis of b, the area, A, and (approximate) circumference, C, are given by these formulas:

$$A = \pi ab$$

$$C = 2\pi\sqrt{\frac{a^2 + b^2}{2}} \quad \text{(approximately)}$$

Write a single program to compute both the area and circumference of an ellipse from input values of a and b. In your program, store the area in R_3 when computed and the circumference in R_4. When all computations are completed, have the program halt to display first the area and then the circumference. Verify that for $a = 2$ and $b = 1$, 6.2832 is the area and 9.9346 is the circumference.

Figure 12–7

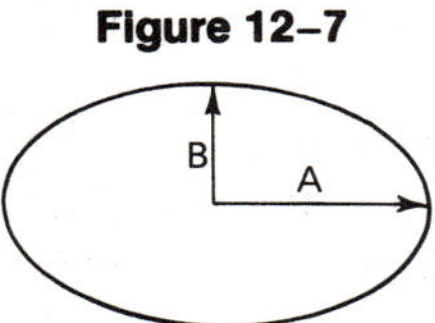

4. a. The formula to compute the area of a rectangular polygon with n sides each of length l is:

$$A = \frac{nl^2}{4\tan\left(\frac{180°}{n}\right)}$$

Write a program for this formula. Verify that for $n = 4$ and $l = 3$, $A = 9.0000$.

b. Show that the area of an equilateral triangle with each side of length 5 is 10.8253.

Figure 12–8

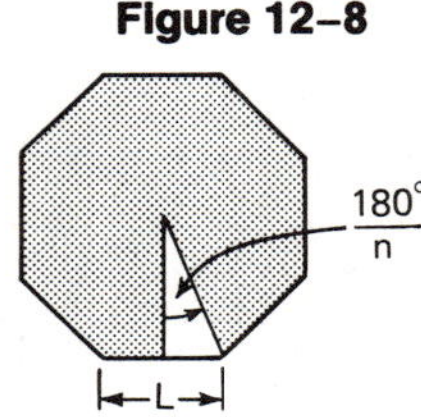

5. On what day of the week were you born? You can find the day of the week corresponding to any date from the formula:

$$R = 7 \times \boxed{g}\ \boxed{\text{FRAC}}\ (N/7)$$

where

$$N = D + Y + \boxed{f}\ \boxed{\text{INT}}\left(\frac{Y-1}{4}\right) - \boxed{f}\ \boxed{\text{INT}}\left(\frac{Y-1}{100}\right) + \boxed{f}\ \boxed{\text{INT}}\left(\frac{Y-1}{400}\right)$$

where D = number of days since the beginning of the year
Y = year (Y must be after 1582 when the present Gregorian calendar system was started)
R = the resulting day of the week, rounded to the nearest integer, according to this code:

Number Code	**Day**
1	Sunday
2	Monday
3	Tuesday
4	Wednesday
5	Thursday
6	Friday
0	Saturday

a. Try this formula out as a program. Check it with January 1, 1900 which was a Monday ($D = 1$, $Y = 1900$, and $R = 2$) and with July 4, 1776 ($D = 186$, $Y = 1776$, and $R = 5$).
b. On what day of the week were you born?
c. When will New Year's day be for the year 2000?

6. Write a program to compute the quantity $\sin^2 \theta + \cos^2 \theta$ for any θ. When you input $\theta = 90°$, you should get value of 1 for $\sin^2 90° + \cos^2 90°$. What happens when you input any other value of θ?
7. If n people are in a group and three of them are to be chosen to form a committee, the formula for determining the number of ways to choose those three people is as follows:

$$\frac{n(n-1)(n-2)}{6}$$

Write a program to determine the number of ways to choose the committee members when $n = 3, 4, 5, 10$, and 100. For $n = 3$, there is obviously only one way to choose the committee.

8. A sphere has a volume and a surface area of:

$$V = \frac{4}{3}\pi r^3 \qquad SA = 4\pi r^2 \qquad \text{where } r = \text{radius}$$

Write a program to find the volume and surface area of a sphere. For $r = 3$, both the volume and the surface area $= 113.0973$.

9. Suppose you plan to cover the outside of a jewelry box with two kinds of velvet. The box itself measures x inches by y inches by z inches. The material for the top and four sides of the box costs 3¢ per square inch while the material for the bottom costs only 2¢ per square inch. Write a program to compute the cost of material for the covering of the box when its length, width, and height are a, y, and z, respectively. Use the formula:

$$\begin{aligned} \text{Cost} &= .03(2xz + 2yz + xy) + .02(xy) \\ &= .06xz + .06yz + .03xy + .02xy \\ &= .06z(x + y) + .05xy \end{aligned}$$

For $x = 2$, $y = 3$, and $z = 4$, the cost is \$1.50.

10. If a new car dealer advertises an automobile at a delivery price of \$5,272.50, how much does this car cost the dealer and how much profit is the dealer making? Usually the dealer pays certain transportation costs (that should be listed on the sales sticker) and about 82 percent of the base price, which is the advertised price less the transportation costs. For example, if there is \$118.50 in transportation costs on a car listed at \$5,272.50, the dealer pays: $(5272.50 - 118.50) \cdot (.82) + 118.50 = 4344.78$.
    a. Program your calculator to accept the input values of the delivery price and the transportation cost. Then calculate the dealer's cost.
    b. Extend your program to output not only the dealer's cost but also the dealer's profit. For a sales sticker of \$5,272.50 and transportation costs of \$118.50, the dealer's profit is \$927.72.
    c. Adapt your program to round all calculations to the nearest cent. Do so by using the key stroke sequence [f] [FIX] [2] in your program.
11. Bayes' Law for probability states that

$$P(\text{B}|\text{A}) = \frac{P(\text{A}|\text{B}) \cdot P(\text{B})}{P(\text{A}|\text{B}) \cdot P(\text{B}) + P(\text{A}|\text{B}') \cdot P(\text{B}')}$$

where $P(\text{A})$ = probability that event A happens
$P(\text{B})$ = probability that event B happens
$P(\text{B}')$ = probability that the complement of event B happens
$P(\text{B}|\text{A})$ = probability that B happens given that A happens
$P(\text{A}|\text{B})$ = probability that A happens given that B happens
$P(\text{A}|\text{B}')$ = probability that A happens given that the complement of B happens

Note that in Bayes' formula, the product $P(\text{A}|\text{B}) \cdot P(\text{B})$ appears twice in the formula. Furthermore, use the formula $P(\text{B}') = 1 - P(\text{B})$ for finding $P(\text{B}')$.

Write a program to compute $P(\text{B}|\text{A})$ from the input values of $P(\text{A}|\text{B})$, $P(\text{A}|\text{B}')$, and $P(\text{B})$. Verify that for $P(\text{A}|\text{B}) = .7$, $P(\text{B}) = .6$, and $P(\text{A}|\text{B}') = .2$, $P(\text{B}|\text{A}) = 0.8400$.

12. Let y be a random variable representing the number of successes on n repeated and independent binomial experiments, where the probability of success on a single experiment is p. Then the expected value $\text{E}(y)$ of y is $\text{E}(y) = np$, and the standard deviation of y is $\text{SD}(y) = \sqrt{np(1 - p)}$.

    Write a program to input n and p and output $\text{E}(y)$ and $\text{SD}(y)$. If $n = 100$ and $p = .5$, then $\text{E}(y) = 50$ and $\text{SD}(y) = 5.0000$.
13. If you shoot a projectile (assuming no air resistance and constant gravitational attraction) with an initial velocity of V_0 feet per second and at an angle θ at a time $t_0 = 0$, then at any later time, the x and y distances of the projectile are given by the formulas in Figure 12–9.

    Write a program to input the initial velocity V_0, the initial angle θ and the time t, and then to compute the x and y coordinates of the projectile at that time. For $V_o = 90$, $\theta = 45°$, and $t = 2$, verify that $x = 127.2792$ and $y = 63.2792$, or $x = 127$ and $y = 63$ when rounded to the nearest foot.

Figure 12–9

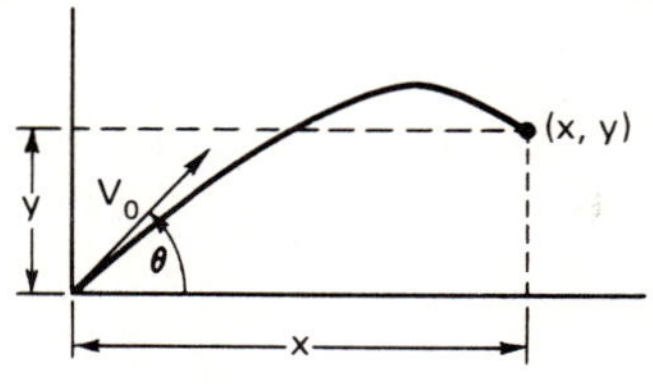

$$x = (V_0 \cos \theta)t(\text{feet})$$

$$y = (V_0 \sin \theta)t - 16t^2(\text{feet})$$

IV

LOOPING AND DECISION MAKING—HP 33E

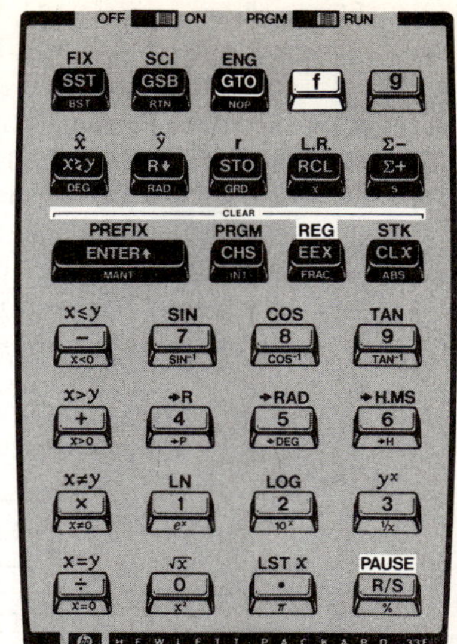

13 Getting Programs to Loop and Generate Sequences

Section 1: Having a Program Loop and Pause

Enter the following program into your calculator:

Figure 13–1

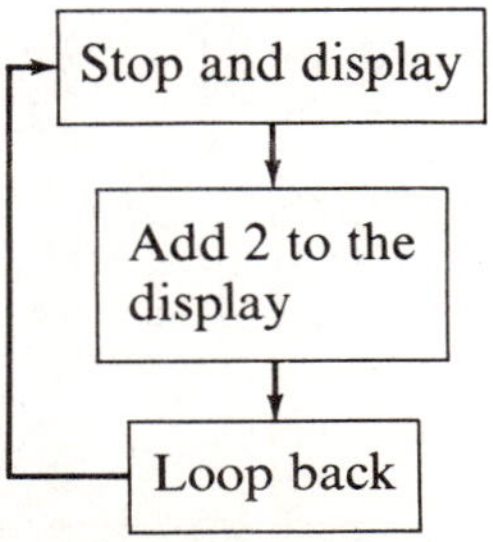

Flow Chart	Program
Stop and display	{ 00 (R/S)
Add 2 to the display	{ 01 ↑ 02 2 03 +
Loop back (→ back to Stop and display)	{ 04 GTO 00

Initialize: [f] [PRGM] [f] [STK]

Now press R/S. Continue pressing the R/S key. You should see the sequence 2, 4, 6, 8, 10, ... The purpose of the GTO 00 instruction in step 04 is to reset the program so that step 00 will be the next step executed. Pressing GTO 00 in the run mode or executing GTO 00 in the program mode always sends the program back to step 00.

Figure 13–2 illustrates another version of the GTO feature of your calculator that does the same kind of looping job but also generates the sequence 2, 4, 6, 8, 10, ... Read through the steps in the program. The instruction GTO 02 in step 05 operates quite like GTO 00, sending the program to step 02 instead of step 00.

Figure 13–2

Flow Chart	Program
Lift the stack	00 (R/S) 01 ↑
Add 2 to the display	02 2 03 +
Stop to display	04 R/S
Loop back	05 GTO 02

Initialize: f STK f PRGM R/S

In general, the GTO n, n instruction sends the program to step n, n where n, n can be any of the 50 program locations from 00 to 49; $n = 0, 1, 2, \ldots, 9$. Furthermore, GTO n, n operates the same way whether pressed in the run mode or executed in the program mode. As such, the GTO n, n instruction can be used in a much more general way than the GTO 00 instruction, to skip a program ahead or loop it back to any step. Figure 13–3 is an example. Enter and run the program.

Figure 13–3

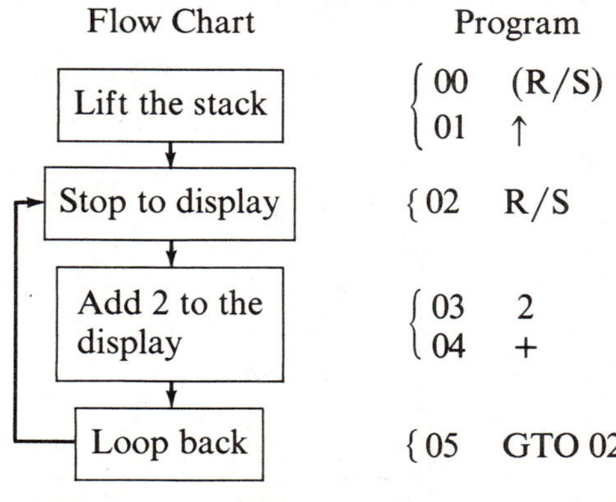

Initialize: f STK f PRGM R/S

When you continue pressing [R/S] you see the sequence 0, 2, 4, 6, 8, ... Read through the steps of the program to see where this program differs slightly from the preceding programs. This program loops back to step 02 instead of back to step 00. Since an extra [R/S] is executed at the beginning of the program, the sequence 0, 2, 4, 6, 8, . . . rather than the sequence 2, 4, 6, 8, . . . , is generated.

With all the programs previously mentioned in this section, it has been necessary to continue pressing the [R/S] key to see each of the terms of the sequence. You can, however, have your calculator display each of the terms automatically for you with the *pause feature*. The [f] [PAUSE] instruction causes the program to stop running for about one second enabling you to view a quantity in the display. After one second, the program automatically continues running. Figure 13–4 illustrates how [f] [PAUSE] can be used; enter this revised version of the last program. You need to press [R/S] only once in order to generate the sequence 0, 2, 4, 6, 8, ... To stop the program, press the [R/S] key.

Figure 13–4

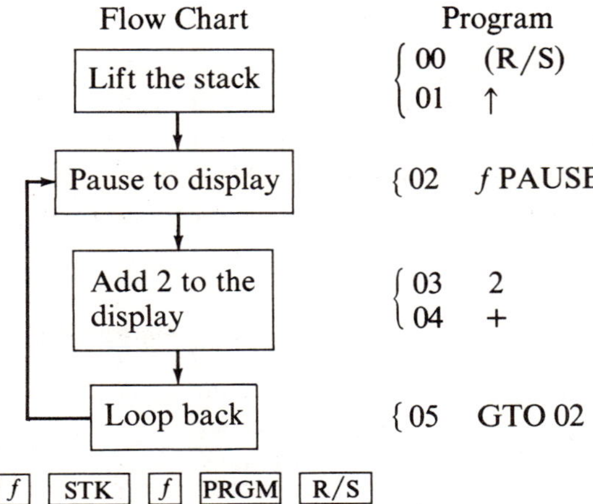

Initialize: [f] [STK] [f] [PRGM] [R/S]

Section 2: Getting Your Calculator to Count

In Section 1 the programs written actually count by twos. How would you program the calculator to display the sequence of consecutive positive integers? In other words, how would you program the calculator to count by ones?

In such a program the central idea is to calculate successive integers by adding 1 to the previous integer during each program loop. To see how this can be done enter and run the program in Figure 13–5. In this program your calculator counts by ones displaying the consecutive integers. You can also get your calculator to count by any other number by merely programming it to add that number during each loop.

Figure 13–5

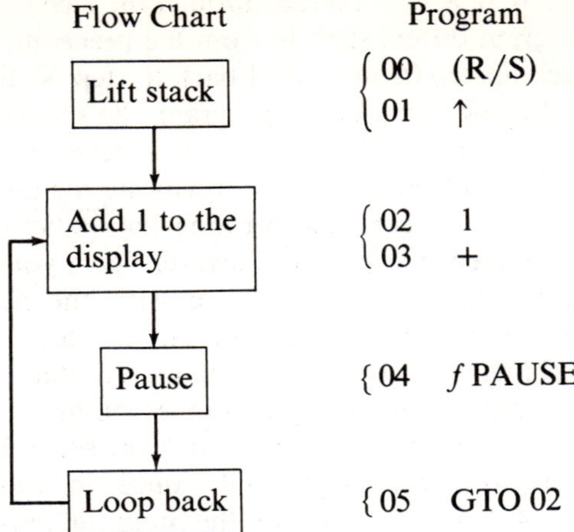

Initialize: [*f*] [STK] [*f*] [PRGM] [R/S]

Moreover, you can get your calculator to "count down," as for a space launching, by programming it to subtract 1 during each loop. If you do so, it is necessary to initialize the program differently. For example, to produce the sequence 59, 58, 57 . . . , you should begin the program with 60 in the display as illustrated in Figure 13–6.

Figure 13–6

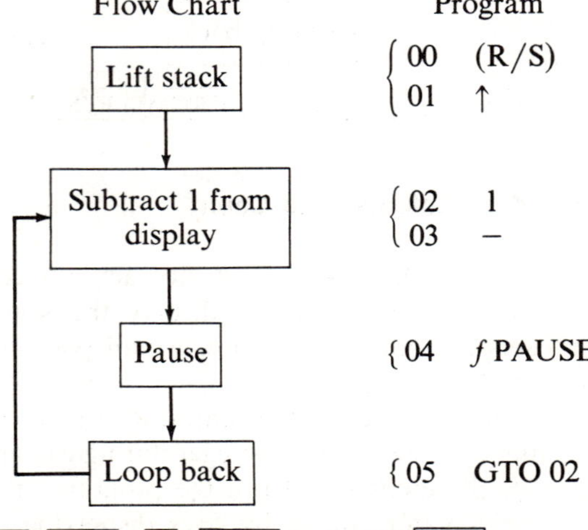

Initialize: [*f*] [STK], [*f*] [PRGM] enter 60 [R/S]

Section 3: Exercises

1. What does the following program do when you enter and run it in your calculator?

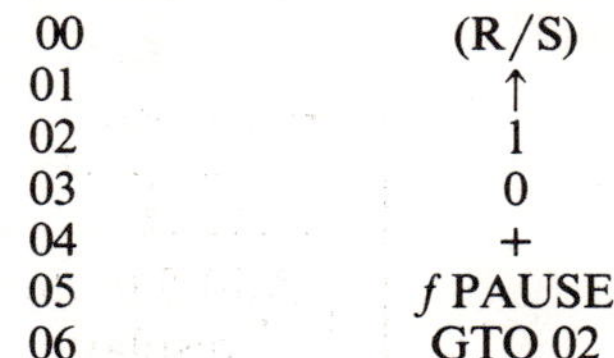

00	(R/S)
01	↑
02	1
03	0
04	+
05	*f* PAUSE
06	GTO 02

Initialize: [*f*] [STK] [*f*] [PRGM] [R/S]

2. What sequence is produced when you change steps 02 and 03 of the program in exercise 1 to become

02	1
03	CHS

3. Write a program to get your calculator to count by fives.
4. Adapt the program from exercise 1 so that it will display the sequence 0, 10, 20, 30, 40, ...
5. Adapt the program from exercise 4 to display the sequence 7, 17, 27, 37, 47, ...
6. Write a program to get your calculator to display the sequence 1,000, 900, 800, 700, ...

Section 4: Sample Programs for Generating Sequences Recursively

Suppose you want your calculator to display the sequence: 3, 8, 13, 18, 23, 28, 33, ... This sequence can be generated by starting with the number 3, adding 5 to get 8, adding 5 to get 13, and so on. Each term is formed by adding 5 to the previous term.

When each term of a sequence is formed by performing arithmetic operations on the previous term (or terms) of the sequence, the sequence is said to be generated *recursively*, or *by recursion*. Recursively generated sequences are particularly easy to program because the repetitious operation of forming each term from the previous term can be done in a loop.

Run the program in Figure 13–7 and see that it generates the sequence 3, 8, 13, 18, 23, 28, 33, ... Notice that the sequence starts at 3 because 3 is placed in the display during the initialization. Notice also that each successive term of the sequence is formed by adding 5 to the previous term during each successive loop.

Figure 13–7

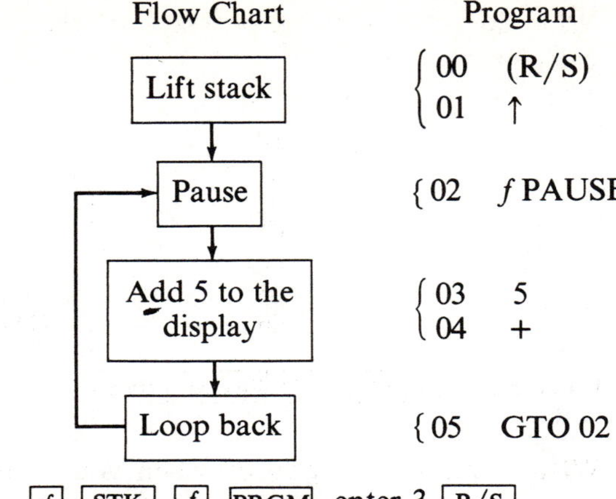

Initialize: [f] [STK] [f] [PRGM] enter 3 [R/S]

Additional examples of programs that generate sequences recursively follow.

Example 1: The Sequence: 1, 2, 5, 14, 41, 122, 365, . . .

Notice that this sequence starts at 1 and that each term is then formed by multiplying the previous term by three and subtracting one, that is, $1 \cdot 3 - 1 = 2$, $2 \cdot 3 - 1 = 5$, $5 \cdot 3 - 1 = 14$, and so on. Can you write a program of your own to generate this sequence before examining the program in Figure 13–8? Sometimes you need to store in memory a previous term that is needed more than once in forming the next term of the sequence.

Figure 13–8

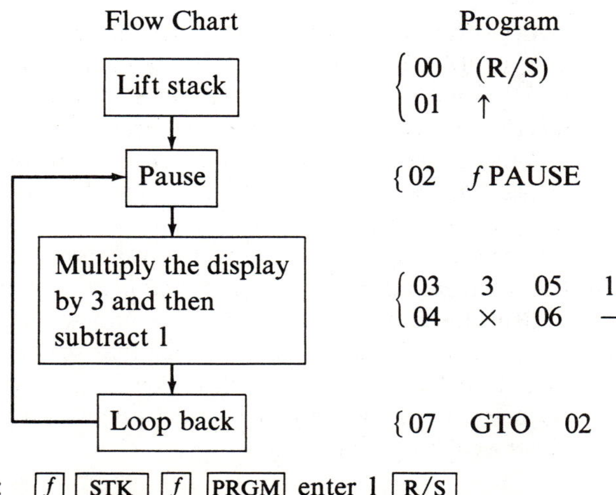

Initialize: [f] [STK] [f] [PRGM] enter 1 [R/S]

Example 2: The Sequence 1, 2, 6, 42, 1806, 3263442, . . .

Notice that this sequence starts at 1. From there the terms are formed as: $1 + 1^2 = 2$, $2 + 2^2 = 6$, $6 + 6^2 = 42$, and so forth. In other words, each term is formed by adding the previous term to its square. Figure 13–9 shows a program for the sequence just discussed. Enter the program in your calculator and run it.

Figure 13–9

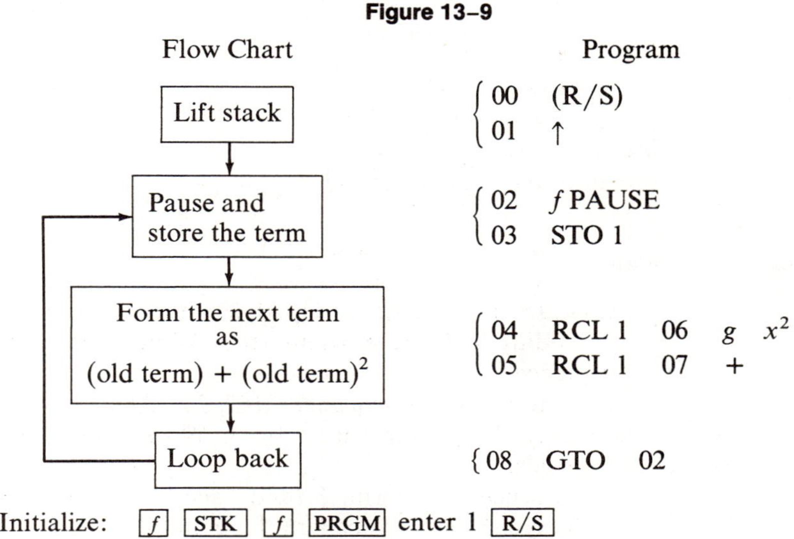

Initialize: [f] [STK] [f] [PRGM] enter 1 [R/S]

As noted, the program illustrates an important feature. Since each previous term must be used twice when forming the new term, storing the previous term at the beginning of the loop becomes convenient. The term can then be recalled as needed.

You may note that step 04 is unnecessary, but it is included to make the program more readable. Delete the step and verify that the program still works. Can you explain why?

Example 3: The Sequence $1^2, 2^2, 3^2, \ldots, n^2, \ldots$

This sequence can be generated recursively with the flow chart and program in Figure 13–10.

Figure 13–10

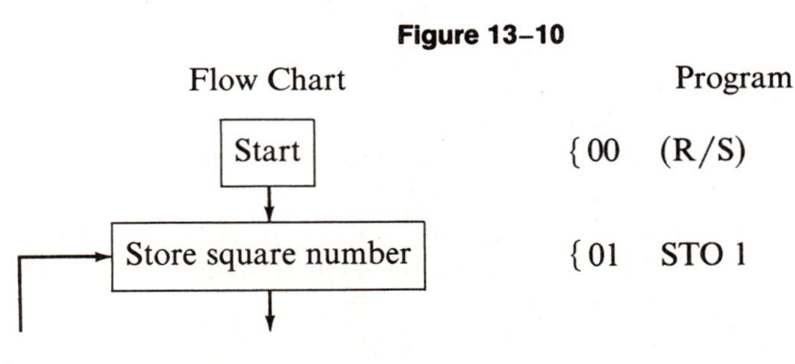

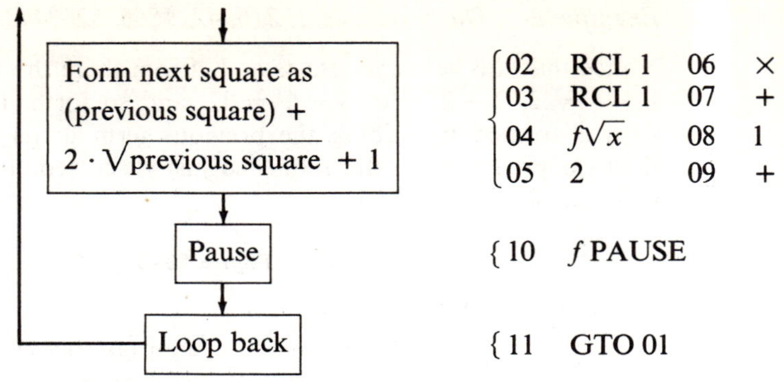

Memory usage: $R_1 = n^2$
Initialization: [f] [STK] [f] [PRGM] [R/S]

Section 5: Problems

1. Consider the sequence 2, 11, 20, 29, 38, . . . where each term is formed by adding 9 to the previous term. Write a program to generate this sequence.
2. Each term of the sequence 2187, 729, 243, 81, 27, . . . is formed by dividing the previous term by 3. Write a program to generate this sequence.
3. A sequence starts with 3, and each subsequent term is formed by multiplying the previous term by 2 and then adding 1.
   a. Program your calculator to generate this sequence. Verify that the sixth term is 127.
   b. Modify your program for this sequence to see which terms are generated when the first term is each of the following:
      i. The positive integer 123
      ii. The negative integer −16
      iii. The fraction 2/3
      iv. The decimal .222
4. What combination of arithmetic operations produces each successive term in these sequences?
   a. 2, 4, 8, 16, 32, 64, 128, . . .
   b. 1/1, 2/3, 4/9, 8/27, 16/81, 32/243, . . .
   c. 1, 3, 7, 15, 31, 63, 127, . . .
   d. −1, −3, −7, −15, −31, −63, −127, . . .
   e. 3, 8, 23, 68, 203, 608, . . .
   f. 2, 4, 16, 256, 65536, . . .
5. Write a program to generate the sequence 15, −27, 57, −111, . . . where each term is formed by first multiplying the previous term by − 2 and then adding 3.
6. Consider the sequence of odd positive integers.
   a. How do you obtain each term of the sequence from the previous term?
   b. Write a program to display this sequence.

7. Write a program to generate each of the following sequences. When you run each program to display many terms, what happens?
   a. The sequence, 2/2, 9/2, 25/4, 57/8, 121/16, . . . , forms each successive term by first dividing the previous term by 2 and then adding 4.
   b. Start with any first term of your choice. Form each term of this sequence by first adding 2 to the previous term and then taking the square root of the result.
8. Write a program to generate either or both of the following sequences. Display many terms and see what happens. Experiment by using different first terms. Do you obtain the same results?
   a. Start with the first term of 6. Generate each term by first dividing 6 by the previous term and then adding 1.
   b. Start with a first term of 5. Generate each subsequent term by subtracting half of the previous term from 1.
9. Write a program to display the sequence formed by squaring the previous term and then subtracting the previous term. Explore what happens when you run your program for each of the following first terms.
   a. 2.1
   b. 1.9
   c. 2.0
10. Enter and run the following program to generate the sequence 3, 6, 30, 870, . . . , recursively.

00	(R/S)
01	*f* PAUSE
02	STO 1
03	*g* x^2
04	RCL 1
05	−
06	GTO 02

Initialize: *f* STK *f* PRGM enter 3 R/S

a. The program should display 3, 6, 30, 870, . . . but does not. What does the program do?

b. What single step of the program is incorrect and needs to be changed so that the program displays the desired result? (Hint: The algebraic computations are correct.)

c. What is register R_1 used for?

d. How is each term of the sequence obtained from the previous term?

e. After the program is corrected (see part b), what sequence is generated by the initialization *f* STK *f* PRGM enter 2 R/S ?

Section 6: Sample Programs for Generating Sequences Nonrecursively

In section 4 you saw how sequences could be generated in a program using recursion. Some sequences are more easily programmed using nonrecursive processes. Consider, for example, the sequence $1^2, 2^2, 3^2, 4^2, \ldots, n^2, \ldots$

presented as example 3 in Section 4. Enter and run the program in Figure 13–11, which also displays the sequence of consecutive squares.

Figure 13–11

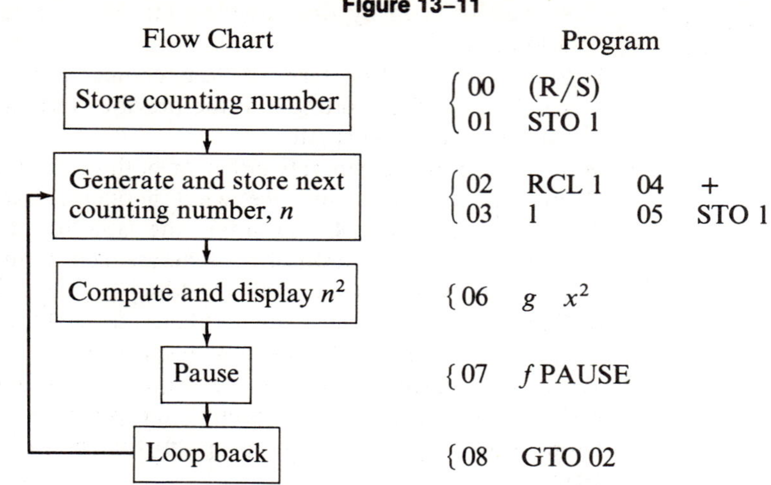

Memory usage: R_1 = counting number, n
Initialize: [f] [STK] [f] [PRGM] [R/S]

Notice in the program that each term is not formed by arithmetic operations on the preceeding terms. Instead, each term is formed in a two-step process. First, each counting number from the sequence 1, 2, 3, 4, . . . , is formed by adding 1 to the previous counting number. Secondly, that counting number is squared to produce the appropriate term in the sequence $1^2, 2^2, 3^2, 4^2, \ldots$. For any sequence, each term has a corresponding counting number that indicates the position of the term in the sequence. For example, 4^2 is the fourth term in the sequence $1^2, 2^2, 3^2, 4^2, \ldots$. The counting number, representing the position of a term in a sequence, is called the *index number*, or simply the *index* of that term.

When each term of a sequence is formed by performing arithmetic operations on its corresponding index number, the sequence is said to be generated *nonrecursively*. Specifically, the program just presented generates the squares nonrecursively because, in general, the nth square is formed by squaring the corresponding index number n.

Figure 13–12 presents another example of a program that uses a nonrecursive approach to generate a sequence. Enter and run this program to verify that it generates the sequence 1, 3, 6, 10, 15, ... Notice in the program the use of [f] [REG] in step 01. This instruction clears each of the memory registers, $R_0, R_1, \ldots, R_7$. Consequently, using the instruction at the beginning of a program effectively enters the number 0 in each memory register. This insures the index register starts with 0. Also notice that arithmetic operations are performed on the counting index in order to generate the sequence 1, 3, 6, 10, ... If n is the index, then the arithmetic operations compute $(n^2 + n)/2$.

Figure 13–12

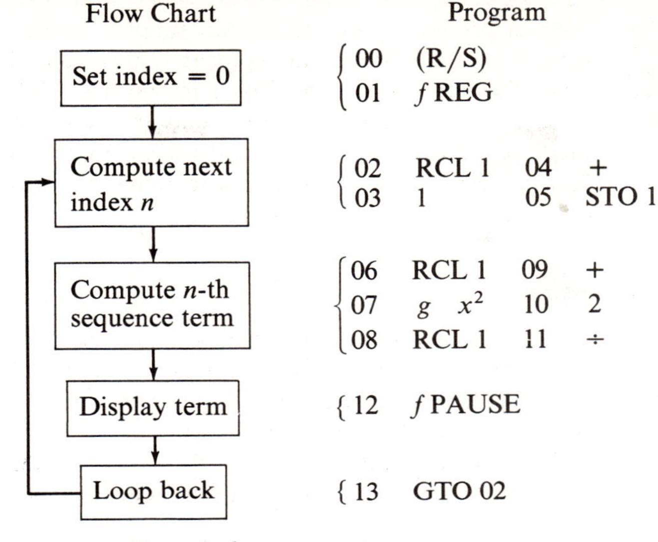

Memory usage: R_1 = index = n
Initialization: [f] [STK] [f] [PRGM] [R/S]

At times in programming you may need to be creative in setting and using the index for a nonrecursively generated sequence.

The next program, in Figure 13–13, is designed to generate the sequence 90, 72, 56, 42, 30, ... Enter it and verify that it does. In this program, the index is set at 10 and decreases by 1 each time through the loop; each term is thereafter computed as $n(n + 1)$.

Figure 13–13

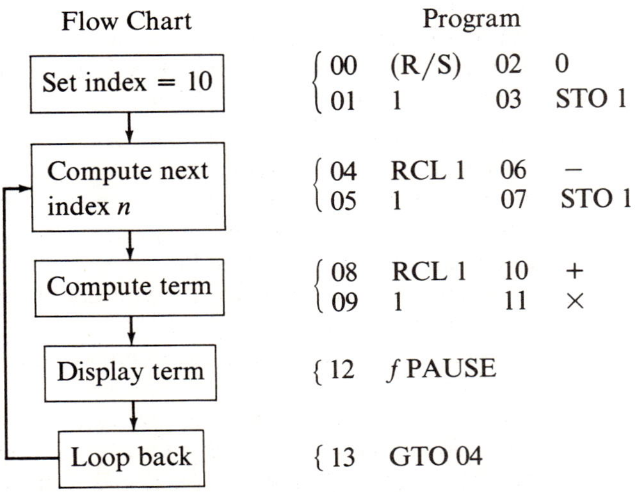

Memory usage: R_1 = index = n
Initialize: [f] [STK] [f] [PRGM] [R/S]

Now suppose that you want a program to display the sequence 90, 56, 30, 12, . . . , (that is, every other term of the sequence generated by the last program presented). Two simple changes in the program accomplish the task. First, set the index at 11 instead of 10 (steps 01–02). Second, place the number 2 instead of 1 in step 05. Make the suggested changes and run the program to verify that the sequence 90, 56, 30, 12, . . . , is displayed. Notice that each term is still computed by $n(n + 1)$, but that the index decreases by 2 each time through the loop thus producing every other term of the original sequence.

Section 7: Problems

1. a. Write a program to display the sequence 2, 5, 10, 17, 26, 37, ... Set the index at 0 and form each term by $n^2 + 1$.
   b. Modify the program in part a by setting the index at 2. What sequence do you obtain?
2. Consider the sequence 1/2, 2, 9/2, 8, 25/2, 18, ...
   a. Write a program to display the sequence. Set the index at 0 and form each term by $(n + 1)^2/2$.
   b. Modify the program in part a to display only the integer sequence terms (that is, 2, 8, 18, . . .).
3. In order to generate each of the following sequences, nonrecursively, where would you set the index and how would you compute the terms?
   a. 0, 5, 10, 15, 20, 25, ...
   b. 0, 3, 8, 15, 24, ...
   c. 8, 15, 24, 35, ...
   d. $2^1, 2^2, 2^3, 2^4$, ...
4. Write a program for each of the following sequences:
   a. 3, 9, 27, 81, ... Set the index at 0 and form each term by 3^n.
   b. 8, 27, 64, 125, ... Set the counting index at 2 and form each term by n^3.
5. Write a program to display the sequence 1, 4, 27, 256, . . . , with index = 1 and terms formed by n^n. How fast does this sequence grow?
6. Write a program to display the sequence with index = 1, first term = 1, and succeeding terms formed by $\sqrt[n]{n}$.
   a. Which term of the sequence is the largest?
   b. What happens as the counting number n grows very large?
7. Write a program to display the sequence with index 0, first term = − 1 and succeeding terms formed by $n^2 - 2^n$.
   a. What does this sequence tell you about the answer to the question, "Which is larger, n^2 or 2^n?"?
   b. What method could you use to answer the question, "Which is larger n^3 or 3^n?"?
8. Write programs to display each sequence according to the information given. What happens in each case as n becomes very large?
   a. First index = 0, first term = 1, and terms formed by $(0.99)^n$.
   b. First index = 0, first term = 1, and terms formed by $(1.01)^n$.
   c. First index = 0, first term = 1, and terms formed by $(1.00)^n$.

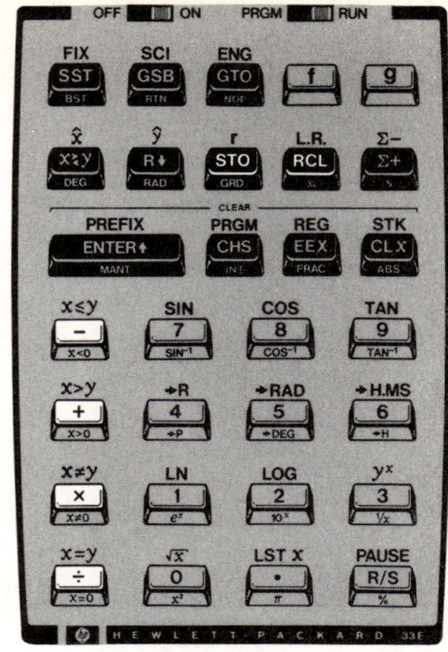

Using Memory Arithmetic to Compute Series

Section 1: A Series Representing the Gambler's Problem

A gambler is offered the following deal. He is to toss a coin repeatedly until the first head comes up. At that time he will receive 1, 4, 9, . . . , n^2 dollars, if the first head appeared on the first, second, third, . . . nth toss. For example, if the first head appears on the fifth toss (that is, the preceding four tosses were all tails), the gambler receives \$25 (\$$5^2$).

How much can the gambler expect to receive, on the average, each time he plays? By considering the probability decision tree shown in Figure 14–1, you can see that the probability associated with the first head coming up on the first, second, third, . . . , nth toss is $1/2$, $1/4$, $1/8$, . . . , $1/2^n$, respectively. Therefore, the amount received if the gambler plays very many games is one dollar half the time, 4 dollars a quarter of the time, 9 dollars an eighth of the time, . . . , n^2 dollars $1/2^n$ of the time, and so forth. Putting this information together gives:

$$\text{Amount received} = \left(1 \cdot \tfrac{1}{2}\right) + \left(4 \cdot \tfrac{1}{4}\right) + \left(9 \cdot \tfrac{1}{8}\right) + \cdots + \left(n^2 \cdot \frac{1}{2^n}\right) + \cdots$$

which can be written as:

$$\sum_{n=1}^{\infty} \left(n^2 \cdot \frac{1}{2^n}\right).$$

The value of this series gives the average amount received, assuming the gambler plays infinitely many times.

Figure 14–1

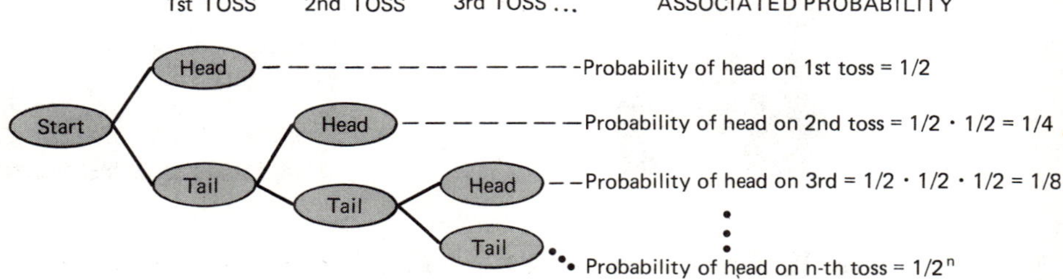

Evaluating this infinite series is rather difficult with standard mathematical techniques, but is not hard to do on your calculator. Your calculator can compute this series by first producing each term of the sequence

$$\left(1 \cdot \tfrac{1}{2}\right), \left(4 \cdot \tfrac{1}{4}\right), \left(9 \cdot \tfrac{1}{8}\right), \ldots, \left(n^2 \cdot \frac{1}{2^n}\right)$$

and then adding each term to a running total,

$$\left(1 \cdot \tfrac{1}{2}\right) + \left(4 \cdot \tfrac{1}{4}\right) + \left(9 \cdot \tfrac{1}{8}\right) + \cdots + \left(n^2 \cdot \frac{1}{2^n}\right)$$

which eventually comes very close to the value of the infinite series

$$\sum_{n=1}^{\infty} \left(n^2 \cdot \frac{1}{2^n}\right).$$

Using a feature of your calculator called *memory arithmetic*, your calculator can efficiently handle the simultaneous calculations of each successive term and the corresponding running total.

In Section 7 of this chapter, after memory arithmetic has been introduced and after the necessary details for computing series as running totals of terms have been explained, the value of the infinite series

$$\sum_{n=1}^{\infty} \frac{n^2}{2^n},$$

the amount the gambler receives, will finally be calculated.

Memory arithmetic is a built-in feature of your calculator that has many applications in addition to computing series. Anytime you have a need to maintain ongoing sequences and/or running totals, memory arithmetic helps you create efficient programs.

Turn your calculator on and key in the program in Figure 14–2. What sequence is displayed?

Figure 14–2

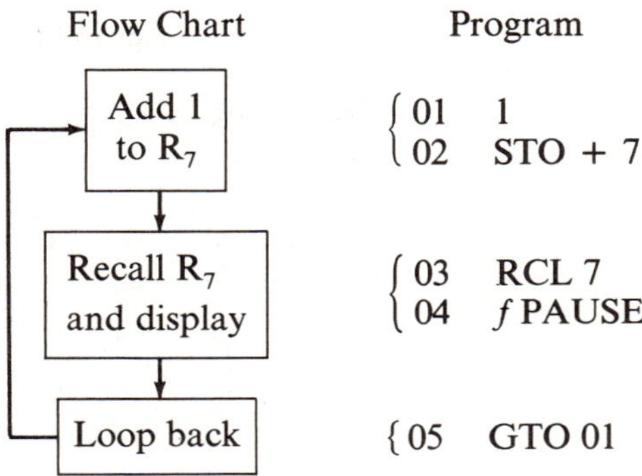

Memory usage: R_7 = counting index
Initialize: [f] [REG] [f] [STK] [f] [PRGM] [R/S]

Step 02 of this program introduces a new feature of your calculator, called *summing* (adding into memory). When the key sequence [STO] [+] [7] is executed, the value in the display is added into memory register 7. In general the key sequence [STO] [+] *m* causes the value in the display to be added into memory register R_m. Effectively this program causes the calculator to count in memory register 7, since the number 1 is added to R_7 each time through the loop.

Your calculator can perform other memory arithmetic as well as addition: it can also subtract from memory, multiply into memory, and divide into memory. The necessary key sequences for accomplishing each of these memory arithmetic operations are described in Table 14–1. Examples of how to use these key sequences are included in the questions at the end of this section.

TABLE 14–1

Key Sequence	*Description*
[STO] [+] *m*	Adds display into memory R_m
[STO] [−] *m*	Subtracts display from memory R_m (and puts the result in R_m)
[STO] [×] *m*	Multiplies display into memory R_m
[STO] [÷] *m*	Divides display into memory R_m

1. In the run mode, store the value 100 in R_6. Next, enter the number 4 in the display. Now key in the sequence [STO] [−] [6].
   a. What is the value that is now in R_6?
      Press [RCL] [6] to verify your answer.
   b. Now enter 6 in the display. Key in the sequence [STO] [−] [6]
      What is the value that is now in R_6?
2. Enter the program from Figure 14–3 into your calculator:

Figure 14–3

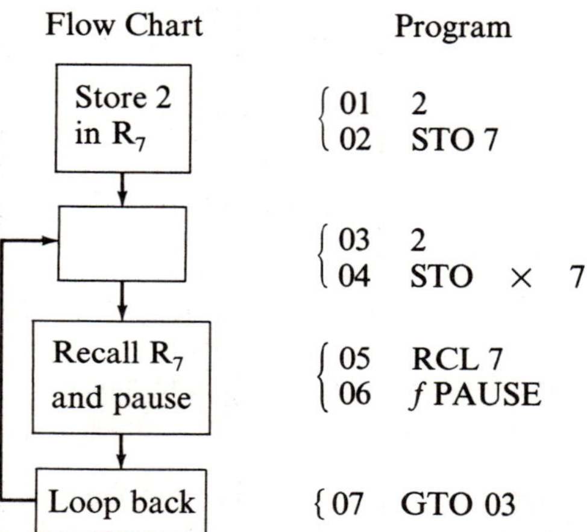

Memory usage: R_7 = sequence term
Initialize: [f] [PRGM] [f] [REG] [f] [STK] [R/S]

   a. What sequence is displayed when this program is run?
   b. What sequence of numbers is generated in memory register R_7?
   c. How is the value in R_7 changed each time through the loop?
   d. What is the effect of the key sequence [2] [STO] [×] [7] in steps 03 and 04? That is, what words best fit in the blank flow chart box?
3. Examine the flow chart and program in Figure 14–4.
   a. What sequence is generated in memory register 5?
   b. What is the effect of the key sequence [1] [0] [STO] [÷] [5] in steps 04–06? What words best describe those instructions in the corresponding flow chart box.
   c. What words in the flow chart describe the effect of the key sequence [6] [g] [10^x] [STO] [5] in steps 01–03?
   d. Notice the use of [f] [PAUSE] successively in steps 08 and 09. This enables the calculator to pause longer than a second.
4. What is a program that generates the sequence 100, 96, 92, 88, 84, 80, 76, . . . , in memory register R_3?

Figure 14–4

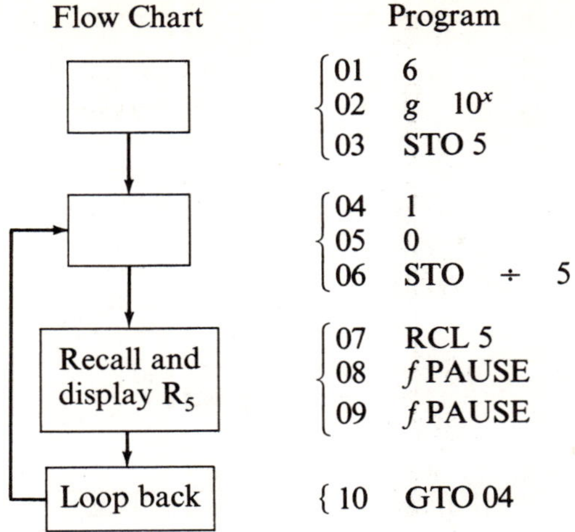

Memory usage: R_5 = sequence term
Initialize: [f] [PRGM] [f] [REG] [f] [STK] [R/S].

Section 4: Generating Sequence Terms in Memory

When programming your calculator to generate the terms of a sequence, you will find memory arithmetic to be a very efficient tool. Memory arithmetic is especially convenient for any sequence term computed recursively using [+] [−] [×] or [÷]. Such a term can be computed directly in memory, leaving the x-register (display) free for other calculations. Also, when each term is computed nonrecursively as a function of a counting index, n, memory arithmetic enables you to generate n directly in memory leaving the x-register (display) available for the computation of the corresponding term.

To demonstrate how memory arithmetic can be used to generate sequence terms, consider the sequence 1, 1/2, 1/4, 1/8, . . . $1/2^n$, . . . , which in decimal form looks like 1.0000, 0.5000, 0.2500, 0.1250, 0.0625, ... The terms of this sequence can be generated either recursively or nonrecursively; programs showing both styles are found in the following examples.

Example 1: A Program to Generate 1, 1/2, 1/4, 1/8, . . . , $1/2^n$, . . . , recursively

Since each term other than the first is half of the previous term, repeatedly dividing 2 into each previous term produces each next term as Figure 14–5 shows. In the program, steps 05 and 06 could be replaced with key strokes [·] [5] [STO] [×] [7] and accomplish the same purpose.

Figure 14–5

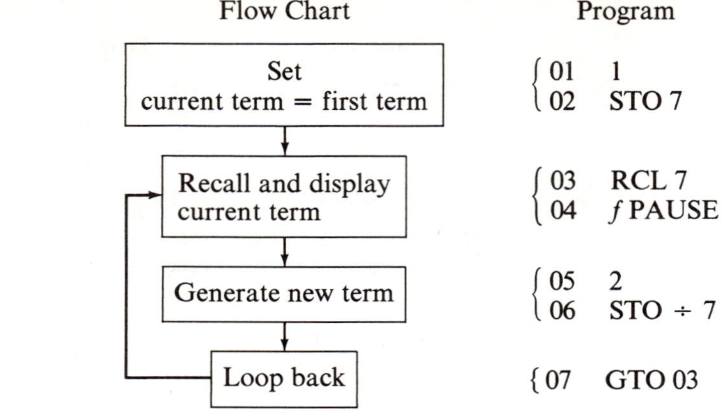

Memory usage: R_7 = term

Initialize: [f] [PRGM] [f] [REG] [f] [STK] [f] [FIX] [9] [R/S]

Example 2: A Program to Generate 1, 1/2, 1/4, 1/8, . . . , $1/2^n$, . . . , Nonrecursively

The next program in Figure 14–6 generates the counting index in R_6 and calculates each corresponding term nonrecursively in the x-register.

Figure 14–6

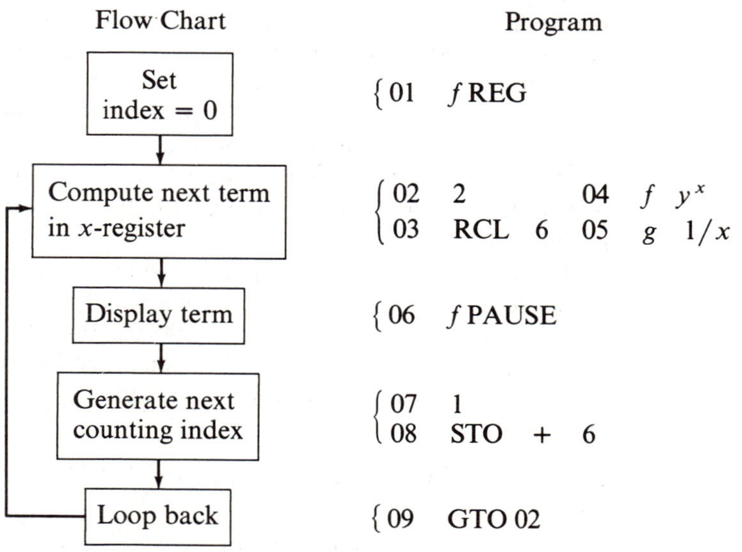

Memory and x-register usage: R_6 = index, x-reg = current term

Initialize: [f] [STK] [f] [PRGM] [f] [FIX] [9] [R/S]

Example 3: A Program to Generate the Sequence 1/2, 4/4, 9/8, 16/16, . . . , $n^2/2^n$, . . .

The terms in the sequence, written as 0.5000, 1.0000, 1.1250, 1.0000, .7813, . . . , can be formed nonrecursively by generating the counting index n in R_6 and computing the corresponding term $n^2/2^n$ in the x-register. A more efficient way, however, is first to generate n in R_6, then to generate the denominator 2^n recursively in R_5, and finally to piece together the information and compute $n^2/2^n$ in the display. Notice how the program in Figure 14-7 uses the more efficient way.

Figure 14–7

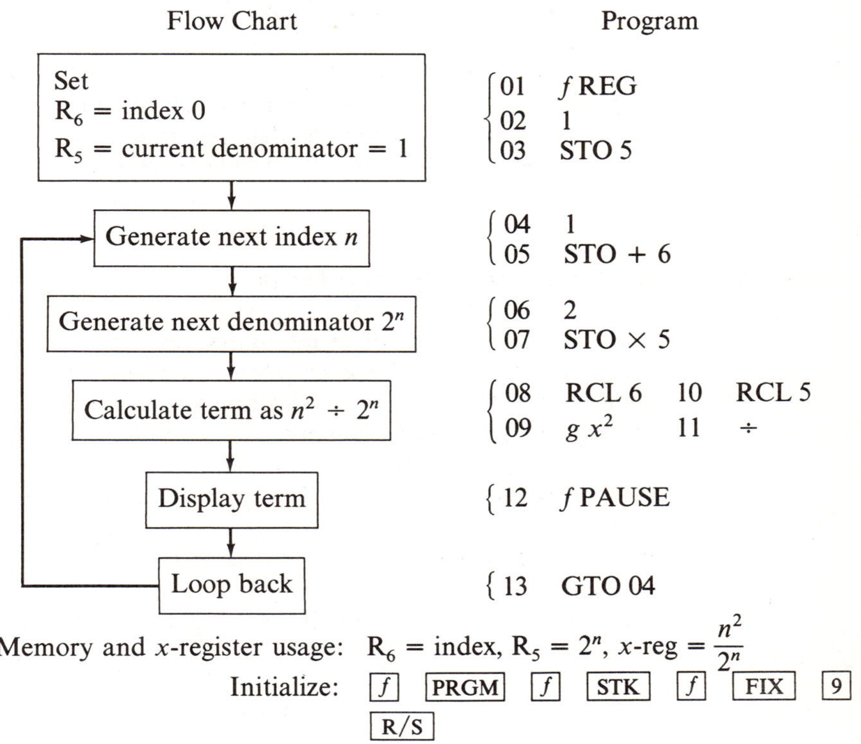

In summary, memory arithmetic is a powerful tool when generating the terms of a sequence, because it enables various calculations to be carried on in memory leaving the x-register (display) free for other calculations.

Section 5: Exercises

1. In the second and third programs in this section, what is the purpose of [f] [REG] as step 01 in the programs?
2. Consider the problem of recursively generating the terms of the sequence 1/3, 1/9, 1/27, . . . , $1/3^n$, . . . in memory R_4.
   a. With what value would you initialize R_4?

b. What key strokes would you repeatedly use to obtain each successive term?

3. Suppose you wish to produce the terms of the sequence

$$\frac{3}{-2}, \frac{5}{-5}, \frac{7}{-8}, \ldots \frac{1+2n}{1-3n},$$

by generating the sequence of numerators 3, 5, 7, 9, . . . $1 + 2n$ recursively in R_2, generating the sequence of denominators recursively in R_3, and forming each fraction in the display.
   a. What repeated key strokes will generate each successive numerator in R_2?
   b. What key strokes will generate each successive denominator in R_3?
   c. What key strokes will then form each fraction in the x-register (display)?

4. The function $\left[\frac{1}{2}n(n+1)+1\right]$ represents the maximum number of pieces that you can obtain when slicing a pancake with n slices. What are the steps of a program that generates the index n in R_3 and the sequence 2, 4, 7, 11, 16, . . . , $\left[\frac{1}{2}n(n+1)+1\right]$, . . . in the x-register (display)?

Section 6: Computing Series as Running Totals

Since series are sums of terms, series can be efficiently computed with memory arithmetic. After each term is calculated, it can be summed into a memory register containing the running total of all the previous terms. In this way, a series can be computed as a running total of its terms. Memory arithmetic is useful both for generating the terms for the series and for computing the running total. For example, consider the series $1/2 + 1/4 + 1/8 + \ldots + 1/2^n$. That the series should total 1 may appear obvious, but can you actually get your calculator to calculate that value?

Figure 14–8 shows a sample program. Run this program and see how many times it pauses before the running total reaches the limiting value of 1.

Figure 14–8

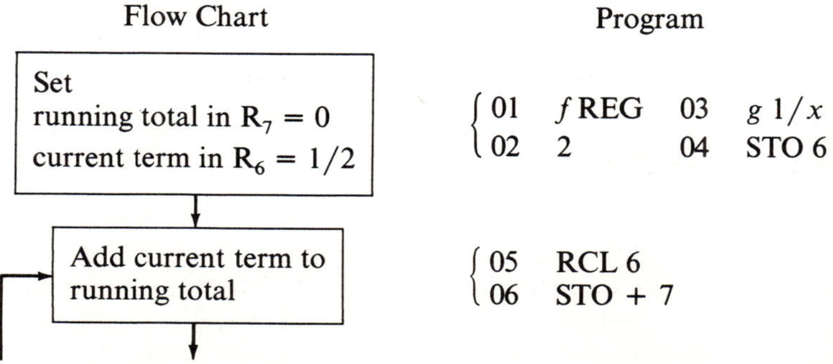

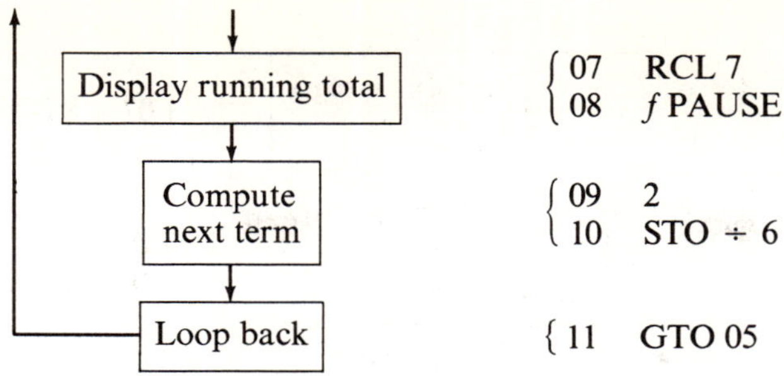

Memory usage: R_6 = term = $\frac{1}{2^n}$,

R_7 = running total

Initialize: [*f*] [STK] [*f*] [PRGM] [*f*] [FIX] [9] [R/S]

As more and more terms are added, the running total becomes closer and closer to the limiting value of the infinite series. Because your calculator only computes with 10 digits, the running total for a convergent infinite series will actually reach a limiting value after a finite number of terms have been totaled.

Section 7: Solving the Gambler's Problem

Now you are prepared to solve the gambler's problem posed in Section 1 of this chapter. Recall that the question was, "How much can the gambler expect to receive, on the average, each time he plays?" In mathematical terms, what is the value of $1/2 + 4/4 + 9/8 + 16/16 + \ldots + n^2/2^n + \ldots$ or more simply,

$$\sum_{n=1}^{\infty} \frac{n^2}{2^n}?$$

You might try writing a program, like the one in Figure 14–9, to evaluate this series before reading further. Run this program to verify that the average amount received is \$6. That means if the gambler has to pay \$10 each time he plays, he should expect to lose \$4 each time on the average.

Figure 14–9

Flow Chart | Program

Set
running total in $R_7 = 0$
index in $R_6 = 1$
current denominator in $R_5 = 2$
current term in x-reg $= 1/2$

01	*f* REG	04	2
02	1	05	STO 5
03	STO 6	06	*g* $1/x$

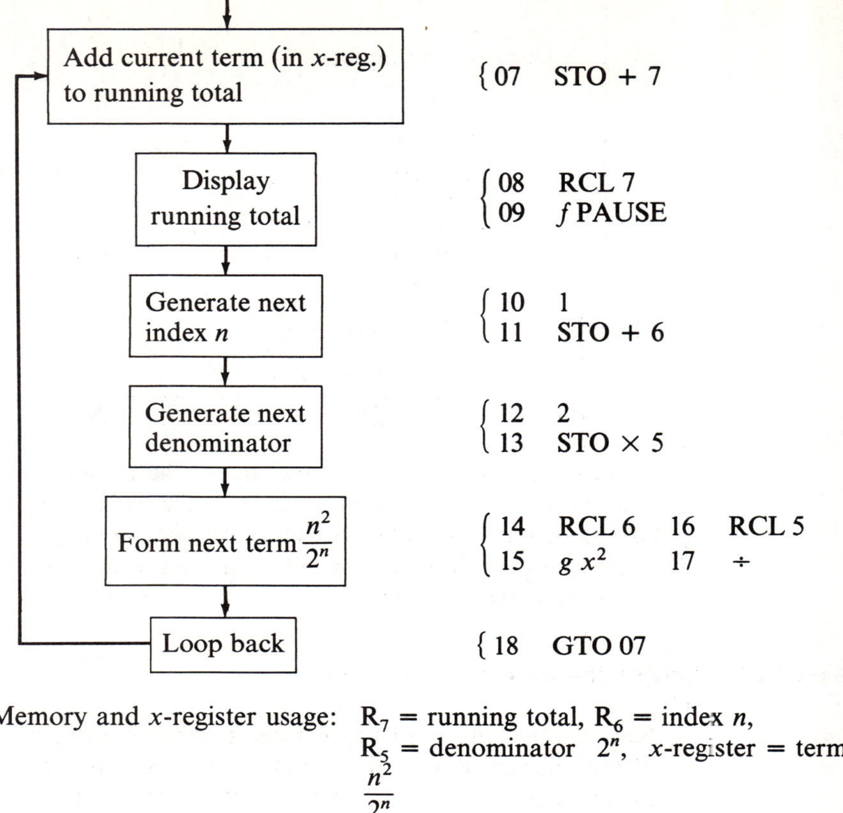

Memory and x-register usage: R_7 = running total, R_6 = index n, R_5 = denominator 2^n, x-register = term $\frac{n^2}{2^n}$

Initialize: [f] [STK] [f] [PRGM] [f] [FIX] [9] [R/S]

Section 8: Problems

In solving these problems, you may find the general flow chart in Figure 14–10 useful for organizing a program to evaluate a series.

Figure 14–10

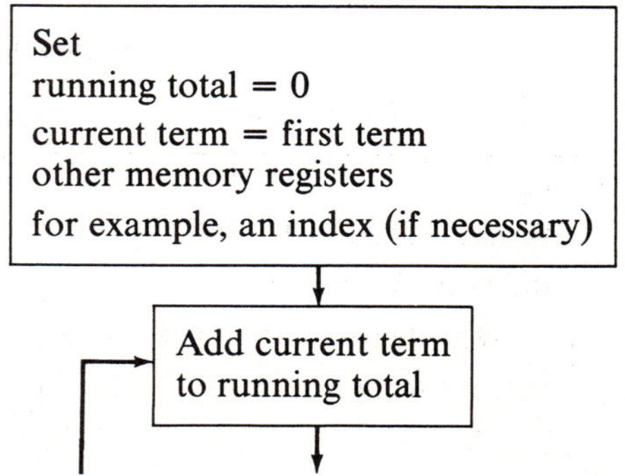

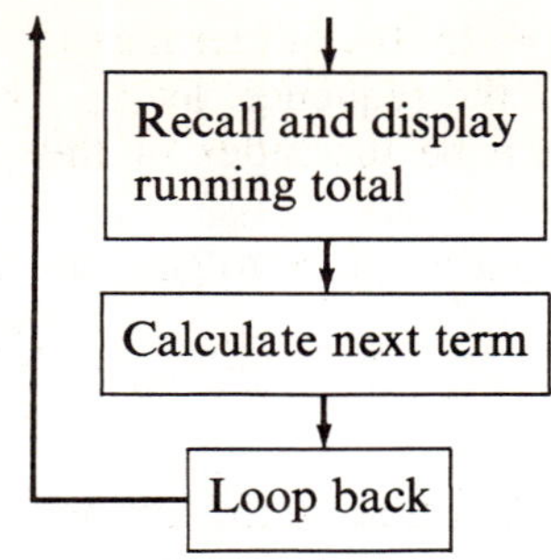

1. The series

$$1 + \frac{1}{3} + \frac{1}{9} + \frac{1}{27} + \cdots + \frac{1}{3^n} + \cdots = \sum_{n=0}^{\infty} \frac{1}{3^n}$$

has the first four partial sums of 1.0000, 1.3333, 1.4444, and 1.4815.
   a. Write a program to evaluate the series.
   b. What is the limiting value?
2. In Sections 1 and 7, the gambler's problem was introduced and solved. The amount received was calculated from the series

$$\sum_{n=1}^{\infty} \frac{n^2}{2^n}.$$

Suppose instead of receiving n^2 dollars when the first head turns up (on the nth toss), the gambler receives n^3 dollars. The average amount received changes to

$$\sum_{n=1}^{\infty} \frac{n^3}{2^n}.$$

   a. Write a program to determine this new expected payoff. The first four partial sums being 0.5000, 2.5000, 5.8750, 9.8750.
   b. How much is the average amount received?
   c. Suppose the gambler has to pay $10 each time to play? What would the gambler's expected profit (or loss) be now?
   d. If the gambler receives only n dollars when the first head turns up (on the nth toss), what is his expected profit?
3. The series

$$\frac{2+3}{6} + \frac{2^2+3^2}{6^2} + \cdots + \frac{2^n+3^n}{6^n} + \cdots = \sum_{n=1}^{\infty} \frac{2^n+3^n}{6^n}$$

has the first four partial sums of 0.8333, 1.1944, 1.3565, and 1.4313.
   a. Write a program to evaluate the series.
   b. What is the limiting value of the series?
4. In the sequence of triangular numbers 1, 3, 6, 10, 15, . . . , each term can be formed by adding the preceding term and the index (sequence position) of the new term. Thus, the 5th term can be formed as

$10 + 5 = 15$, the 6th term as $15 + 6 = 21$, and so on. Let t_n be the nth term of the sequence, let t_{n-1} be the terms preceding the nth term, and let n be the index of the nth term. Then, $t_n = t_{n-1} + n$, where $t_1 = 1$.

a. Write a program to generate the series

$$\sum_{n=1}^{\infty} \frac{6t_n + 1}{t_n^3}.$$

The first three terms of the series are 7.0000, 7.7037, and 7.8750.

b. What is the limiting value of the series in part a?

5. Given the information in problem 4,

a. Write a program to generate the series

$$\sum_{n=1}^{\infty} \frac{20t_n^2 + 10t_n + 1}{t_n^5}.$$

The first term is 31.0000.

b. What is the limiting value of the series in part b?

6. a. As graphed in Figure 14–11, a ball is dropped from a point 5 meters above flat surface. Each time the ball hits the ground after falling a certain distance, it rebounds to a height of 80 percent of that distance. Write a program to find the total distance the ball travels from the series.

$$5 + 2(.80)^1 5 + 2(.80)^2 5 + 2(.80)^3 5 + \ldots .$$

The first few terms are 5.0000, 13.0000, and 19.4000.

b. How far does the ball travel?

Figure 14–11

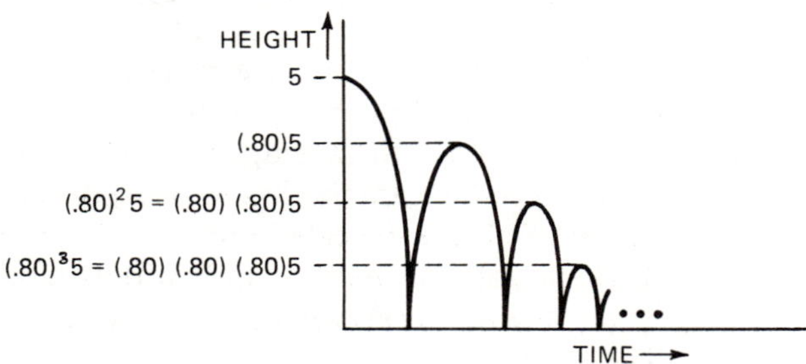

7. The Riemann zeta function is defined by

$$\zeta(s) = \sum_{n=1}^{\infty} \frac{1}{n^s} \qquad \text{for each } s > 1.$$

a. Write a program that allows you to input a value of s (where $s > 4$) and then compute $\zeta(s)$. Check your program by evaluating $\zeta(10)$. The answer should be 1.000994576, which is $\pi^{10}/93{,}555$. To see this value, include the key strokes [*f*] [FIX] [9] in the initialization.

b. Find $\zeta(8)$ and $\zeta(6)$. These values should correspond to $\pi^8/9450$ and $\pi^6/945$ respectively.

c. Why has the restriction that $s > 4$ been included in this problem?

8. The series

$$1 - \frac{1}{2^6} + \frac{1}{3^6} - \frac{1}{4^6} + \cdots + (-1)^{n+1} \cdot \frac{1}{n^6} + \cdots$$

should equal

$$\frac{31}{32} \cdot \frac{\pi^6}{945}$$

However, the series causes some programming problems since it has alternating signs. One approach is to compute $(-1)^{n+1}$ using the [y^x] key when forming each term. On the HP33E, [y^x] functions properly for $y \leqslant 0$ as long as x is an integer.

Another approach is to avoid using [y^x] to produce the alternating signs. Instead use a memory location, say R_3, for the appropriate sign ($+1$ or -1), which can then be multiplied onto the appropriate term. Initialize R_3 with an appropriate sign ($+1$ or -1) and then repeat the key strokes [1] [CHS] [STO] [×] [3] in order to alternately change the sign.

Evaluate the series by this latter method. After computing the term $1/n^6$, in the display, multiply it by the $+1$ or -1 from R_3, and then sum the result into the running total.

Verify that the first three terms are 1, .984375000, and .985746742. Include [f] [FIX] [9] in the initialization.

9. What is the value of the series

$$2\sqrt{3}\left(1 - \frac{1}{3 \cdot 3} + \frac{1}{5 \cdot 3^2} - \frac{1}{7 \cdot 3^3} + \frac{1}{9 \cdot 3^4} - \cdots\right)?$$

The first three terms are 3.4641016, 3.0792014, and 3.1561815. In the initialization include the sequence [f] [FIX] [7].

10. Write a program to show that for any value of $0° < x < 180°$ or $0 < x < \pi$ radians,

$$\frac{\pi}{4} = \sin x + \frac{\sin 3x}{3} + \frac{\sin 5x}{5} + \cdots + \frac{\sin(2n-1)x}{2(n-1)} + \cdots,$$

Include [f] [FIX] [7] in the initialization.

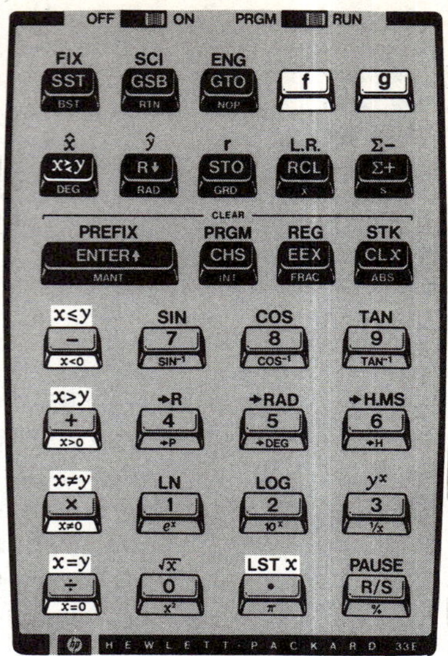

Programming Your Calculator to Make Decisions

Section 1: Learning About the Test Registers

Your Hewlett-Packard calculator has a stack of four registers, the *x*-, *y*-, *z*-, and *t*-registers. All four of these registers can be used for temporary storage of algebraic calculations. The *x*- and *y*-registers, however, can also be used as test registers in two ways. First, the *x*-register can be used alone, when you wish to compare the value in the *x*-register with the number zero. Or, both the *x*- and *y*-registers can be used, when you wish to compare the value in the *x*-register with that in the *y*-register.

Figure 15–1

Flow Chart	Program
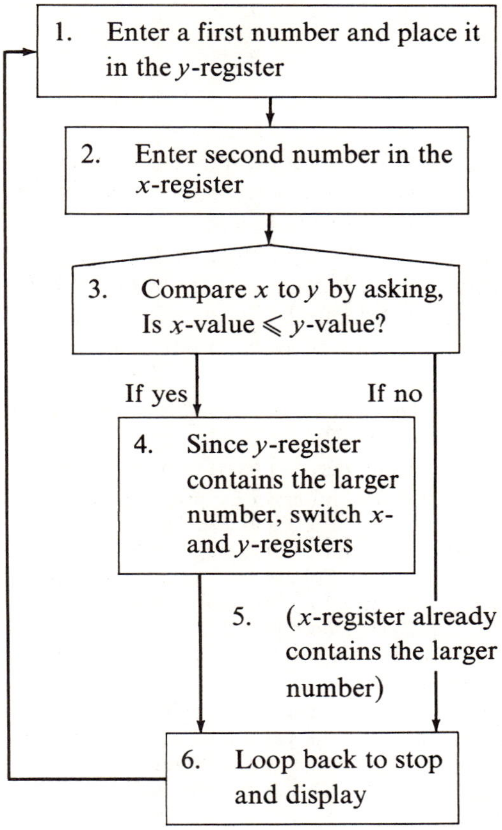 1. Enter a first number and place it in the y-register	00 (R/S) 01 ↑
2. Enter second number in the x-register	02 R/S
3. Compare x to y by asking, Is x-value $\leqslant$ y-value?	03 f $x \leqslant y$
If yes: 4. Since y-register contains the larger number, switch x- and y-registers	04 $x \gtrless y$ *
If no: 5. (x-register already contains the larger number)	
6. Loop back to stop and display	05 GTO 00

Initialization: [f] [PRGM] enter first number, [R/S] enter second number, [R/S]

Notice in Figure 15–1 that a new shape has been introduced to surround the decision-making step in the flow chart. This shape always indicates that the flow of the program branches in either of two directions depending on the decision the calculator makes in that step. Now run the program. Let 100 be the first number and 25 the second. You should see "100.0000" in the display.

Now enter 500, press [R/S] enter 100 and press [R/S]. You should see "500.0000" in the display. What do you see in the display if you enter 2

*The symbol $x \gtrless y$ represents the "x exchange y" key on the calculator.

press [R/S] enter 85 and press [R/S]? What result do you obtain for each of the following pairs of numbers?

a. 36, 360
b. 900, 20
c. 8, 3
d. 65, 1
e. 0, 1065

What decision is your program making? In each case, after the two numbers you entered are compared, the larger is placed in the x-register and displayed when the program stops.

To understand what is happening in this program, follow the step-by-step explanation below. Notice that the number before each of the items corresponds to the same number on the flow chart, indicating which parts of the program are discussed in each paragraph.

1. The first number entered is placed in the y-register (step 01) and the calculator stops (step 02).
2. Next the second number is entered into the x-register.
3. When you restart the program by pressing [R/S], the program encounters the instruction [f] [$x \leq y$] (step 03). This instruction causes the calculator to decide whether the value in the x-register (display) is less than or equal to the value in the y-register. Effectively, the calculator decides whether yes or no is the answer to the question, "Is the x-register value less than or equal to the y-register value?" Depending on the answer, the calculator goes (branches) to either the next memory location or to the one after that and continues execution from there.
4. If the answer is yes (that is the x-register value is less than or equal to the y-register value), then the calculator proceeds to the next memory location (step 04). There it executes the instruction [$x \gtrless y$], which exchanges the x- and y-registers. Thus, the program places the larger value from the y-register into the x-register.
5. If the answer is no (that is, the x-register value is not less than or equal to the y-register value), then the calculator goes to the program step immediately after the next instruction; it skips step 04 and goes to step 05. Thus the larger value already in the x-register is left in the x-register.
6. Whatever decision is made in step 03, the calculator eventually comes to step 05 where it is instructed to loop back to the permanent [R/S] in step 00 in order to stop and display the larger of the two numbers originally entered.

Section 3: Using Comparison Tests to Make Decisions

In the last section your calculator made a decision by comparing two numbers, one in the y-register and the other in the x-register. In fact the only way your calculator can make a decision is by comparing the value in the x-register to the value in the y-register. Your calculator can make a total of eight specific comparison tests, as shown in Table 15–1.

TABLE 15–1

KEY SEQUENCE		COMPARISON TEST
f	$x \leq y$	*Is* $x \leq y$?
f	$x > y$	*Is* $x > y$?
f	$x \neq y$	*Is* $x \neq y$?
f	$x = y$	*Is* $x = y$?
g	$x < 0$	*Is* $x < 0$?
g	$x > 0$	*Is* $x > 0$?
g	$x \neq 0$	*Is* $x \neq 0$?
g	$x = 0$	*Is* $x = 0$?

For each of these tests the procedure is identical. If the answer to the test question is "yes," the calculator proceeds to the next instruction, as usual. If, however, the answer to the question is "no," the calculator skips the next instruction and goes (branches) to the instruction following that one.

To illustrate the use of these comparison tests in getting your calculator to make decisions, consider the following examples.

Example 1

For a specific value of x, is $x^2 - 2x - 3 = 0$? First have your program compute the value of $x^2 - 2x - 3$ for a specific x. Then with the comparison test [g] [$x = 0$], your program will be able to decide whether $x^2 - 2x - 3 = 0$ or not.

You can see how this is accomplished in the program in Figure 15–2, which is designed to display either x if $x^2 - 2x - 3 = 0$ or $\pi =$ 3.141592654 otherwise. Verify that for $x = 6$, the program displays π, and for $x = 3$, it displays"3.0000."

Figure 15–2

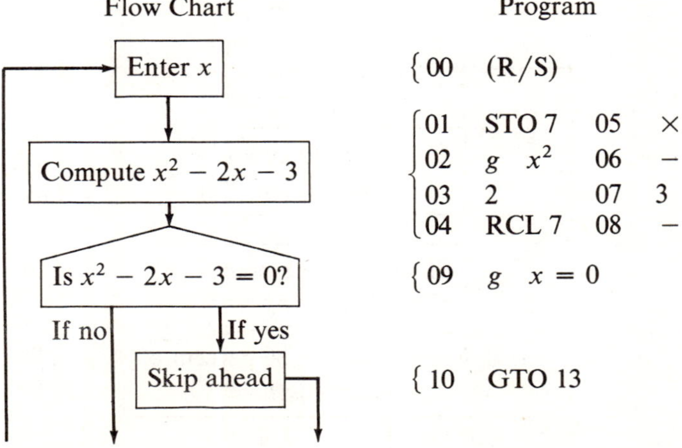

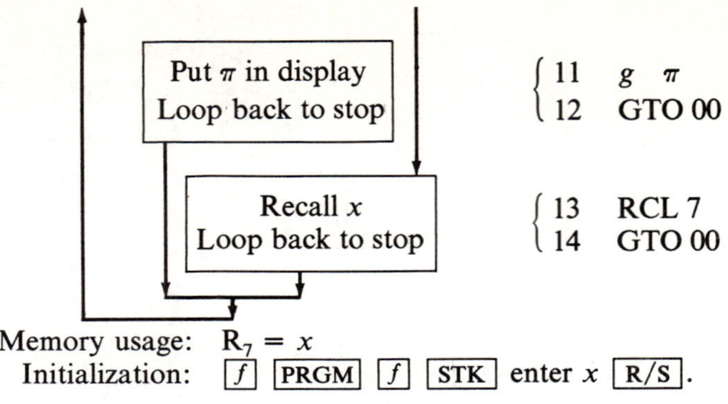

Memory usage: $R_7 = x$
Initialization: [f] [PRGM] [f] [STK] enter x [R/S].

Example 2

Suppose you are working for a bank that offers home mortgages at 8 1/4 percent depending on whether a customer places 30 percent or more of the cost of the house as a down payment. For less than a 30 percent down payment, the mortgage rate is 8 1/2 percent.

How can you program your calculator to answer the question, "For a given house cost and customer's down payment, is the down payment greater than or equal to 30 percent of the house cost?"

First compute 30 percent of the house cost and place it in the y-register. Next place the customer's down payment in the x-register. Finally, with the comparison test [f] [$x \leqslant y$], your program will be able to decide whether the down payment is greater than or equal to 30 percent of the house cost.

You can see how this comparison test is used in the program in Figure 15–3. If the down payment is 30 percent or more of the house cost, the program stops and displays "8.2500" representing the fact that the 8 1/4 percent mortgage rate applies. Otherwise the program stops and displays "8.5000".

Figure 15–3

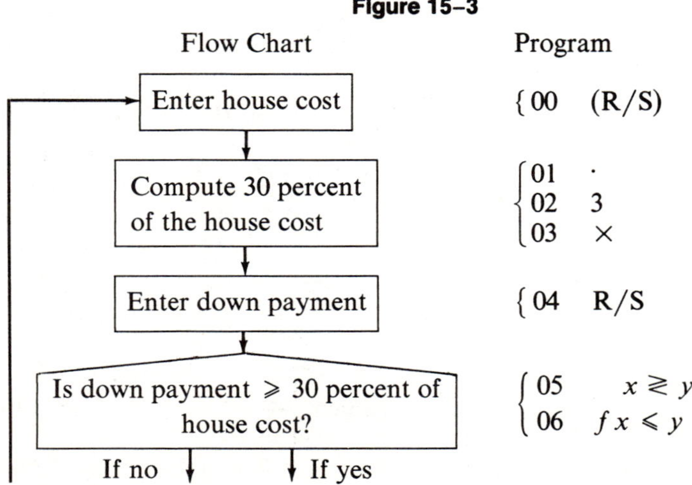

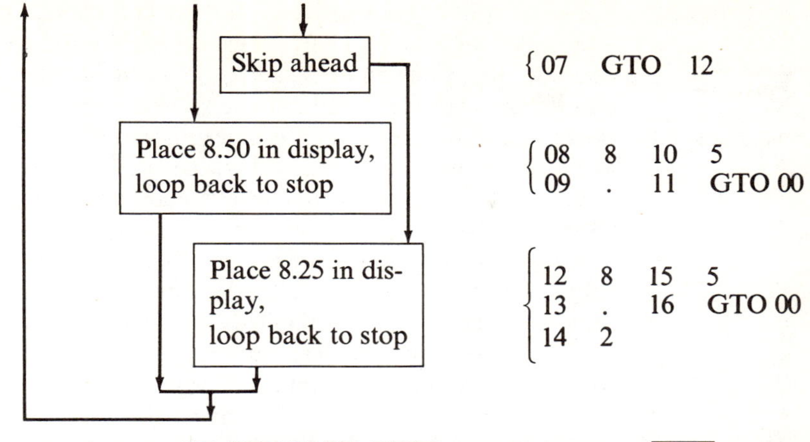

Initialization: [f] [PRGM] [f] [STK] enter house cost [R/S] customer's down payment, [R/S]

Verify that for a house costing $50,000 with a customer putting $10,000 down, the program shows "8.5000" in the display.

Section 4: Problems

1. A certain bank has "now" accounts where the balance at the end of a month earns interest at the monthly rate of 1/2 percent as long as the balance is more than $200. Otherwise the balance earns no interest. Write a program to accept a monthly balance as input, and decide whether that amount is more than $200. If it is, add 1/2 percent of that amount and display the new balance. If it is not, merely display the balance. Test your program by entering a balance of $500. You should obtain $502.50 in the display.
2. Postal rates (effective May, 1978) for first and second class are:

CLASS	RATE	
1	15¢ for first ounce plus 13¢	for each additional ounce or fraction thereof.
2	10¢ for first 2 ounces plus 6¢	

In other words, if z is the weight in ounces rounded up to the nearest integer equal or greater than the actual weight, the rates are:

CLASS	RATE	
1	$.15 + .13(z - 1)$	for $z = 1, 2, 3, \cdots$
2	$.10 + .06(z - 2)$	for $z = 2, 3, 4, \cdots$

Write a program to compute the correct postal rate from two input numbers: the rounded-up weight, z, and the number 1 or 2 indicating the class. Use this data to verify that your program works: For $z = 5$, the class 1 postal rate is 67¢ and the class 2 postal rate is 28¢.

3. Faced with a set of numbers, how do you choose the smallest? One process is to systematically examine each number in the set. First examine the first number and choose it as the smallest number examined so far. Next examine the second number; if it is smaller than the first, choose the second number instead of the first as the smallest so far. Continue examining each successive number, choosing it if it is smaller than the previously chosen smallest number. After examining all the numbers, the smallest of all of them will have been chosen.

   Write a program to find the smallest of a set of numbers by the above process. Initially store the first number in R_1. After that, accept each next number as input, decide whether the new number is smaller than the previous smallest number saved in R_1, and replace the contents of R_1 with the new number if appropriate. At the end, recall the contents from R_1 to display the smallest number.
4. A point (x_0, y_0) is on a line if the coordinates x_0 and y_0 satisfy the equation of the line. For example, the point (7, 32) is on $y = 5x - 3$ since $32 = (5 \cdot 7) - 3$. Write a program to decide whether or not a point is on the line $y = 5x - 3$. In case the point is on the line, display the number 1; otherwise, display 0. These points are on the line: (3, 12), (5, 22), (−3, −18). These points are not on the line: (−2, 5), (6, 20), (−2, 3).
5. Write a program to decide whether a number is between 14.5 and 25.5. If it is, display the number. If not, display π.
6. United Parcel Service has a maximum package size requirement that the length plus girth may not exceed 108 inches. If the length, width, and height of a rectangular box are l, w, and h, the girth (or the distance around the box) is $(2w + 2h)$. Write a program to accept input values for l, w, and h (in inches), calculate the length plus girth and compare it with 108. If the size of a package is too large, display 0; if its size is acceptable, display 1. To check your program: for $l = 20$, $w = 14$, and $h = 30$, a 1 should appear in the display; and $l = 30$, $w = 14$, and $h = 30$, a 0 should appear in the display.

Figure 15–4

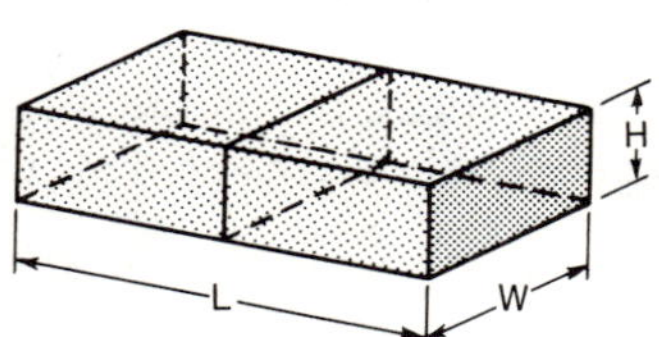

7. Not only does United Parcel Service have a maximum size for packages, they also have a maximum weight of 50 pounds. Write a program to accept input values for length, width, height, and weight, and decide whether the package can or cannot be sent by U.P.S.

8. A quadratic equation $ax^2 + bx + c = 0$ has the roots

$$x_1, x_2 = \frac{-b \pm \sqrt{d}}{2a}.$$

When $d \geqslant 0$, the roots are real and are

$$x_1 = \frac{-b + \sqrt{d}}{2a}, \qquad x_2 = \frac{-b - \sqrt{d}}{2a}.$$

When $d < 0$, the roots are complex and are

$$x_1 = u + vi, \qquad x_2 = u - vi \qquad \text{where } i = \sqrt{-1} \quad \text{and}$$

$$u = -b/2a, \quad v = \sqrt{-d}\,/2a$$

Write a program to allow for the input numbers a, b, and c. Compute d and test for real or complex roots. If the roots are real, display x_1 and x_2; and if the roots are complex, display u and v. Test your program with

a. for $x^2 - 2x - 8 = 0$; $d = 36$ and $x_1, x_2 = +4$ or -2

b. for $9x^2 - 3x - 2 = 0$; $d = 81$; and $x_1, x_2 = +\frac{2}{3}, -\frac{1}{3}$

c. for $x^2 + 2x + 3 = 0$; $d = -8$, and $x_1, x_2 = -1 \pm \sqrt{2}\, i$

Section 5: Making Decisions Involving Whole Numbers

As you have seen, the eight comparison tests shown in Table 15–1 can be used to make decisions in a program. Often which comparison test will make a particular decision is obvious. Sometimes, it is not obvious—namely when the corresponding comparison test for a decision requires some special knowledge about your calculator, mathematics, or both.

Consider, for instance, how you would test to see whether a number is a whole number. Every number has an integer part and a fractional part. For example, 3.157 has an integer part of 3 and a fractional part of .157, while 7 has an integer part of 7 and a fractional part of 0. Notice that a number is a whole number when its fractional part is 0 or when it is the same as its integer part.

Using the [g] [INT] and [g] [FRAC] instructions on your calculator, you can find the integer and fractional parts of a number, respectively. You can therefore test to see whether a number is a whole number by either comparing its integer part to itself or its fractional part to zero.

Determining whether a number is or is not a whole number can be useful in making a variety of other decisions. For example, deciding whether a number, n, is divisible by four (or d) can be accomplished by testing whether the quotient $n/4$ (or n/d) is a whole number or not. Similarly, deciding whether a number is a perfect square (or perfect kth power) can be accomplished by testing whether the square root (or kth root) is a whole number or not.

For your interest, the two programs following illustrate the ideas just presented. The first decides whether a number, n, is divisible by four by comparing the fractional part of the quotient $n/4$ to zero. The second program decides whether a number is a perfect square by taking the square root of the number and then comparing the square root to its integer part.

Program 1

Figure 15–5 contains a program that generates the sequence of counting numbers 1, 2, 3, 4, . . . , pauses to show those terms that are not divisible by 4, and stops to display those terms that are.

Figure 15–5

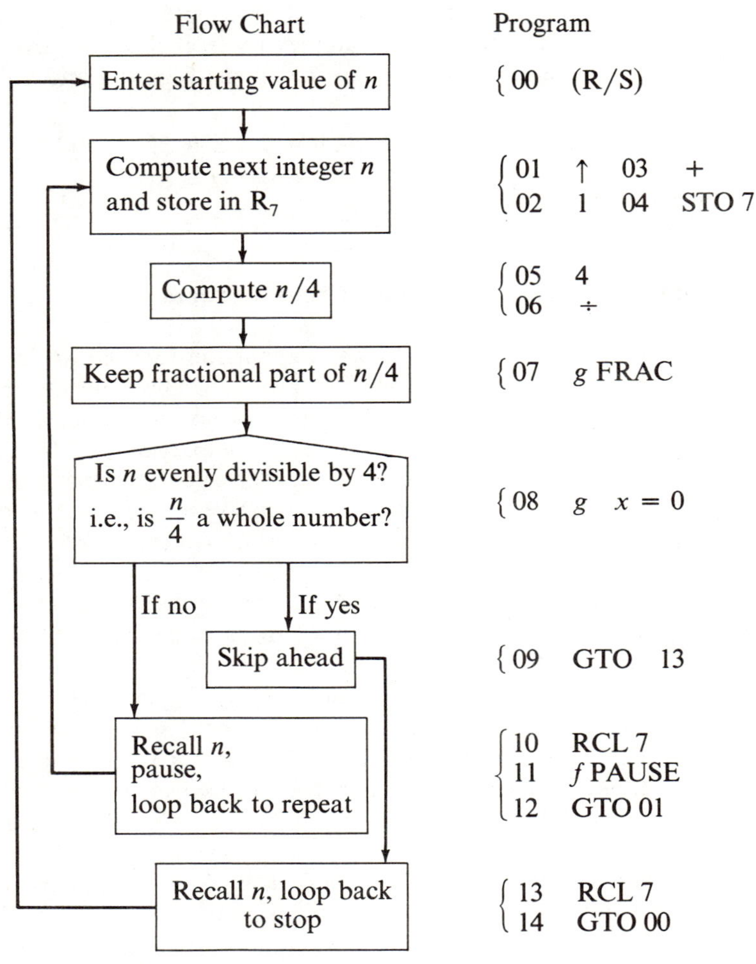

Memory usage: $R_7 = n$
Initialize: [f] [PRGM] [f] [STK] enter first value of n (i.e., 0) [R/S]
Comment: When the calculator stops to display on integer evenly divisible by four, press [R/S] to restart the program.

Program 2

The program in Figure 15–6 generates the sequence of counting numbers 1, 2, 3, 4, . . . , pauses to shown those terms that are not perfect squares, and stops to display those terms that are.

Figure 15–6

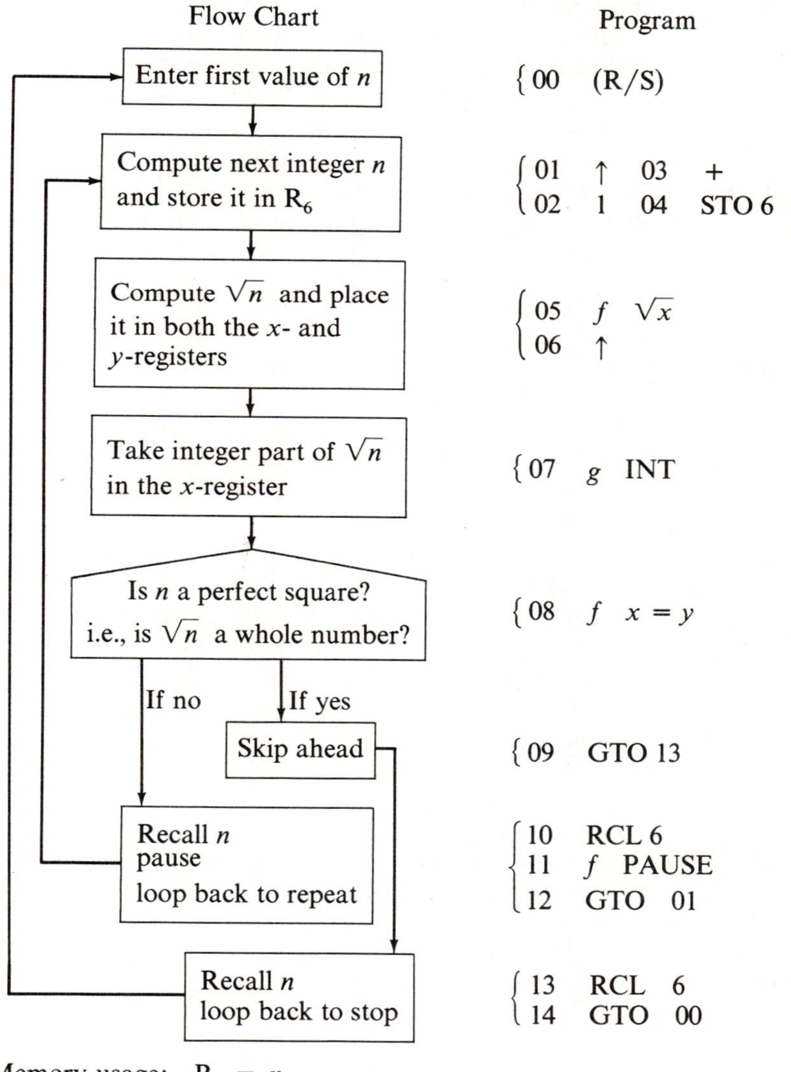

Memory usage: $R_6 = n$

Initialize: [f] [PRGM] [f] [STK] enter first value of n (i.e., 0), [R/S]

Comment: When the calculator stops to display an integer that is a perfect square, press [R/S] to restart the program.

If you are testing to see whether a number is a whole number, you may at times obtain unexpected results, due to the way your calculator is engineered to make various computations. For example, if you compute the cube root of 125, in spite of the fact that the display shows 5.0000, the actual value computed internally by the calculator differs from 5. in the last one or two decimal places. (See the owner's manual of your calculator for details.) So, in a program that tests whether the cube root of 125 is a whole number, the calculator will conclude that it is not whole! If your calculator computes a value involving only [+] [−] [×] [÷] or [x^2] you need not worry about obtaining unexpected results of this type. However, you should expect them with other functions, especially with [y^x].

For your interest, a sequence of key strokes avoids this difficulty. This sequence of nine program instructions rounds off the number in the display to 8 significant digits: enter [↑] [*f*] [log] [*g*] [INT] [2] [+] [*g*] [10^x] [+] [*f*] [LAST *X*] [−]. Include this sequence in a program after computing a value and before performing any of the tests [*f*] [$x \neq y$], [*f*] [$x = 0$], [*g*] [$x \neq 0$], or [*g*] [$x = 0$].

Section 6: Problems

1. Write a program to accept any year between 1901 and 2099 as input and decide whether that year is a leap year. If it is, display the year as a positive number. If it is not a leap year, display the year as a negative number.
2. a. Write a program to decide whether a number is both less than 100 and a perfect cube. If it is, have your calculator display the number, otherwise, display 0. Test your program for 4, 100, and 125, which should give 0 in the display, and then for 27 which should give 27 in the display.
   b. What happens when you test your program for a negative number? Why?
3. Write a program to decide whether a number is between −100 and 100 and is a perfect cube.
4. Write a program to generate the sequence of multiples of three. Have your program pause to display each multiple and stop for each multiple of three that is a perfect square.
5. A Pythagorean triple is a triple of integers (a, b, c) that represent the lengths of the three sides of a right triangle. Necessarily, $c^2 = \sqrt{a^2 + b^2}$.

Figure 15–7

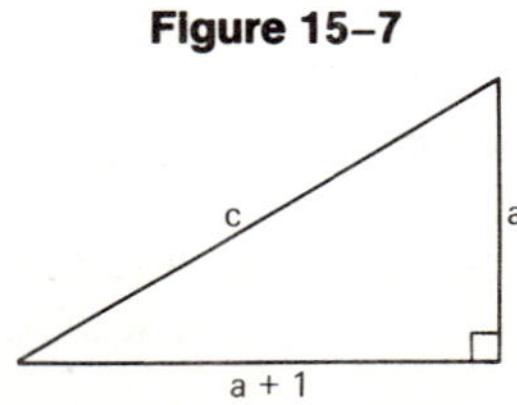

Find all pythagorean triples of the form shown in Figure 15–7: a, $a + 1$, and $c = \sqrt{a^2 + (a + 1)^2} = \sqrt{2a^2 + 2a + 1}$, where a, $a + 1$, and c are all integers. Have your program begin with $a = 1$, increment a by 1 each time through the loop, and stop to display c when c is integral. (Hint: (3, 4, 5) is the first triple of this type. There are four solutions with c less than 1,000. Can you find them all?)

6. The triangular numbers T_n can be defined recursively $T_n = T_{n-1} + n$ with $T_1 = 1$. For which n is T_n a perfect square? For $n < 2{,}000$, there are exactly 5 solutions. Can you find them all?
7. Many problems of a puzzle nature involve dividing numbers by other numbers and can be solved directly with the use of your calculator.

   Find the smallest positive whole number with a remainder of 5 when divided by 6 and a remainder of 8 when divided by 11. (Hint: You are looking for a number n so that $n = 6k + 5$ and $n = 11l + 8$. Write a program to let $l = 1, 2, 3, \ldots,$ compute n, solve for k, and test whether k is an integer. Have the program stop at the first instance when k is integral and then display n.

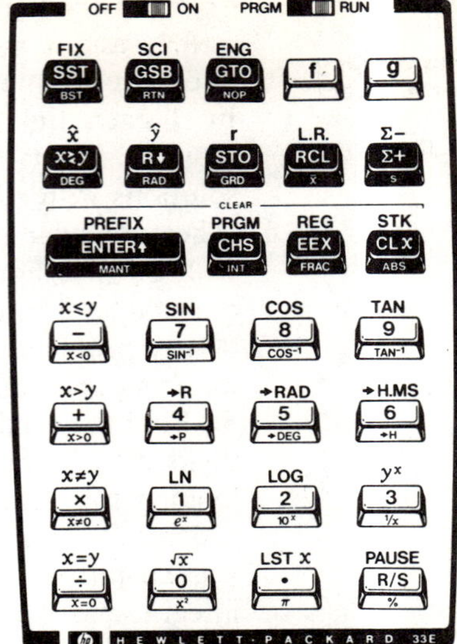

Programming Finite Loops

Section 1: Having Your Calculator End Loops

A square-based pyramid is formed using cannonballs with a single cannonball on top and a square number on each layer as shown in Figure 16–1. How many cannonballs are there in 10 layers? How many layers can be made from 10,000 cannonballs?

Rephrased in mathematical language these questions become:

1. How large is

$$\sum_{k=1}^{10} k^2 = 1^2 + 2^2 + 3^2 + \ldots + 10^2?$$

and

2. What is the largest value of n so that

$$\sum_{k=1}^{n} k^2 = 1^2 + 2^2 + \ldots + n^2 \leqslant 10{,}000?$$

Figure 16–1

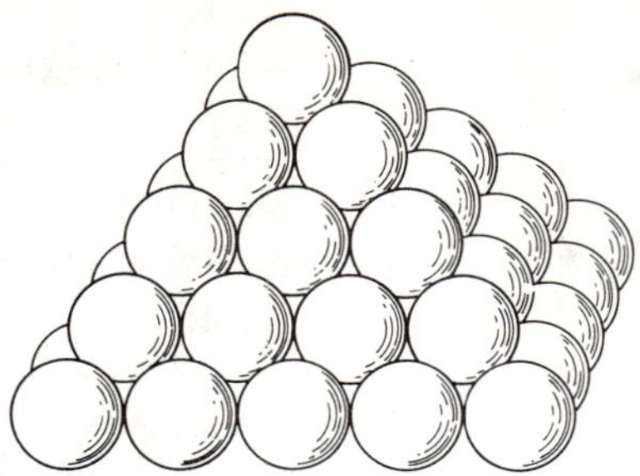

You could answer each of these questions by setting up an infinite loop to calculate $1^2 + 2^2 + 3^2 + \ldots$ as a running total. During each loop the calculator computes the next integer k, adds k^2 to the running total, and displays the current running total. Then you can answer question 1 by counting the loops and stopping the calculator after the 10th loop. Similarly, you can answer the second question by counting the loops and stopping the calculator just as the total goes over 10,000. (In this case you have counted one loop too many (that is, $n + 1$ loops), so you must subtract one from the number of loops counted to get n, the answer.)

Nonetheless, your calculator can do the watching, counting, and the decision-making for you. By including within the loop a comparison test to check whether it is time to end the loop, you can convert an infinite loop into a finite one.

For the first cannonball question, have the program loop to compute the running total $1^2 + 2^2 + 3^2 + \ldots$. Include in the loop a comparison test to decide when the number of times through the loop has reached 10. At that time have the program stop to display the current running total, the answer to the first question. You will find a flow chart and program to do the Cannonball Problem in the next section.

For the second question, use the same type of loop as in the previous program. Include in this loop a comparison test to determine when the running total becomes at least 10,000. At this time the number of completed loops minus 1 answers the question.

All loops you program are infinite loops unless you include in the loop a comparison test to decide when to terminate it. Sections 2 and 3 of this chapter present examples and problems for which the terminating condition is simply, "Has the number of completed loops reached a predetermined number yet?" Sections 4 and 5 go on to present examples and problems of other conditions for terminating a loop.

Section 2: Calculating Finite Sums or Products

How can you set up a finite loop to calculate a finite sum, such as $1^2 + 2^2 + 3^2 + \ldots + n^2$, or a finite product like $n! = (n)(n-1)(n-2)\ldots(2)(1)$?

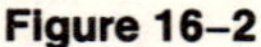

Figure 16–2

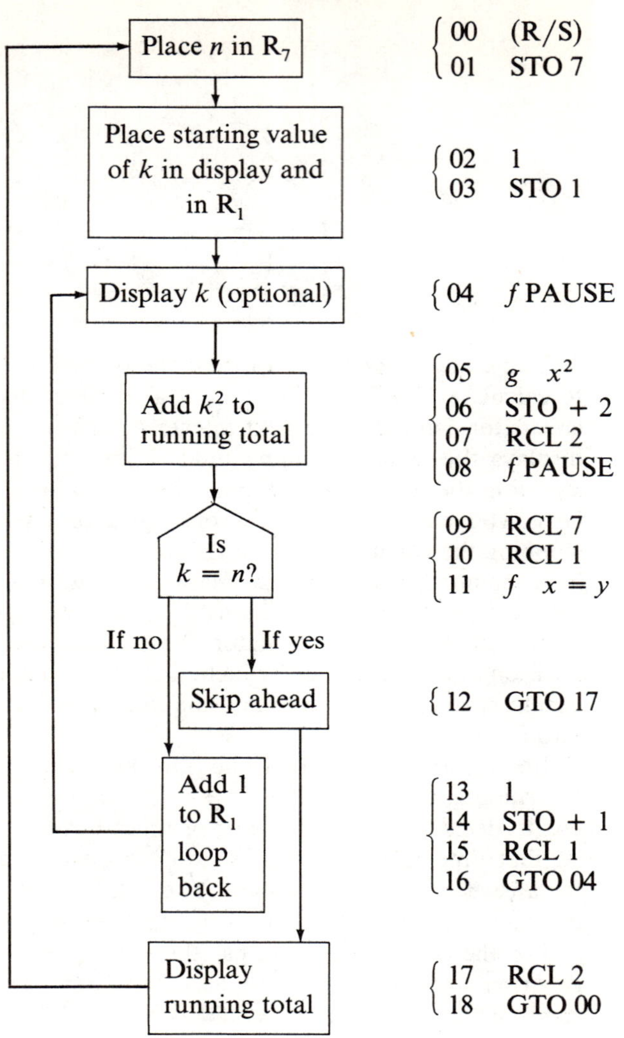

Memory usage: $R_1 = k$, $R_2 =$ sum, $R_7 = n$

Initialization: [f] [PRGM] [f] [REG] [f] [STK] enter n [R/S]

Comment: Notice the pauses in steps 04 and 08 which show k and the running total as the program proceeds. If either of these pauses is not desired, delete step 04 or delete steps 07 and 08.

Example 1: The Cannonball Problem

As mentioned in the previous section, the calculation of the sum $1^2 + 2^2 + 3^2 + \ldots + 10^2$ in the Cannonball Problem can be set up as a loop designed to compute a running total. To make the loop finite, include within the loop a comparison test to see whether the loop has been processed 10 times yet. How would you set up a finite loop to compute $1^2 + 2^2 + 3^2 + \ldots + n^2$ where n may be different each time you run the program, but will be known at the start of the program each time you run it? You may want to try to program this on your own before reading further.

Figure 16–2 contains a flow chart and corresponding program to enter the value of n and then compute $1^2 + 2^2 + 3^2 + \ldots + n^2$ for the Cannonball Problem. Run this program for $n = 10$ to verify that the number of cannonballs in 10 layers is 385. Then modify your program to show that for $n = 30$, the number of cannonballs is just less than 10,000.

Example 2: Computing n!

The next flow chart and program in Figure 16–3 compute $n!$ from an entered value of n. The computation is performed from left to right according to $n! = (n)(n - 1)(n - 2) \ldots (3)(2)(1)$. Initially the value of n is used as the current factor and the current factor is reduced by one each time through the loop. The current factor is compared to the number one after multiplying the factor onto the running product. When the current factor becomes 1 the product is complete.

Figure 16–3

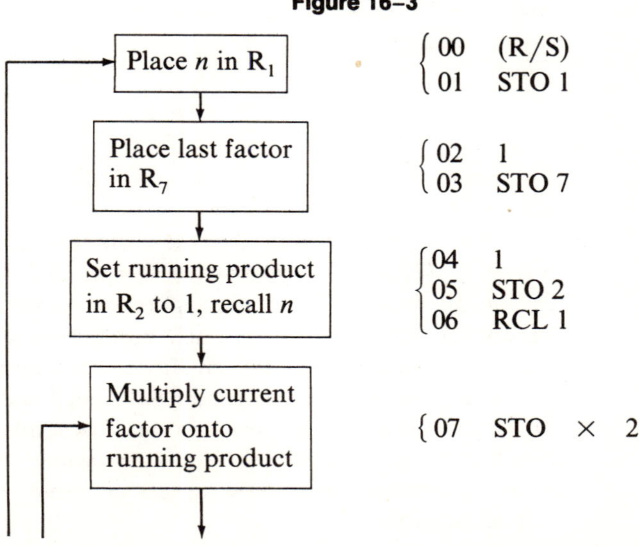

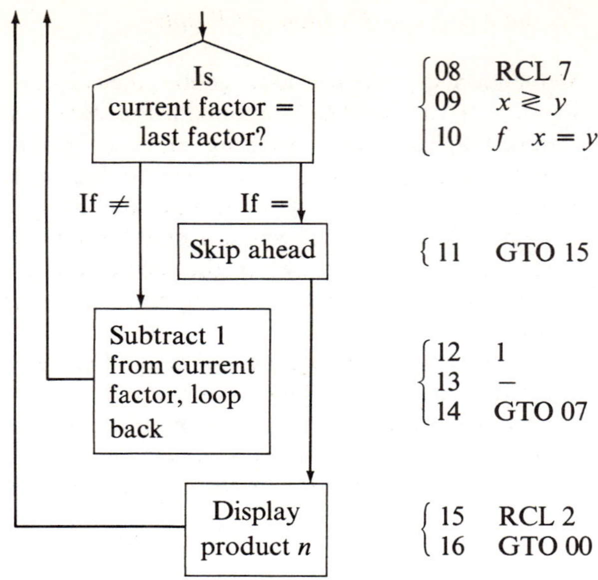

Memory usage: R_7 = end factor = 1, $R_1 = n$
R_2 = running product

Initialize: [f] [PRGM] [f] [REG] [f] [STK] enter n [R/S]

Section 3: Problems

1. How many cannonballs are there in a triangular-based pyramid with 1 cannonball on the top, 3 on the second layer, 6 on the third layer, $k(k + 1)/2$ balls on the kth layer, and n layers all together? When n = 1, 2, 3, 4 the correct numbers are 1, $1 + 3 = 4$, $1 + 3 + 6 = 10$, and $1 + 3 + 6 + 10 = 20$. How many cannonballs are there in 10 layers? 20 layers? 50 layers?
2. Find

$$\sum_{k=1}^{n} [3k(k - 1) + 1]$$

for values of n equal to 2, 3, 4, and 5. Do you recognize the sequence that is generated?
3. The Fibonacci numbers are the numbers in the sequence $f(0) = 0$, $f(1) = 1$, $f(2) = f(1) + f(0) = 1 + 0 = 1$, and $f(k) = f(k - 1) + f(k - 2)$ for all $k > 1$. Write a program to compute a running total of Fibonacci numbers, display each number as it is calculated, and then display the sum of the first ten Fibonacci numbers.
4. Permutations are finite products. Specifically, $P_y^n = n(n - 1)(n - 2) \ldots (n - y + 1)$. The permutation P_y^n is similar to $n!$ but differs in the fact that the last factor is $(n - y + 1)$ instead of 1.
   a. Write a program to allow inputs of y and n and then compute the permutation P_y^n.

b. How many ways could you choose a committee of a president, vice-president, secretary, and treasurer from a group of 10 people? This number is symbolized by P_4^{10}. What is its value?

c. How many ways could 5 out of a group of 12 people seat themselves in five chairs placed in a row? In other words, what is P_5^{12}?

5. When y objects are chosen from a collection of n objects, but the order of choosing the objects is irrelevant, the number of choices is called the number of combinations of y chosen from n, symbolized by C_y^n—specifically, $C_y^n = P_y^n/y!$ But the computation can be more efficiently performed as a product of fractions:

$$C_y^n = \frac{n}{y} \cdot \frac{n-1}{y-1} \cdot \frac{n-2}{y-2} \cdots \frac{n-y+2}{2} \cdot \frac{n-y+1}{1}$$

a. Program your calculator to compute C_y^n with given input values of y and n.

b. How many ways can you choose 4 people out of 10 when order is unimportant?

c. If you have a collection of 10 different coins, how many different subcollections of 6 coins could you choose?

6. The efficient formula for calculating a value of e, the base of the natural logarithms is:

$$e = 1 + \frac{1}{1!} + \frac{1}{2!} + \frac{1}{3!} + \frac{1}{4!} + \ldots .$$

Find the sum of the first 20 terms of this series.

Section 4: Ending a Loop When a Condition is Met

With the use of the comparison tests, you can set up a program loop that ends when any of a number of different types of conditions is met. Presenting an exhaustive list of such conditions is impractical since they depend upon the context of an individual problem and on the particular approach you use to solve the problem. Instead, two characteristic examples are given in this section.

Example 1: Finding the Maximum of a Finite Number of Possibilities—the Volume of the Box Problem

If a piece of paper 22 cm. by 28 cm. is marked off into centimeter squares, has an x-cm. square cut off each corner, and is then folded into an open box (see Figure 16–4), what value of x yields the box with the maximum volume?

The volume is given by $V(x) = (22 - 2x)(28 - 2x)(x)$, and x may take on the (whole) values 1, 2, . . . , 10. Notice that if $x = 11$, the box has no width since 11 is half of 22. Consequently, x cannot exceed 10.

A program to find the x value corresponding to the maximum volume can test each possible value of x, saving x if $V(x)$ is larger than the volume

Figure 16–4

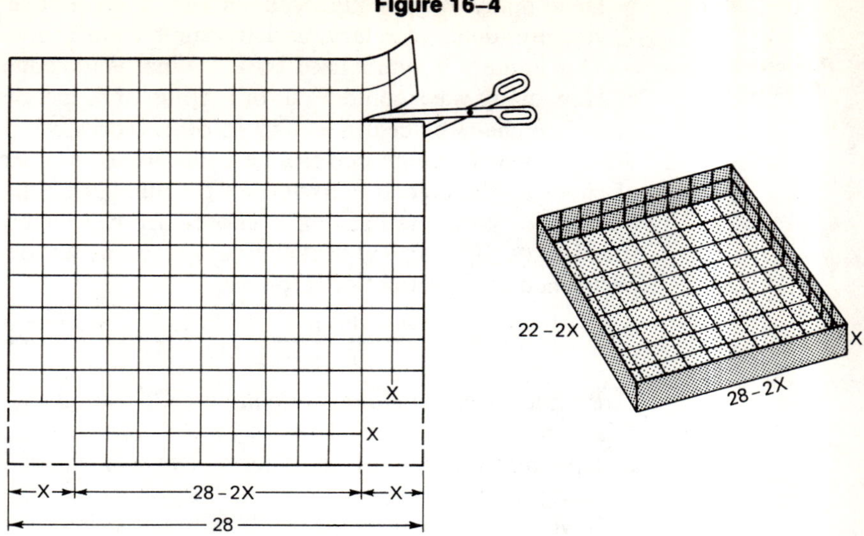

for any previous x value. The looping in the program ends when all values of x have been tested. Therefore, this program is similar to those described in Sections 2 and 3 in the sense that the program stops after the loop has been processed a predetermined number of times (ten in this case).

Here is a flow chart and program to solve this problem.

Figure 16–5

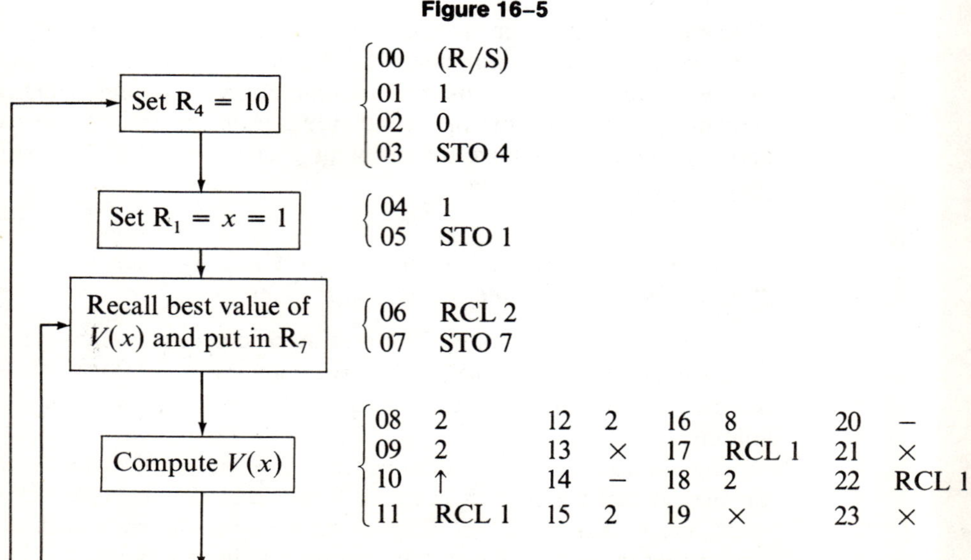

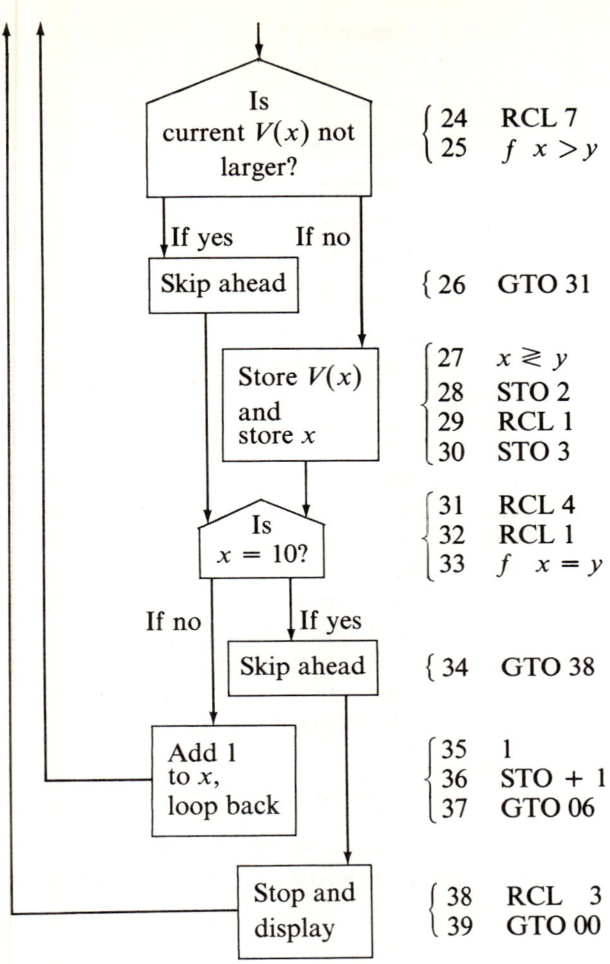

Memory usage: $R_1 = x$, $R_2 = R_7 =$ best $V(x)$, $R_3 =$ best x, $R_4 = 10$
Initialize: [f] [PRGM] [f] [REG] [f] [STK] [R/S]
Comment: The best x is 4. To see the best $V(x)$ press [RCL] [2] or [RCL] [7]

Example 2: Finding a First Value When a Condition is Met—the Stacking Problem

Suppose you have a large collection of *n* congruent unit length objects, such as bricks, books, or cards. If you stack them so that the one on top extends as far to the right of the bottom one as possible (see Figure 16–6), can the top one overhang more than one unit length to the right? If so, how many objects are necessary to achieve this condition?

Figure 16–6

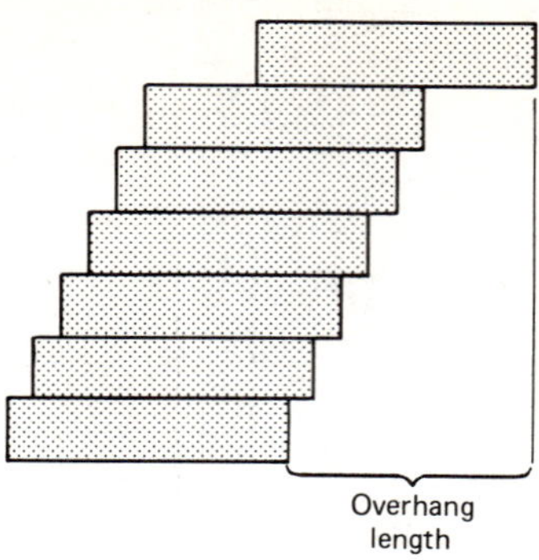

Considering physics, the maximum overhang length occurs if the center of mass of the top object is balanced over the right edge of the next object down. If the center of mass is to the right of that point, the object will fall; if the center of mass is to the left, the overhang is not maximal. Similarly the center of mass of the top two objects needs to balance on top of the right edge of the third. In general, the center of mass of the top $n - 1$ objects needs to balance on top of the right edge of the nth object. This describes a way to actually build such a stack from the top down and mathematically leads to the overhang length of

$$\sum_{k=1}^{n} \frac{1}{2k}$$

for n objects stacked for the maximal overhang length.

Now the mathematical question becomes: For what first value of n (if any) does

$$\sum_{k=1}^{n} \frac{1}{2k} > 1?$$

A flow chart and program for the stacking problem are found in Figure 16–7. The program loops for each consecutive value of k, starting at $k = 1$, computes $\frac{1}{2k}$ and adds $\frac{1}{2k}$ to a running total. The looping ends when the running total first exceeds the value 1. Then, the current value of k, representing the desired number of objects, is displayed.

According to this program only 4 objects are necessary so that

$$\sum_{k=1}^{n} \frac{1}{2k} > 1.$$

Is it possible to find an n so that

$$\sum_{k=1}^{n} \frac{1}{2k} > 2?$$

Change the initialization in the program to [f] [PRGM] [f] [REG] [f] [STK] enter 2 [R/S] and see if you obtain 31.

Figure 16–7

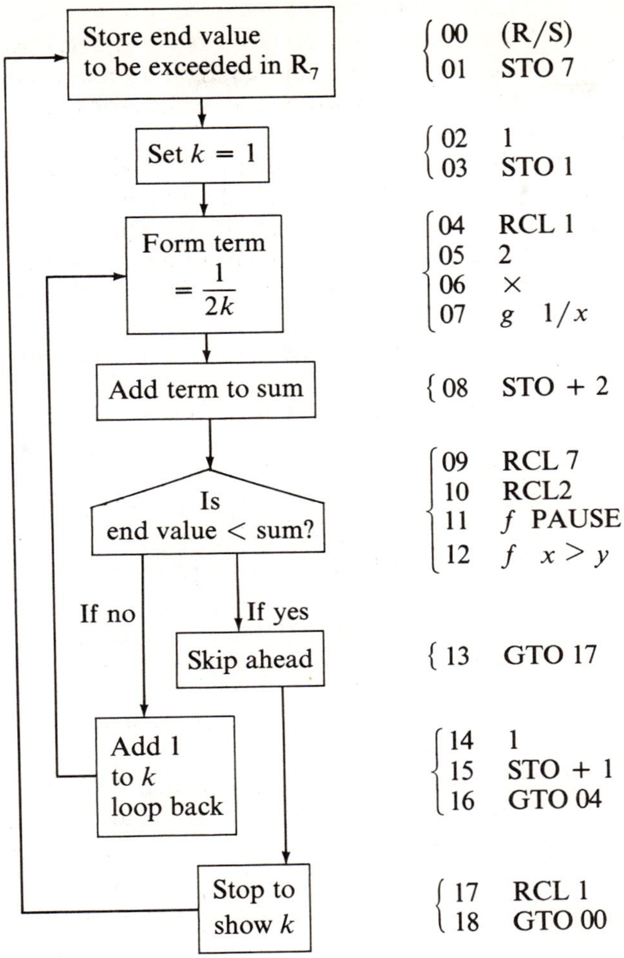

Memory usage: R_7 = end value to be exceeded, $R_1 = k$, R_2 = SUM
Initialize: [f] [PRGM] [f] [REG] [f] [STK] enter 1 [R/S]

Section 5: More Problems

1. Write a program to generate the values $\sqrt[1]{1}$, $\sqrt[2]{2}$, $\sqrt[3]{3}$, $\sqrt[4]{4}$, . . . , $\sqrt[30]{30}$, that is, the values $\sqrt[n]{n}$ for n going from 1 to 30. Have your program find and display the maximum of these values.
2. a. Write a program to compute the fourth root of $n = 1, 2, 3, 4, \ldots$, and to stop and display the first one exceeding π.
   b. How would you change the program to allow for any number rather than just π to be used for the test value?

3. Suppose you paint k faces of a cube red and the other $6 - k$ faces blue. Then, when the paint has dried, you toss the cube three times hoping to obtain red on the top face twice and blue once in any order. How many faces should you paint red and how many blue so that what you wish to obtain has the maximum possible probability? (Hint: $k = 0, 1, 2, 3, 4, 5$ or 6.)
4. What is the largest number of levels you can build in a square-based pyramid made from 10,000 cannonballs? (See Section 1 if you need to.)
5. At a local school benefit dance, students paid \$4 a couple and others paid \$5 a couple to attend. In total, \$77 was collected. Phrased mathematically, this last sentence becomes: for positive integers x and y, $4x + 5y = 77$.
   a. Find all four integer pairs (x, y) that solve the equation $4x + 5y = 77$.
   b. If the number of students and the number of other people who came to the dance were as close together as possible, how many of each came?
6. Jack's beanstalk was most unusual. Someone said that on the first day it grew to a short height and then grew according to the following pattern. On the second day it increased its height by $\frac{1}{2}$, on the third day by $\frac{1}{3}$ and on the fourth day by $\frac{1}{4}$, and so on. How long did it take for Jack's beanstalk to reach 100 times its height on the first day?
   Caution: The answer is *not* given by the first n for which
   $$\sum_{k=1}^{n} 1/n \geqslant 100.$$
7. At a special fund-raising banquet, 100 senators, congresspersons, and lobbyests showed up. Senators paid \$75 each; congresspersons paid \$99; and lobbyests, \$40 each. If \$7,869 was collected, how many of each came to the banquet? (Hint: If S, C, and L represent the respective numbers of senators, congresspersons, and lobbyests, then
   $$S + C + L = 100 \text{ people}$$
   $$\$75S + \$99C + \$40L = \$7{,}869$$
   Since there are at most 100 senators from 50 states, set up a loop with S as an index, letting S go from 1 to 100. By solving the two equations algebraically for C and L, you obtain
   $$C = \frac{(3{,}869 - 35S)}{59}$$
   $$S = \frac{(2{,}031 - 24S)}{59}$$
   In the program, compute C and L from these formulas and test to see whether each is an integer. Stop to display any integer triple solution for S, C, and L.

APPENDIX A

ANSWER KEYS—TI 57 AND EC 4000

1.4.1a

Stops the program so you can input the value of n.

1.4.1b

Permits the calculation of $n + 1$ before squaring.

1.4.1c

Stops the program so you can see the output value of $2(n + 1)^2$.

1.4.2a

Display flashes, indicating an error condition, with the value of n entered.

1.4.2b

Returns the "memorized" program back to the first step.

1.4.3

No . . . the LRN key stroke cannot be memorized because it is a "switch" that changes the calculator from one mode (learn or run) to the other.

1.4.4

STEP	PROGRAM
00	2
01	×
02	R/S
03	x^2
04	+
05	1
06	=
07	R/S

Initialize: CLR, RST, R/S, enter n, R/S

1.6.1a

Detailed Flow Chart

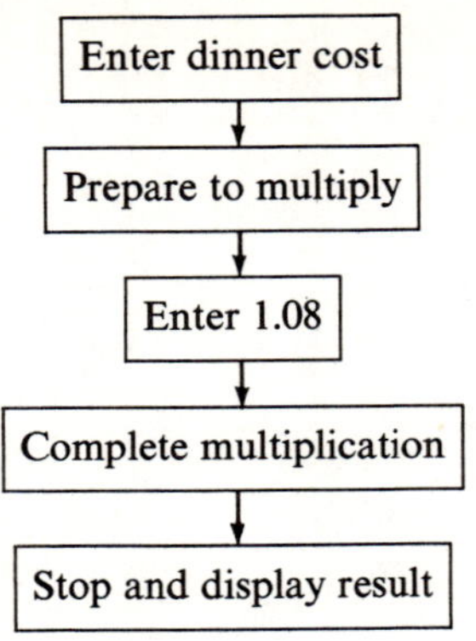

1.6.1b

STEP	PROGRAM
00	R/S
01	×
02	1
03	.
04	0
05	8
06	=
07	R/S

Initialize: CLR, RST, R/S, enter dinner cost, R/S

1.6.2

Detailed Flow Chart

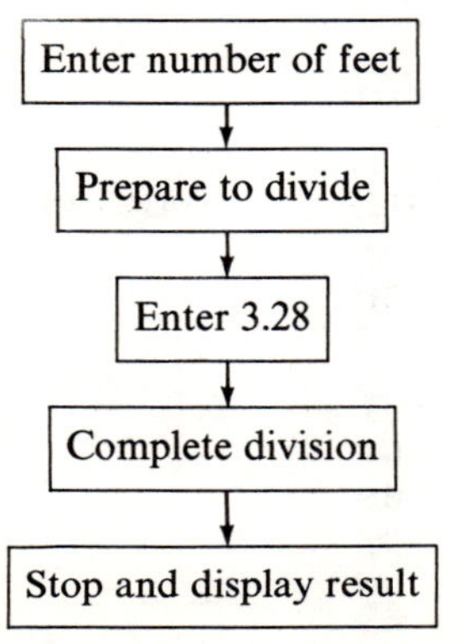

1.6.3a

General Flow Chart

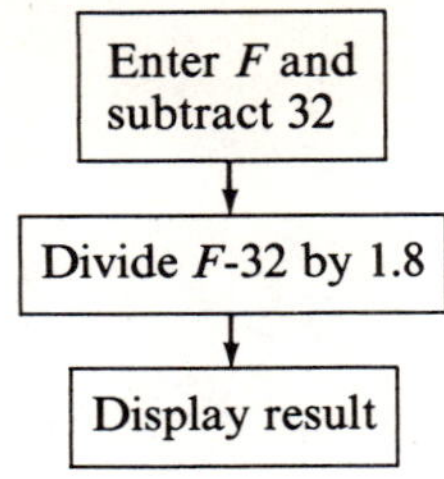

1.6.3b

STEP	PROGRAM
00	(
01	R/S
02	−
03	3
04	2
05	)
06	÷
07	1
08	.
09	8
10	=
11	R/S

Initialize: CLR, RST, R/S, enter F, R/S

1.6.4a

Detailed Flow Chart

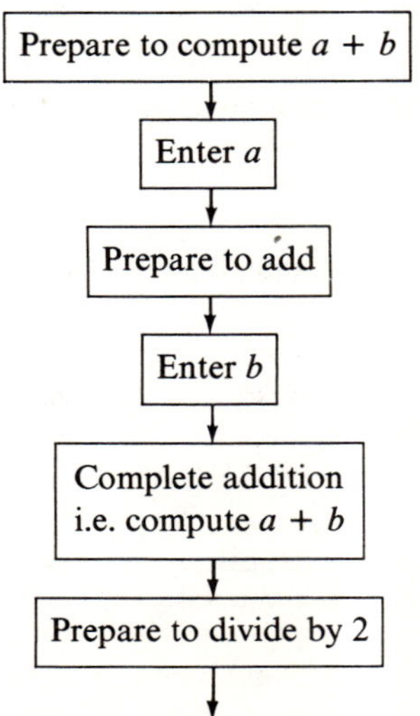

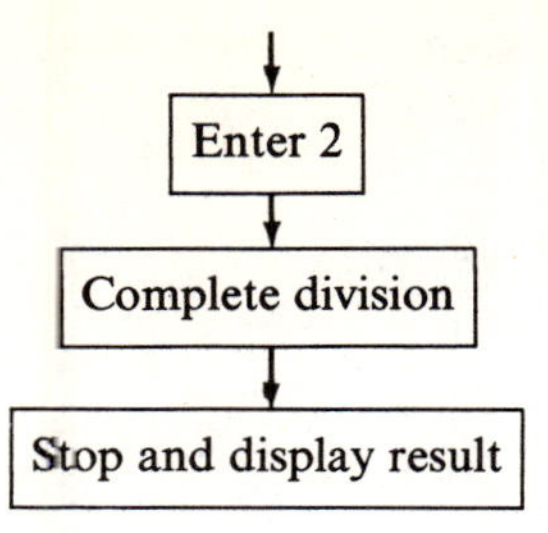

1.6.4b

STEP	PROGRAM
00	(
01	R/S
02	+
03	R/S
04	)
05	÷
06	2
07	=
08	R/S

Initialize: CLR, RST, R/S, enter a, R/S, enter b, R/S

1.6.5

General Flow Chart

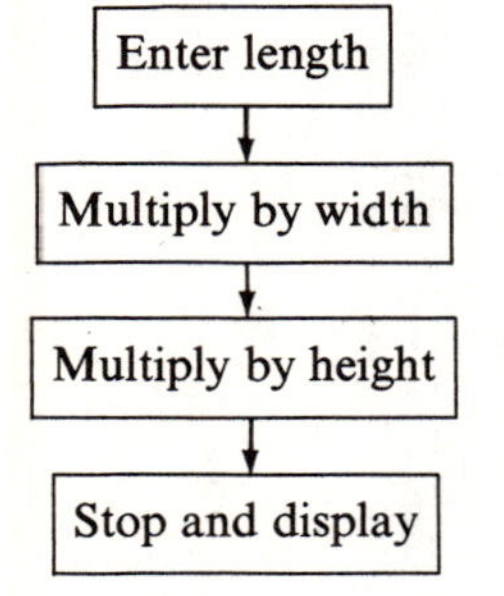

Detailed Flow Chart

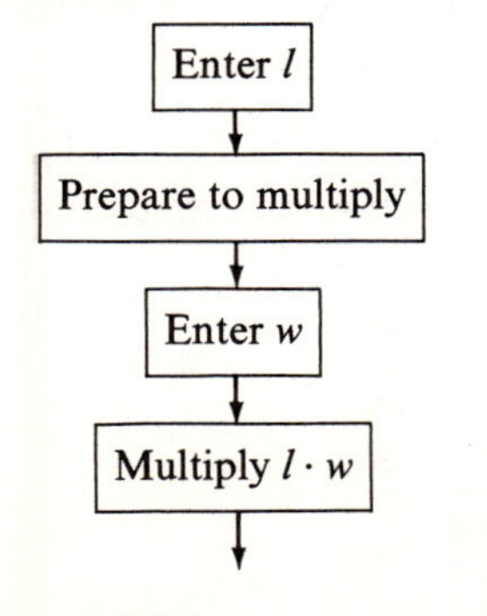

Prepare to multiply

Enter h

Multiply $(l \cdot w) \cdot h$

Stop and display

STEP	PROGRAM
00	R/S
01	×
02	R/S
03	=
04	×
05	R/S
06	=
07	R/S

Initialize: CLR, RST, R/S, enter l, R/S, enter w, R/S, enter h, R/S

1.6.6a

STEP	PROGRAM
00	(
01	R/S
02	×
03	2
04	+
05	8
06	−
07	2
08	)
09	÷
10	2
11	−
12	R/S
13	=
14	R/S

Initialize: CLR, RST, R/S, enter n, R/S, re-enter n, R/S

1.6.6b

3

1.7.1

STEP	PROGRAM
00	R/S
01	÷
02	.
03	6
04	2
05	=
06	R/S

Initialize: CLR, RST, R/S, enter number of miles, R/S

Comments: 5 mi. = 8.0645161 km.
8 mi. = 12.903226 km.
31 mi. = 50 km.
500 mi. = 806.45161 km.
3000 mi. = 4838.7097 km.

1.7.2

STEP	PROGRAM
00	R/S
01	×
02	2
03	.
04	8
05	5
06	=
07	R/S

Initialize: CLR, RST, R/S, enter number of hours, R/S

Comments: 12 hrs. gives $34.20
14 hrs. gives $39.90
18 hrs. gives $51.30
22 hrs. gives $62.70

1.7.3a

Two programs for $C = (F + 40) \times \frac{5}{9} - 40$ are presented. Both are correct. However, program A illustrates an important point. For $F = 32$, you will not obtain the expected result, 0; rather, "−3.−09" will be in the display. This value is very close to 0 and differs from it only in the 9th decimal place. There are times when your calculator computes unexpected results because of round-off errors. Such errors are rarely a problem, as you can usually recognize what the correct result should be. Still, you should be aware of this phenomenon. Consult your owner's manual for further details on the accuracy of your calculator's computations.

STEP	PROGRAM A
00	R/S
01	+
02	4
03	0
04	=
05	×
06	(
07	5
08	÷
09	9
10	)
11	=
12	−
13	4
14	0
15	=
16	R/S

Initialize: CLR, RST, R/S, enter *F*, R/S

STEP	PROGRAM B
00	(
01	(
02	R/S
03	+
04	4
05	0
06	)
07	×
08	5
09	)
10	÷
11	9
12	−
13	4
14	0
15	=
16	R/S

Initialize: CLR, RST, R/S, enter *F*, R/S

1.7.3b

STEP	PROGRAM
00	(
01	(
02	R/S
03	+
04	4
05	0
06	)

STEP	PROGRAM
07	×
08	9
09	)
10	÷
11	5
12	−
13	4
14	0
15	=
16	R/S

Initialize: CLR, RST, R/S, enter *C*, R/S

1.7.4

STEP	PROGRAM
00	R/S
01	×
02	R/S
03	×
04	.
05	0
06	3
07	=
08	R/S

Initialize: CLR, RST, R/S, enter *l*, R/S enter *w*, R/S

1.7.5

STEP	PROGRAM
00	5
01	.
02	8
03	9
04	×
05	(
06	2
07	×
08	R/S
09	+
10	2
11	×
12	R/S
13	)
14	=
15	R/S

Initialize: CLR, RST, R/S, enter *l*, R/S, enter *w*, R/S

1.7.6a

STEP	PROGRAM
00	(
01	R/S
02	+
03	R/S
04	+
05	R/S
06	)
07	÷
08	3
09	=
10	R/S

Initialize: CLR, RST, R/S, enter *a*, R/S, enter *b*, R/S, enter *c*, R/S

1.7.6b

Within the parentheses, include an additional R/S, + sequence to add the fourth number. Then be sure to divide by 4 rather than 3.

1.7.7

STEP	PROGRAM
00	R/S
01	+
02	R/S
03	=
04	÷
05	2
06	=
07	×
08	R/S
09	=
10	R/S

Initialize: CLR, RST, R/S, enter b_1, R/S, enter b_2, R/S, enter *h*, R/S

1.7.8a

STEP	PROGRAM
00	R/S
01	×
02	(
03	1
04	+
05	.
06	0

STEP	PROGRAM
07	6
08	=
09	R/S

Initialize: CLR, RST, R/S, enter n, R/S

1.7.8b

$106.00

1.7.8c

With $106.00 in display, press RST, R/S to obtain $112.36

1.7.8d

Repeat the sequence RST, R/S enough times to obtain $133.82

1.7.9a

STEP	PROGRAM
00	3
01	6
02	0
03	÷
04	R/S
05	=
06	R/S

Initialize: CLR, RST, R/S, enter l, R/S

1.7.9b

72, 45, 36, 24

1.7.9c

18, 20

2.2.1

No answer required.

2.2.2

$49.89

2.2.3

$153.25

2.2.4

$54,575,904.00

2.2.5

STEP	PROGRAM
00	1
01	.
02	0
03	6
04	y^x
05	R/S
06	=
07	×
08	1
09	0
10	0
11	=
12	R/S

Initialize: CLR, RST, R/S, enter n, R/S

2.4.1

Program 2

2.4.2

Program 2

2.4.3

Sequence 1 evaluates $10^{(1+n)}$.
Sequence 2 evaluates $1 + 10^n$.
Sequence 3 evaluates $1 + n$.

2.4.4

Initialization sequence a gives $3^5 = 243$ while sequence b gives $5^3 = 125$.

2.6.1

STEP	PROGRAM
00	(
01	R/S
02	+
03	R/S
04	+
05	R/S
06	)
07	÷
08	3
09	=
10	R/S

Initialize: CLR, RST, R/S, enter a, R/S, enter b, R/S, enter c, R/S

2.6.2

STEP	PROGRAM
00	R/S
01	×
02	R/S
03	=
04	$\sqrt{x}$
05	R/S

Initialize: CLR, RST, R/S, enter a, R/S, enter b, R/S

2.6.3

STEP	PROGRAM
00	R/S
01	×
02	R/S
03	×
04	R/S
05	=
06	INV y^x
07	3
08	=
09	R/S

Initialize: CLR, RST, R/S, enter a, R/S, enter b, R/S, enter c, R/S

2.6.4

STEP	PROGRAM
00	$1/x$
01	+
02	R/S
03	$1/x$
04	=
05	$1/x$
06	R/S

Initialize: CLR, RST, enter R_1, R/S, enter R_2, R/S

2.6.5a

STEP	PROGRAM
00	R/S
01	2nd sin (or 2nd cos or 2nd tan)
02	$1/x$
03	R/S

Initialize: CLR, RST, R/S, enter θ, R/S

2.6.5b

STEP	PROGRAM
00	9
01	0
02	−
03	R/S
04	=
05	2nd tan
06	R/S

Initialize: CLR, RST, R/S, enter θ, R/S

2.6.6

STEP	PROGRAM
00	2
01	y^x
02	R/S
03	−
04	1
05	=
06	R/S

Initialize: CLR, RST, R/S, enter n, R/S

2.6.7

STEP	PROGRAM
00	.
01	1
02	3
03	×
04	(
05	3
06	2

STEP	PROGRAM
07	+
08	(
09	R/S
10	−
11	3
12	2
13	)
14	2nd Int
15	=
16	R/S

Initialize: CLR, RST, R/S, enter *n*, R/S

2.6.8

STEP	PROGRAM
00	−
01	R/S
02	=
03	2nd $\|x\|$
04	R/S

Initialize: CLR, RST, enter year, R/S, enter second year, R/S

2.6.9

STEP	PROGRAM
00	1
01	+
02	(
03	R/S
04	2nd log
05	)
06	2nd Int
07	=
08	R/S

Initialize: CLR, RST, R/S, enter *n*, R/S

2.6.10

STEP	PROGRAM
00	(
01	3
02	×
03	R/S
04	÷
05	(
06	4
07	×
08	2nd π
09	)
10	)
11	INV y^x
12	3
13	=
14	R/S

Initialize: CLR, RST, R/S, enter *V*, R/S

2.6.11a

STEP	PROGRAM
00	(
01	R/S
02	×
03	R/S
04	+
05	4
06	×
07	R/S
08	×
09	R/S
10	+
11	R/S
12	×
13	R/S
14	)
15	×
16	R/S
17	÷
18	6
19	=
20	R/S

Initialize: CLR, RST, R/S, enter *a*, R/S, enter *b*, R/S, enter *a*, R/S, enter *b*, R/S, enter *a*, R/S, enter *b*, R/S, enter *h*, R/S

Here is a second, shorter program giving the same result. It is based on the following algebra, which leads to the familiar formula for the volume of a rectangular prism:

$$V = (ab + 4ab + ab) \cdot \frac{h}{6}$$

$$= (6ab) \cdot \frac{h}{6}$$

$$= abh$$

STEP	PROGRAM
00	×
01	R/S
02	×
03	R/S
04	=
05	R/S

Initialize: CLR, RST, enter a, R/S, enter b, R/S, enter h, R/S

2.6.11b

STEP	PROGRAM
00	4
01	×
02	2nd π
03	×
04	(
05	R/S
06	÷
07	2
08	)
09	x^2
10	+
11	2nd π
12	×
13	R/S
14	x^2
15	=
16	×
17	R/S
18	÷
19	6
20	=
21	R/S

Initialize: CLR, RST, R/S, enter r, R/S, enter r, R/S, enter h, R/S

2.6.11c

STEP	PROGRAM
00	(
01	R/S
02	x^2
03	+
04	4
05	×
06	(
07	(
08	R/S
09	+
10	R/S
11	)
12	÷
13	2
14	)
15	x^2
16	+
17	R/S
18	x^2
19	)
20	×
21	R/S
22	÷
23	6
24	=
25	R/S

Initialize: CLR, RST, R/S, enter a, R/S, enter a, R/S, enter b, R/S, enter b, R/S, enter c, R/S

2.6.12a

STEP	PROGRAM
00	×
01	2
02	=
03	2nd sin
04	×
05	R/S
06	x^2
07	=
08	÷
09	3
10	2
11	=
12	R/S

Initialize: CLR, RST, enter θ, R/S, enter V_0, R/S

2.6.12b

No answer required.

2.6.12c

45°, 253.1 feet when rounded to the nearest tenth of a foot.

3.5.1

No answer necessary.

3.5.2

No answer necessary.

3.5.3

A corrected program for computing $(A - 5)/(B + 5)$ is as follows:

STEP	PROGRAM
00	(
01	R/S
02	−
03	5
04	)
05	÷
06	(
07	R/S
08	+
09	5
10	)
11	=
12	R/S

Initialize: CLR, RST, R/S, enter a, R/S, enter b, R/S

4.3.1

STEP	PROGRAM
00	STO 1
01	RCL 1
02	×
03	(
04	RCL 1
05	+
06	1
07	)
08	×
09	(
10	2
11	×
12	RCL 1
13	+
14	1
15	)
16	÷
17	6
18	=
19	R/S

Memory: $R_1 = n$
Initialize: CLR, RST, enter n, R/S

4.3.2

STEP	PROGRAM
00	STO 1
01	RCL 1
02	×
03	(
04	RCL 1
05	+
06	1
07	)
08	÷
09	2
10	=
11	x^2
12	R/S

Memory: $R_1 = n$
Initialize: CLR, RST, enter n, R/S

4.3.3

STEP	PROGRAM
00	STO 1
01	R/S
02	STO 2
03	RCL 1
04	×
05	RCL 2
06	×
07	2nd π
08	=
09	STO 3
10	2
11	×
12	2nd π
13	×
14	(

STEP	PROGRAM
15	(
16	(
17	RCL 1
18	x^2
19	+
20	RCL 2
21	x^2
22	)
23	÷
24	2
25	)
26	$\sqrt{x}$
27	)
28	=
29	STO 4
30	2nd Fix 2
31	RCL 3
32	R/S
33	RCL 4
34	R/S

Memory: $R_1 = a$, $R_2 = b$, $R_3 = A$, $R_4 = C$
Initialize: CLR, RST, enter a, R/S, enter b, R/S (see area), R/S, (see circumference)

4.3.4

STEP	PROGRAM
00	STO 1
01	R/S
02	STO 2
03	RCL 1
04	×
05	RCL 2
06	x^2
07	÷
08	(
09	4
10	×
11	(
12	1
13	8
14	0
15	÷
16	RCL 1
17	)
18	2nd tan

STEP	PROGRAM
19	)
20	=
21	R/S

Memory: $R_1 = n$, $R_2 = l$
Initialize: CLR, RST, enter n, R/S, enter l, R/S

4.3.5a

STEP	PROGRAM
00	STO 1
01	R/S
02	STO 2
03	−
04	1
05	=
06	STO 3
07	÷
08	4
09	0
10	0
11	=
12	2nd Int
13	−
14	(
15	RCL 3
16	÷
17	1
18	0
19	0
20	)
21	2nd Int
22	+
23	(
24	RCL 3
25	÷
26	4
27	)
28	2nd Int
29	+
30	RCL 2
31	+
32	RCL 1
33	=
34	÷
35	7
36	=
37	INV 2nd Int

STEP	PROGRAM
38	×
39	7
40	=
41	+
42	.
43	1
44	=
45	2nd Int
46	R/S

Memory: $R_1 = D$, $R_2 = Y$, $R_3 = Y - 1$
Initialize: CLR, RST, enter D, R/S, enter Y, R/S

4.3.5b

Variable answers.

4.3.5c

Saturday.

4.3.6

STEP	PROGRAM
00	STO 1
01	RCL 1
02	2nd sin
03	x^2
04	+
05	RCL 1
06	2nd cos
07	x^2
08	=
09	R/S

Memory: $R_1 = \theta$
Initialize: CLR, RST, enter θ, R/S
Comments: For any value of θ, $\sin^2\theta + \cos^2\theta = 1$.

4.3.7

STEP	PROGRAM
00	STO 1
01	×
02	(
03	RCL 1
04	−
05	1
06	)
07	×
08	(
09	RCL 1
10	−
11	2
12	)
13	=
14	÷
15	6
16	−
17	R/S

Memory: $R_1 = n$
Initialize: CLR, RST, enter n, R/S
Comments: For n = 3, 4, 5, 10, and 100, the corresponding values are 1, 4, 10, 120, and 161,700.

4.3.8

STEP	PROGRAM
00	STO 1
01	4
02	÷
03	3
04	×
05	2nd π
06	×
07	RCL 1
08	y^x
09	3
10	=
11	R/S
12	4
13	×
14	2nd π
15	×
16	RCL 1
17	x^2
18	=
19	R/S

Memory: R_1 = radius
Initialize: CLR, RST, enter r, R/S, (see volume), R/S (see surface area)

4.3.9

STEP	PROGRAM
00	STO 1
01	R/S
02	STO 2
03	R/S
04	STO 3
05	.
06	0
07	6
08	×
09	RCL 3
10	×
11	(
12	RCL 1
13	+
14	RCL 2
15	)
16	+
17	.
18	0
19	5
20	×
21	RCL 1
22	×
23	RCL 2
24	=
25	R/S

Memory: $R_1 = x$, $R_2 = y$, $R_3 = z$
Initialize: CLR, RST, 2nd Fix 2, enter x, R/S, enter y, R/S, enter z, R/S

4.3.10a

STEP	PROGRAM
00	STO 1
01	R/S
02	STO 2
03	(
04	RCL 1
05	−
06	RCL 2
07	)
08	×
09	.
10	8
11	2
12	+
13	RCL 2
14	=
15	R/S

Memory: R_1 = delivery price, R_2 = transportation cost
Initialize: CLR, RST, enter delivery price, R/S, enter transportation costs, R/S

4.3.10b

Augment the program with:

STEP	PROGRAM
16	STO 3
17	RCL 1
18	−
19	RCL 3
20	=
21	R/S

4.3.10c

Include in the initialization, or insert between steps 02 and 03, the instruction 2nd Fix 2.

4.3.11

STEP	PROGRAM
00	STO 1
01	R/S
02	STO 2
03	R/S
04	STO 3
05	RCL 1
06	×
07	RCL 2
08	=
09	STO 4
10	1
11	−
12	RCL 2
13	=
14	STO 5
15	(
16	RCL 4
17	÷
18	(
19	RCL 4
20	+
21	(

STEP	PROGRAM
22	RCL 3
23	×
24	RCL 5
25	)
26	)
27	=
28	STO 6
29	R/S

Memory: R_1 = P(A|B), R_2 = P(B), R_3 = P(A|B′), R_4 = P(A|B) · P(B), R_5 = 1 − P(B) = P(B′), R_6 = P(B|A)
Initialize: CLR, RST, enter P(A|B), R/S, enter P(B), R/S, enter P(A|B′), R/S

4.3.12

STEP	PROGRAM
00	STO 1
01	R/S
02	STO 2
03	RCL 1
04	×
05	RCL 2
06	=
07	STO 3
08	(
09	RCL 3
10	×
11	(
12	1
13	−
14	RCL 2
15	)
16	)
17	$\sqrt{x}$
18	STO 4
19	RCL 3
20	R/S
21	RCL 4
22	R/S

Memory: $R_1 = n$, $R_2 = p$, $R_3 = np$, R_4 = SD(y)
Initialize: CLR, RST, enter n, R/S, enter p, R/S, (wait to see E[y]), R/S

4.3.13

STEP	PROGRAM
00	STO 1
01	R/S
02	STO 2
03	R/S
04	STO 3
05	RCL 1
06	×
07	RCL 2
08	2nd cos
09	×
10	RCL 3
11	=
12	STO 4
13	RCL 1
14	×
15	RCL 2
16	2nd sin
17	×
18	RCL 3
19	−
20	1
21	6
22	×
23	RCL 3
24	x^2
25	=
26	STO 5
27	RCL 4
28	R/S
29	RCL 5
30	R/S

Memory: $R_1 = V_0$, $R_2 = \theta$, $R_3 = t$, $R_4 = x$, $R_5 = y$
Initialize: CLR, RST, enter V_0, R/S, enter θ, R/S, enter t, R/S, (wait to see x), R/S

5.3.1

Displays the multiples of 10.

5.3.2

Displays the negative integers.

5.3.3

STEP	PROGRAM
00	2nd Lbl 2
01	+
02	5
03	=
04	2nd Pause
05	GTO 2

Initialize: CLR, RST, R/S

5.3.4

STEP	PROGRAM
00	2nd Pause
01	2nd Lbl 5
02	+
03	1
04	0
05	=
06	2nd Pause
07	GTO 5

Initialize: CLR, RST, R/S

5.3.5

Initialize the program in problem 5.3.4 with CLR, RST, 7, R/S or, using the 2nd Ins instruction at step 00, insert 7 in the program.

5.3.6

STEP	PROGRAM
00	1
01	0
02	0
03	0
04	2nd Pause
05	2nd Lbl 4
06	−
07	1
08	0
09	0
10	=
11	2nd Pause
12	GTO 4

Initialize: CLR, RST, R/S

5.5.1

STEP	PROGRAM
00	2
01	2nd Pause
02	2nd Lbl 1
03	+
04	9
05	=
06	2nd Pause
07	GTO 1

Initialize: CLR, RST, R/S

5.5.2

STEP	PROGRAM
00	2nd Pause
01	2nd Lbl 1
02	÷
03	3
04	=
05	2nd Pause
06	GTO 1

Initialize: CLR, RST, 2187, R/S

5.5.3a

STEP	PROGRAM
00	2nd Pause
01	2nd Lbl 4
02	×
03	2
04	+
05	1
06	=
07	2nd Pause
08	GTO 4

Initialize: CLR, RST, 3, R/S

5.5.3b

To modify the program for each part, change the initialization to include the appropriate first sequence term. The sequences obtained are:

i. 123, 247, 495, 991, 1,983, . . .

ii. $-16, -31, -61, -121, -241, \ldots$

iii. .6666667, 2.3333333, 5.6666667, 12.333333, 25.666667, . . .

iv. .222, 1.444, 3.888, 8.776, 18.552, . . .

5.5.4

If t is the previous term, then the successive term of each sequence is formed as follows:

a. $2t$ b. $2t/3$ c. $2t + 1$ d. $2t - 1$
e. $3t - 1$ f. t^2

5.5.5

STEP	PROGRAM
00	1
01	5
02	2nd Pause
03	2nd Lbl 1
04	×
05	2
06	+/−
07	=
08	+
09	3
10	=
11	2nd Pause
12	GTO 1

Initialize: CLR, RST, R/S

5.5.6a

Add 2

5.5.6b

STEP	PROGRAM
00	1
01	2nd Pause
02	2nd Lbl 2
03	+
04	2
05	=
06	2nd Pause
07	GTO 2

Initialize: CLR, RST, R/S

5.5.7a

STEP	PROGRAM
00	1
01	2nd Pause
02	2nd Lbl 1
03	÷
04	2
05	=
06	+
07	4
08	=
09	2nd Pause
10	GTO 1

Initialize: CLR, RST, R/S
Comments: The sequence approaches a limiting value of 8.

5.5.7b

STEP	PROGRAM
00	2nd Pause
01	2nd Lbl 1
02	+
03	2
04	=
05	$\sqrt{x}$
06	2nd Pause
07	GTO 1

Initialize: CLR, RST, enter any number larger than -2, R/S
Comments: The sequence approaches a limiting value of 2.

5.5.8a

STEP	PROGRAM
00	6
01	2nd Pause
02	2nd Lbl 2
03	STO 1
04	6
05	÷
06	RCL 1
07	=
08	+
09	1

STEP	PROGRAM
10	=
11	2nd Pause
12	GTO 2

Memory: R_1 = previous term
Initialize: CLR, RST, R/S
Comments: The sequence approaches a limiting value of 3.

5.5.8b

STEP	PROGRAM
00	5
01	2nd Pause
02	2nd Lbl 3
03	STO 1
04	1
05	−
06	(
07	RCL 1
08	÷
09	2
10	)
11	=
12	2nd Pause
13	GTO 3

Memory: R_1 = previous term
Initialize: CLR, RST, R/S
Comments: The sequence approaches a limiting value of 0.6666667 or 2/3.

5.5.9

STEP	PROGRAM
00	2nd Pause
01	2nd Lbl 1
02	STO 1
03	x^2
04	−
05	RCL 1
06	=
07	2nd Pause
08	GTO 1

Memory: R_1 = previous term
Initialize: CLR, RST, enter first term, R/S

Comments:

a. For 2.1, the sequence terms get larger and larger and eventually overflow, producing a flashing display.
b. For 1.9, the sequence produces alternating positive and negative terms that slowly approach a limiting value of 0.
c. For 2.0, the sequence stays at a limiting value of 2.0.

5.5.10a

It shows the first two sequence terms 3 and 6 and then flashes with a 6 in the display.

5.5.10b

Either step 02 or step 10 is incorrect. The GTO *n* used with 2nd Lbl *n* must have the same value for *n*.

5.5.10c

R_1 = previous term.

5.5.10d

Each new term is formed by squaring the previous term and subtracting the previous term from that result.

5.5.10e

All twos.

5.7.1a

STEP	PROGRAM
00	INV 2nd C.t
01	2nd Lbl 2
02	+
03	1
04	=
05	STO 1
06	x^2
07	+
08	1
09	=
10	2nd Pause
11	RCL 1
12	GTO 2

Memory: R_1 = index
Initialize: CLR, RST, R/S

5.7.1b

By inserting 2, STO 1 after step 00, you obtain the sequence 10, 17, 26, 37, ...

5.7.2a

STEP	PROGRAM
00	INV 2nd C.t
01	2nd Lbl 2
02	RCL 1
03	+
04	1
05	=
06	STO 1
07	x^2
08	÷
09	2
10	=
11	2nd Pause
12	GTO 2

Memory: R_1 = index
Initialize: CLR, RST, R/S

5.7.2b

Change step 04 to 2 instead of 1.

5.7.3a

If during each loop you first compute the nth term and then add 1 to the index, n, the following answers apply:

Index = 0, form term as $5n$.

5.7.3b

Index = 1, form term as $n^2 - 1$; or, index = 0, form term as $n(n + 2)$.

5.7.3c

Index = 3, form term as $n^2 - 1$; or, index = 2, form term as $n(n + 2)$.

5.7.3d

Index = 1, form term as 2^n.

5.7.4a

STEP	PROGRAM
00	INV 2nd C.t
01	2nd Lbl 3
02	+
03	1
04	=
05	STO 1
06	3
07	y^x
08	RCL 1
09	=
10	2nd Pause
11	RCL 1
12	GTO 3

Memory: R_1 = index
Initialize: CLR, RST, R/S

5.7.4b

STEP	PROGRAM
00	2
01	STO 1
02	2nd Lbl 3
03	y^x
04	3
05	=
06	2nd Pause
07	RCL 1
08	+
09	1
10	=
11	STO 1
12	GTO 3

Memory: R_1 = index
Initialize: CLR, RST, R/S

5.7.5

STEP	PROGRAM
00	1
01	STO 1
02	2nd Lbl 3
03	RCL 1
04	y^x
05	RCL 1
06	=
07	2nd Pause
08	RCL 1
09	+

STEP	PROGRAM
10	1
11	=
12	STO 1
13	GTO 3

Memory: R_1 = index
Initialize: CLR, RST, R/S
Comments: The sequence grows quickly. For $n = 57$, n^n results in an overflow condition indicated by flashing nines.

5.7.6

STEP	PROGRAM
00	1
01	STO 1
02	2nd Lbl 2
03	RCL1
04	INV y^x
05	RCL 1
06	=
07	2nd Pause
08	RCL 1
09	+
10	1
11	=
12	STO 1
13	GTO 2

Memory: R_1 = index
Initialize: CLR, RST, R/S
Comments:
a. The third term, 1.4422496, when $n = 3$ is the largest.
b. As n grows very large $\sqrt[n]{n}$ gets smaller and smaller approaching a value of 1.

5.7.7

STEP	PROGRAM
00	INV 2nd C.t
01	2nd Lbl 1
02	STO 1
03	x^2
04	−
05	(
06	2
07	y^x
08	RCL 1
09	)
10	EE
11	INV EE
12	=
13	2nd Pause
14	RCL 1
15	+
16	1
17	=
18	GTO 1

Memory: R_1 = index
Initialize: CLR, RST, R/S
Comments: The sequence EE, INV EE in steps 10–11 rounds the calculation to the number of digits shown in the display.
a. Since the result of $n^2 - 2^n$ is negative, except for $n = 2$, 3, and 4, you may conclude that 2^n is greater than n^2 except for $n = 2$ and $n = 4$ when $n^2 = 2^n$ and for $n = 3$ when $3^2 > 2^3$.
b. Generate the sequence $n^3 - 3^n$. If the terms of the sequence are negative, then $3^n > n^3$, otherwise $n^3 \geqslant 3^n$.

5.7.8a

STEP	PROGRAM
00	STO 1
01	RCL 2
02	y^x
03	RCL 1
04	=
05	2nd Pause
06	RCL 1
07	+
08	1
09	=
10	RST

Memory: R_1 = index, R_2 = number to be raised to a power
Initialize: RST, .99, STO 2, CLR, R/S
Comments: The generated sequence is 1, .99, .9801, .970299, . . . and as n becomes very large, $(.99)^n$ becomes very close to zero.

5.7.8b

Change the initialization to RST, 1.01, STO 2, CLR, R/S. This gives the sequence 1, 1.01, 1.0201, 1.030301, . . . which becomes very large when n grows very large. The sequence increases towards $9.99999999 \times 10^{99}$.

5.7.8c

Change the initialization to RST, 1, STO 2, CLR, R/S. This sequence is constant: 1., 1., 1., 1., 1., ...

6.3.1a

96

6.3.1b

90

6.3.2a

4, 8, 16, 32, 64, . . .

6.3.2b

4, 8, 16, 32, 64, . . .

6.3.2c

It is multiplied by 2.

6.3.2d

Multiplies 2 into R_1 and, in effect, doubles the value of R_1.

6.3.3a

10^8, 10^7, 10^6, 10^5, . . .

6.3.3b

Divides 10 into R_1.

6.3.3c

Stores 10^9 in R_1.

6.3.4

STEP	PROGRAM
00	1
01	0
02	4
03	STO 1
04	2nd Lbl 1
05	−
06	4
07	INV SUM 1
08	RCL 1
09	2nd Pause
10	GTO 1

Memory: R_1 = difference
Initialize: CLR, INV 2nd C.t, RST, R/S

6.5.1

INV 2nd C.t clears all memory registers filling them with 0.

6.5.2a

$1/3^0 = 1.$

6.5.2b

3, $1/x$, 2nd Prd 4. You can check to see that this works by following the given keystrokes in a program with RCL 4, $1/x$, 2nd Pause, which will show the denominator of the term.

6.5.3a

2, SUM 2 if 1 is placed in R_2 at the start.

6.5.3b

3, +/−, SUM 3 if 1 is placed in R_3 at the start.

6.5.3c

RCL 2, ÷, RCL 3, =

6.5.4

STEP	PROGRAM
00	INV 2nd C.t
01	2nd Lbl 1
02	1
03	SUM 3
04	RCL 3
05	×
06	(
07	RCL 3
08	+
09	1
10	)
11	÷
12	2
13	+
14	1

STEP	PROGRAM
15	=
16	2nd Pause
17	GTO 1

Memory: R_3 = index
Initialize: CLR, RST, R/S

6.8.1a

STEP	PROGRAM
00	INV 2nd C.t
01	1
02	2nd Lbl 1
03	SUM 2
04	RCL 2
05	2nd Pause
06	1
07	SUM 1
08	3
09	y^x
10	RCL 1
11	=
12	$1/x$
13	GTO 1

Memory: R_1 = index, R_2 = total
x-register: term
Initialize: RST, CLR, R/S

6.8.1b

The limiting value is 1.5.

6.8.2a

STEP	PROGRAM
00	INV 2nd C.t
01	1
02	STO 2
03	2
04	STO 3
05	$1/x$
06	2nd Lbl 1
07	SUM 1
08	RCL 1
09	2nd Pause
10	1
11	SUM 2
12	2
13	2nd Prd 3
14	RCL 2
15	y^x
16	3
17	=
18	÷
19	RCL 3
20	=
21	GTO 1

Memory: R_1 = running total, R_2 = index, R_3 = denominator 2^n
x-register: term $n^3/2^n$
Initialize: CLR, RST, R/S

6.8.2b

The average amount received is the limiting value of \$26.

6.8.2c

Since $26 - 10 = 16$, the gambler's expected *gain* is \$16.

6.8.2d

By pressing 2nd Nop at steps 15, 16, and 17 of the program in 6.8.2a, you can compute the limiting value of the sum of $n/2^n$ which is 2. Hence, $12 - 10 = 8$ and the gambler's *loss* is \$8.

6.8.3a

STEP	PROGRAM
00	INV 2nd C.t
01	1
02	STO 3
03	2nd Lbl 1
04	1
05	SUM 2
06	6
07	2nd Prd 3
08	2
09	y^x
10	RCL 2
11	+
12	3
13	y^x
14	RCL 2
15	=
16	÷

STEP	PROGRAM
17	RCL 3
18	=
19	SUM 1
20	RCL 1
21	2nd Pause
22	GTO 1

Memory: R_1 = running total, R_2 = index, $R_3 = 6^n$
Initialize: CLR, RST, R/S

6.8.3b

The limiting value is 1.5.

6.8.4a

STEP	PROGRAM
00	INV 2nd C.t
01	2nd Lbl 1
02	1
03	SUM 2
04	RCL 3
05	+
06	RCL 2
07	=
08	STO 3
09	×
10	6
11	+
12	1
13	=
14	÷
15	(
16	RCL 3
17	y^x
18	3
19	)
20	=
21	SUM 1
22	RCL 1
23	2nd Pause
24	GTO 1

Memory: R_1 = running total, R_2 = index, $R_3 = t_n$
Initialize: CLR, RST, R/S

6.8.4b

The limiting value of the series is 8. If you wish to see this value in the x-register, include the sequence 2nd Fix 3 in the initialization of the program in 6.8.4a.

6.8.5a

STEP	PROGRAM
00	INV 2nd C.t
01	2nd Lbl 1
02	1
03	SUM 2
04	RCL 3
05	+
06	RCL 2
07	=
08	STO 3
09	x^2
10	×
11	2
12	0
13	+
14	RCL 3
15	×
16	1
17	0
18	+
19	1
20	=
21	÷
22	RCL 3
23	y^x
24	5
25	=
26	SUM 1
27	RCL 1
28	2nd Pause
29	GTO 1

Memory: R_1 = running total, R_2 = index $R_3 = t_n$
Initialize: CLR RST, R/S

6.8.5b

The limiting value of the series is 32.

6.8.6a

STEP	PROGRAM
00	INV 2nd C.t
01	5
02	2nd Lbl 1
03	SUM 1
04	RCL 1
05	2nd Pause
06	1
07	SUM 2
08	2
09	×
10	(
11	.
12	8
13	y^x
14	RCL 2
15	)
16	×
17	5
18	=
19	GTO 1

Memory: R_1 = running total, R_2 = index
x-register: term
Initialize: CLR, RST, R/S

6.8.6b

The ball will travel about 45 meters.

6.8.7a

STEP	PROGRAM
00	STO 3
01	2nd Lbl 1
02	1
03	SUM 2
04	RCL 2
05	y^x
06	RCL 3
07	=
08	$1/x$
09	SUM 1
10	RCL 1
11	2nd Pause
12	GTO 1

Memory: R_1 = running total, R_2 = index, $R_3 = s$
Initialize: CLR INV 2nd C.t, RST, enter s, R/S
Comments: INV 2nd C.t is part of the initialization rather than in the program. If the sequence is included in program, it would clear the t-registers, not the rest of the memory registers when encountered.

6.8.7b

For $s = 8$ you obtain 1.0040774 and for $s = 6$ you obtain 1.0173431.

6.8.7c

For values of $s \leqslant 4$, the number of times through the loop to evaluate the function is excessive. For $s = 4$, it takes more than 200 iterations. For $s = 2$, your calculator would require more than 9 hours to obtain $\pi^2/6$.

6.8.8

STEP	PROGRAM
00	INV 2nd C.t
01	1
02	STO 2
03	STO 3
04	2nd Lbl 1
05	SUM 1
06	RCL 1
07	2nd Pause
08	1
09	SUM 2
10	+/−
11	2nd Prd 3
12	RCL 2
13	y^x
14	6
15	=
16	$1/x$
17	×
18	RCL 3
19	=
20	GTO 1

Memory: R_1 = running total, R_2 = index, $R_3 = s$
x-register: term
Initialize: CLR, RST, R/S
Comments: The value of the series is .9855511 which is $(31/32)(\pi^6/945)$.

6.8.9

STEP	PROGRAM
00	INV 2nd C.t
01	1
02	+/−
03	STO 2
04	STO 3
05	3
06	$\sqrt{x}$
07	×
08	2
09	=
10	STO 4
11	2nd Lbl 1
12	1
13	SUM 2
14	+/−
15	2nd Prd 3
16	2
17	×
18	RCL 2
19	+
20	1
21	=
22	×
23	(
24	3
25	y^x
26	RCL 2
27	)
28	=
29	$1/x$
30	×
31	RCL 4
32	×
33	RCL 3
34	=
35	SUM 1
36	RCL 1
37	2nd Pause
38	GTO 1

Memory: R_1 = running total, R_2 = index, R_3 = sign, $R_4 = 2\sqrt{3}$
Initialize: CLR, RST, R/S
Comments: The limiting value of the series is $\pi = 3.1415927$.

6.8.10

STEP	PROGRAM
00	STO 6
01	1
02	STO 5
03	2nd Lbl 1
04	RCL 6
05	×
06	RCL 5
07	=
08	2nd sin
09	÷
10	RCL 5
11	=
12	SUM 4
13	RCL 4
14	2nd Pause
15	2nd Pause
16	2
17	SUM 5
18	GTO 1

Memory: $R_6 = x$, $R_5 = 2n - 1$, R_4 = running total
Initialize: CLR INV 2nd C.t, RST, enter x, R/S
Comments: $\pi/4 = .7853982$ and it will take your calculator a considerable length of time to approach this limit.

7.4.1

STEP	PROGRAM
00	2
01	0
02	0
03	$x \gtrless t$*
04	R/S
05	STO 1
06	INV 2nd $x \geqslant t$
07	R/S
08	×
09	.
10	0
11	0

*The symbol $x \gtrless y$ represents the "x exchange t" key on the calculator.

STEP	PROGRAM
12	5
13	=
14	+
15	RCL 1
16	=
17	R/S

Memory: R_1 = balance
Initialize: CLR, RST, R/S, enter balance, R/S

7.4.2

STEP	PROGRAM
00	STO 1
01	1
02	$x \gtrless t$
03	R/S
04	2nd $x = t$
05	GTO 1
06	.
07	1
08	0
09	+
10	.
11	0
12	6
13	×
14	(
15	RCL 1
16	−
17	2
18	)
19	=
20	GTO 2
21	2nd Lbl 1
22	.
23	1
24	5
25	+
26	.
27	1
28	3
29	×
30	(
31	RCL 1
32	−
33	1
34	)
35	=
36	2nd Lbl 2
37	R/S

Memory: $R_1 = z$
Initialize: CLR, RST, enter z, R/S, enter class, R/S

7.4.3

STEP	PROGRAM
00	STO 1
01	2nd Lbl 1
02	R/S
03	STO 7
04	RCL 1
05	INV 2nd $x \geqslant t$
06	GTO 1
07	$x \gtrless t$
08	STO 1
09	GTO 1

Memory: R_1 = number, R_7 = t-register
Initialize: CLR, RST, enter number, R/S
Comments: To display smallest number in a set, continue the enter number and R/S key sequence until all numbers have been considered.

7.4.4

STEP	PROGRAM
00	STO 1
01	R/S
02	STO 2
03	$x \gtrless t$
04	5
05	×
06	RCL 1
07	−
08	3
09	=
10	2nd $x = t$
11	GTO 2

STEP	PROGRAM
12	0
13	GTO 1
14	2nd Lbl 2
15	1
16	2nd Lbl 1
17	R/S

Memory: $R_1 = x$, $R_2 = y$
Initialize: CLR, RST, enter x, R/S, enter y, R/S

7.4.5

STEP	PROGRAM
00	2
01	5
02	.
03	5
04	STO 7
05	R/S
06	STO 1
07	2nd $x \geqslant t$
08	GTO 1
09	STO 7
10	1
11	4
12	.
13	5
14	2nd $x \geqslant t$
15	GTO 1
16	RCL 1
17	GTO 2
18	2nd Lbl 1
19	0
20	2nd Lbl 2
21	R/S

Memory: R_1 = number, R_7 = t-register
Initialize: CLR, RST, R/S, enter number, R/S

7.4.6

STEP	PROGRAM
00	STO 1
01	R/S
02	STO 2
03	R/S
04	STO 3
05	RCL 1
06	+
07	2
08	×
09	RCL 2
10	+
11	2
12	×
13	RCL 3
14	=
15	$x \gtrless t$
16	1
17	0
18	8
19	2nd $x \geqslant t$
20	GTO 1
21	0
22	GTO 2
23	2nd Lbl 1
24	1
25	2nd Lbl 2
26	R/S

Memory: $R_1 = l$, $R_2 = w$, $R_3 = h$, R_7 = t-register
Initialize: CLR, R/S, enter l, R/S, enter w, R/S, enter h, R/S

7.4.7

STEP	PROGRAM
00	STO 1
01	R/S
02	STO 2
03	R/S
04	STO 3
05	R/S
06	STO 4
07	$x \gtrless t$
08	5
09	0
10	INV 2nd $x \geqslant t$
11	GTO 1
12	2nd Nop
13	RCL 1
14	+

STEP	PROGRAM
15	2
16	$\times$
17	RCL 2
18	+
19	2
20	$\times$
21	RCL 3
22	=
23	$x \gtrless t$
24	1
25	0
26	8
27	2nd $x \geqslant t$
28	GTO 2
29	2nd Lbl 1
30	0
31	GTO 3
32	2nd Lbl 2
33	1
34	2nd Lbl 3
35	R/S

Memory: $R_1 = l$, $R_2 = w$, $R_3 = h$, $R_4 =$ weight, $R_7 = t$-register

Initialize: CLR, R/S enter l, RS, enter w, R/S, enter h, R/S, enter weight, R/S

Comments: If a package can be sent by U.P.S., a 1 appears in the display, otherwise a 0 appears. Notice the 2nd Nop instruction in step 12; it was used to delete an unwanted instruction discovered in the program during the preparation of this answer key.

7.4.8

STEP	PROGRAM
00	RCL 6
01	SUM 3
02	SUM 3
03	RCL 5
04	x^2
05	−
06	4
07	$\times$
08	RCL 6
09	$\times$
10	RCL 4
11	=
12	STO 2
13	2nd $x \geqslant t$
14	GTO 1
15	RCL 5
16	+/1
17	÷
18	RCL 3
19	=
20	R/S
21	RCL 2
22	+/−
23	$\sqrt{x}$
24	÷
25	RCL 3
26	GTO 2
27	2nd Lbl 1
28	RCL 2
29	$\sqrt{x}$
30	STO 1
31	RCL 5
32	+/−
33	+
34	RCL 1
35	=
36	÷
37	RCL 3
38	=
39	R/S
40	RCL 5
41	+/−
42	−
43	RCL 1
44	=
45	÷
46	RCL 3
47	2nd Lbl 2
48	=
49	R/S

Memory: $R_6 = a$, $R_5 = b$, $R_4 = c$, $R_3 = 2a$, $R_2 = d$, $R_1 = \sqrt{d}$, $R_7 = 0$

Initialize: CLR, INV 2nd C.t, RST, enter a, STO 6, enter b, STO 5, enter c, STO 4, R/S, (wait to see x_1 or u), R/S (wait to see x_2 or v)

Comments: For complex roots, your calculator stops first to display u and then v. Thus, to form the roots merely form $x_1, x_2 = u \pm vi$.

7.6.1

STEP	PROGRAM
00	STO 1
01	÷
02	4
03	=
04	STO 7
05	2nd Int
06	2nd $x = t$
07	GTO 1
08	RCL 1
09	+/−
10	GTO 2
11	2nd Lbl 1
12	RCL 1
13	2nd Lbl 2
14	R/S

Memory: R_1 = year n, R_7 = t-register = $n/4$
Initialize: RST, CLR, input year n, R/S

7.6.2a

STEP	PROGRAM
00	STO 1
01	STO 7
02	1
03	0
04	0
05	INV 2nd $x \geqslant t$
06	GTO 1
07	$x \gtrless t$
08	INV y^x
09	3
10	=
11	EE
12	INV EE
13	INV 2nd Int
14	$x \gtrless t$
15	0
16	2nd $x = t$
17	GTO 2
18	2nd Lbl 1
19	0
20	GTO 3
21	2nd Lbl 2
22	RCL 1
23	2nd Lbl 3
24	R/S

Memory: $R_1 = n$, R_7 = t-register
Initialize: CLR, RST, enter n, R/S
Comments: Notice the EE, INV EE sequence in steps 11 and 12. It rounds calculations to the number of digits in the display.

7.6.2b

You obtain a flashing display since INV y^x may only be used for positive numbers.

7.6.3

In the program for problem 7.6.2a in this section, insert 2nd $|x|$ between steps 00 and 01.

7.6.4

STEP	PROGRAM
00	3
01	SUM 1
02	RCL 1
03	2nd Pause
04	$\sqrt{x}$
05	INV 2nd Int
06	INV 2nd $x = t$
07	RST
08	RCL 1
09	R/S
10	RST

Memory: R_1 = multiple of 3, R_7 = t-register
Initialize: CLR, INV 2nd C.t, RST, R/S
Comments:
1. When the calculator stops to display multiples of 3 that are perfect squares, press R/S to continue.
2. The use of RST in step 10 returns the program to step 00 automatically.

7.6.5

STEP	PROGRAM
00	1
01	SUM 1
02	2
03	×
04	RCL 1
05	x^2
06	+
07	2

STEP	PROGRAM
08	×
09	RCL 1
10	+
11	1
12	=
13	$\sqrt{x}$
14	EE
15	INV EE
16	STO 7
17	2nd Int
18	INV 2nd $x = t$
19	RST
20	$x \gtrless t$
21	R/S
22	RST

Memory: R_1 = index a, R_7 = t-register
Initialize: CLR, INV 2nd C.t, RST, R/S
Comments: 1. When c is displayed, you can see a by pressing RCL 1 and compute b as a-1.
2. The other triples are (20, 21, 29); (119, 120, 169); and (696, 697, 985).
3. Notice the use of the special rounding sequence in steps 14 and 15.

7.6.6

STEP	PROGRAM
00	1
01	SUM 1
02	RCL 1
03	SUM 2
04	RCL 2
05	$\sqrt{x}$
06	EE
07	INV EE
08	STO 7
09	2nd Int
10	INV 2nd $x = t$
11	RST
12	RCL 2
13	R/S
14	RST

Memory: $R_1 = n$, $R_2 = T_n$, $R_7 = t$-register
Initialize: INV 2nd C.t, RST, R/S
Comments: 1. Notice the use of the rounding sequence in steps 06 and 07.
2. The first three triangular numbers that are perfect squares are 1, 36 and 1225.

7.6.7

STEP	PROGRAM
00	1
01	SUM 1
02	1
03	1
04	×
05	RCL 1
06	+
07	3
08	=
09	÷
10	6
11	=
12	STO 7
13	2nd Int
14	INV 2nd $x = t$
15	RST
16	1
17	1
18	×
19	RCL 1
20	+
21	8
22	=
23	R/S
24	RST

Memory: $R_1 = k$, $R_7 = t$-register
Initialize: CLR, INV 2nd C.t, RST, R/S
Comments: The smallest is 41 and the next is 107.

8.3.1

STEP	PROGRAM
00	STO 7
01	1
02	STO 1
03	2nd Lbl 1
04	RCL 1
05	SUM 2
06	RCL 2
07	SUM 3
08	RCL 1

STEP	PROGRAM
09	2nd $x = t$
10	GTO 2
11	1
12	SUM 14
13	GTO 1
14	2nd Lbl 2
15	RCL 3
16	R/S

Memory: $R_7 = n$, $R_1 = k$, $R_2 = t_k$, $R_3 =$ sum

Initialize: CLR, INV 2nd C.t, RST, enter n, R/S

Comments: 10 layers use 220 cannonballs; 20 layers use 1540, and 50 layers use 22,100.

8.3.2

STEP	PROGRAM
00	STO 7
01	1
02	STO 1
03	2nd Lbl 1
04	3
05	×
06	RCL 1
07	×
08	(
09	RCL 1
10	−
11	1
12	)
13	+
14	1
15	=
16	SUM 2
17	RCL 1
18	2nd $x = t$
19	GTO 2
20	1
21	SUM 1
22	GTO 1
23	2nd Lbl 2
24	RCL 2
25	R/S

Memory: $R_7 = n$, $R_1 = k$, $R_2 =$ sum

Initialize: CLR, INV 2nd C.t, RST, enter n, R/S

Comments: By inserting RCL 2, 2nd Pause between steps 16 and 17, you can display each term of the sequence for any n. The sequence displayed happens to be n^3.

8.3.3

STEP	PROGRAM
00	STO 7
01	1
02	STO 1
03	2nd Lbl 1
04	RCL 3
05	2nd Exc 2
06	SUM 3
07	RCL 2
08	2nd Pause
09	SUM 4
10	RCL 1
11	2nd $x = t$
12	GTO 2
13	1
14	SUM 1
15	GTO 1
16	2nd Lbl 2
17	RCL 4
18	R/S

Memory: $R_7 = n$, $R_1 = k$, $R_2 = f(k)$, $R_3 = f(k + 1)$, $R_4 =$ sum

Initialize: CLR, INV 2nd C.t, 1, STO 3, RST, enter $n = 10$, R/S

Comments: The sum of the first 10 Fibonacci numbers is 143.

8.3.4a

STEP	PROGRAM
00	STO 1
01	−
02	R/S
03	+
04	1
05	=
06	STO 7
07	1
08	STO 2
09	2nd Lbl 1
10	RCL 1
11	2nd Prd 2
12	2nd $x = t$
13	GTO 2
14	1
15	INV SUM 1
16	GTO 1
17	2nd Lbl 2
18	RCL 2
19	R/S

Memory: $R_7 = n - y + 1$, $R_1 = n$, $R_2 =$ running product

Initialize: CLR, INV 2nd C.t, RST, enter n, R/S, enter y, R/S

8.3.4b

5040

8.3.4c

95040

8.3.5a

STEP	PROGRAM
00	STO 1
01	R/S
02	STO 2
03	1
04	STO 3
05	STO 7
06	2nd Lbl 1
07	RCL 1
08	÷
09	RCL 2
10	=
11	2nd Prd 3
12	RCL 2
13	2nd $x = t$
14	GTO 2
15	1
16	INV SUM 2
17	INV SUM 1
18	GTO 1
19	2nd Lbl 2
20	RCL 3
21	R/S

Memory: $R_7 = 1$, $R_1 =$ numerator, $R_2 =$ denominator, $R_3 =$ running product

Initialize: CLR, INV 2nd C.t, RST, enter n, R/S, enter y, R/S

Comments: For $y > n$, you will obtain 0 in the display.

8.3.5b

210

8.3.5c

210

8.3.6

STEP	PROGRAM
00	−
01	1
02	=
03	STO 7
04	1
05	STO 1
06	STO 2
07	STO 3
08	2nd Lbl 1
09	RCL 1
10	INV 2nd Prd 2
11	RCL 2
12	SUM 3
13	RCL 1
14	2nd $x = t$
15	GTO 2
16	1
17	SUM 1
18	GTO 1
19	2nd Lbl 2
20	RCL 3
21	R/S

Memory: $R_7 = n$, $R_1 = k$, $R_2 = 1/k!$, R_3 = running total

Initialize: CLR, INV 2nd C.t, RST, enter $n = 20$, R/S

Comments: For $n = 20$, the sum is 2.7182818. What is the smallest value of n for which the sum is 2.7182818?

8.5.1

STEP	PROGRAM
00	STO 4
01	1
02	STO 1
03	2nd Lbl 1
04	RCL 2
05	STO 7
06	RCL 1
07	INV y^x
08	RCL 1
09	=
10	INV 2nd $x \geqslant t$
11	GTO 2
12	STO 2
13	RCL 1
14	STO 3
15	2nd Lbl 2

STEP	PROGRAM
16	RCL 4
17	STO 7
18	RCL 1
19	2nd $x \geqslant t$
20	GTO 3
21	1
22	SUM 1
23	GTO 1
24	2nd Lbl 3
25	RCL 2
26	R/S
27	RCL 3
28	R/S

Memory: $R_7 = t$-register, $R_1 = k$, $R_2 =$ largest $\sqrt[k]{k}$, $R_3 =$ best k
Initialize: INV 2nd C.t, RST, enter 30, R/S
Comments: $\sqrt[3]{3}$ is maximum, i.e., 1.4422496.

8.5.2a

STEP	PROGRAM
00	2nd π
01	STO 7
02	1
03	STO 1
04	2nd Lbl 1
05	RCL 1
06	INV y^x
07	4
08	=
09	$x \gtrless t$*
10	INV 2nd $x \geqslant t$
11	GTO 2
12	$x \gtrless t$
13	1
14	SUM 1
15	GTO 1
16	2nd Lbl 2
17	RCL 1
18	R/S

Memory: $R_7 = \pi$, $R_1 = k$
Initialize: CLR, INV 2nd C.t, RST, R/S
Comments: $k = 98$ is the first integer such that $\sqrt[4]{k} > \pi$

8.5.2b

Delete step 00, change the initialization to INV 2nd C.t, RST, enter end test value, R/S

8.5.3

STEP	PROGRAM
00	6
01	STO 4
02	0
03	STO 1
04	2nd Lbl 1
05	RCL 2
06	STO 7
07	RCL 1
08	x^2
09	$\times$
10	(
11	6
12	$-$
13	RCL 1
14	)
15	$\div$
16	7
17	2
18	=
19	INV 2nd $x \geqslant t$
20	GTO 2
21	STO 2
22	RCL 1
23	STO 3
24	2nd Lbl 2
25	RCL 4
26	STO 7
27	RCL 1
28	2nd $x \geqslant t$
29	GTO 3
30	1
31	SUM 1
32	GTO 1
33	2nd Lbl 3
34	RCL 3
35	R/S
36	RCL 2
37	R/S

Memory: $R_4 = 6$, $R_1 = k$, $R_2 =$ best probability, $R_3 =$ best k
Initialize: CLR, INV 2nd C.t, RST, R/S

*The symbol $x \gtrless y$ represents the "x exchange t" key on the calculator.

Comments: To see the probability, press R/S or RCL 2. The maximal probability occurs for $k = 4$ and $P(k) = 4/9 = 0.44444444$.

8.5.4

STEP	PROGRAM
00	STO7
01	1
02	STO 1
03	2nd Lbl 1
04	RCL 1
05	x^2
06	SUM 2
07	RCL 2
08	2nd Pause
09	$x \gtrless t$
10	INV 2nd $x \geqslant t$
11	GTO 2
12	$x \gtrless t$
13	1
14	SUM 1
15	GTO 1
16	2nd Lbl 2
17	RCL 1
18	−
19	1
20	=
21	R/S

Memory: R_7 = 10,000 = end test value, R_1 = k = number of layers, R_2 = sum

Initialize: INV 2nd C.t, RST, enter 10,000, R/S.

Comments: The number of layers is 30. Press $x \gtrless t$ to see the number in 31 layers, (i.e., 10416). Subtract 31^2 to see 9455 cannonballs used. Subtract from 10,000 to see 545 unused cannonballs.

8.5.5a

STEP	PROGRAM
00	4
01	×
02	2nd π
03	×
04	(
05	R/S
06	÷

8.5.5a

STEP	PROGRAM
07	STO 7
08	RCL 1
09	×
10	5
11	=
12	2nd $x \geqslant t$
13	GTO 3
14	7
15	7
16	−
17	5
18	×
19	RCL 1
20	=
21	÷
22	4
23	=
24	EE
25	INV EE
26	STO 2
27	2nd C.t
28	INV 2nd Int
29	INV 2nd $x = t$
30	GTO 2
31	RCL 2
32	R/S
33	RCL 1
34	R/S
35	2nd Lbl 2
36	1
37	SUM 1
38	GTO 1
39	2nd Lbl 3
40	R/S

Memory: R_7 = t-register, R_4 = 77 + 1, R_1 = y, R_2 = ‘x

Initialize: CLR, INV 2nd C.t, RST, R/S

Comments: $x = 18$, $y = 1$; $x = 13$, $y = 5$; $x = 8$, $y = 9$; or $x = 3$, $y = 13$. Notice the use of the roundoff sequence EE, INV EE. The use of 2nd C.t in step 27 clears only the t-register. To see all solutions, continue pressing R/S.

8.5.5b

$x = 8$, $y = 9$ by inspection

8.5.6

STEP	PROGRAM
00	1
01	0
02	0
03	STO 7
04	1
05	STO 1
06	STO 2
07	2nd Lbl 1
08	1
09	SUM 1
10	RCL 2
11	+
12	RCL 2
13	÷
14	RCL 1
15	=
16	2nd Pause
17	STO 2
18	INV 2nd $\geqslant t$
19	GTO 1
20	RCL 1
21	R/S

Memory: $R_7 = 100$, $R_1 = k$, $R_2 =$ height
Initialize: CLR, INV 2nd C.t, RST, R/S
Comments: The sequence of heights proceeds 1.5, 2, 2.5, 3, 3.5, . . . so the height is 100 times the original on the 199th day.

8.5.7

STEP	PROGRAM
00	RCL 2
01	−
02	RCL 4
03	×
04	RCL 1
05	=
06	÷
07	RCL 0
08	=
09	EE
10	INV EE
11	STO 6
12	STO 7
13	2nd Int
14	INV 2nd $x = t$
15	GTO 1
16	RCL 3
17	−
18	RCL 5
19	×
20	RCL 1
21	=
22	÷
23	RCL 0
24	=
25	EE
26	INV EE
27	STO 7
28	2nd Int
29	INV 2nd $x = t$
30	GTO 1
31	R/S
32	RCL 6
33	R/S
34	RCL 1
35	R/S
36	2nd Lbl 1
37	1
38	0
39	0
40	STO 7
41	RCL 1
42	2nd $x \geqslant t$
43	GTO 2
44	1
45	SUM 1
46	RST
47	2nd Lbl 2
48	0
49	R/S

Memory: $R_0 = 59$, $R_1 = S$, $R_2 = 3869$, $R_3 = 2031$, $R_4 = 35$, $R_5 = 24$, $R_6 = C$
Initialize: RST, enter 59, STO 0, enter 1, STO 1, enter 3869, STO 2, enter 2031, STO 3, enter 35, STO 4, enter 24, STO 5, R/S
Comments: The solution is unique $L = 21$, $C = 46$, and $S = 33$. Notice the use of the special roundoff sequence EE, INV EE.

APPENDIX B

ANSWER KEY– HP 33E

9.4.1a

Allows for input value of n.

9.4.1b

Separates n from the entered digit 1.

9.4.1c

Stops program in order to display the result.

9.4.2

STEP	PROGRAM
00	(R/S)
01	g x^2
02	2
03	×
04	1
05	+
06	GTO 00

Initialize: f PRGM, enter n, R/S

9.6.1a

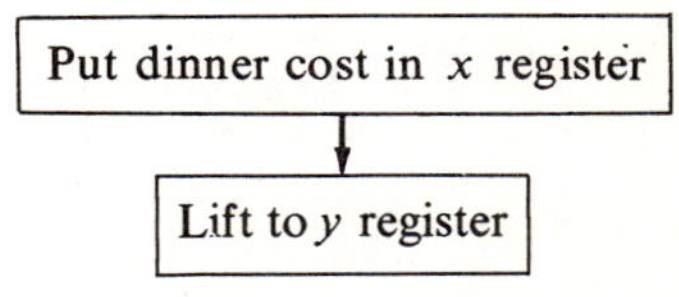

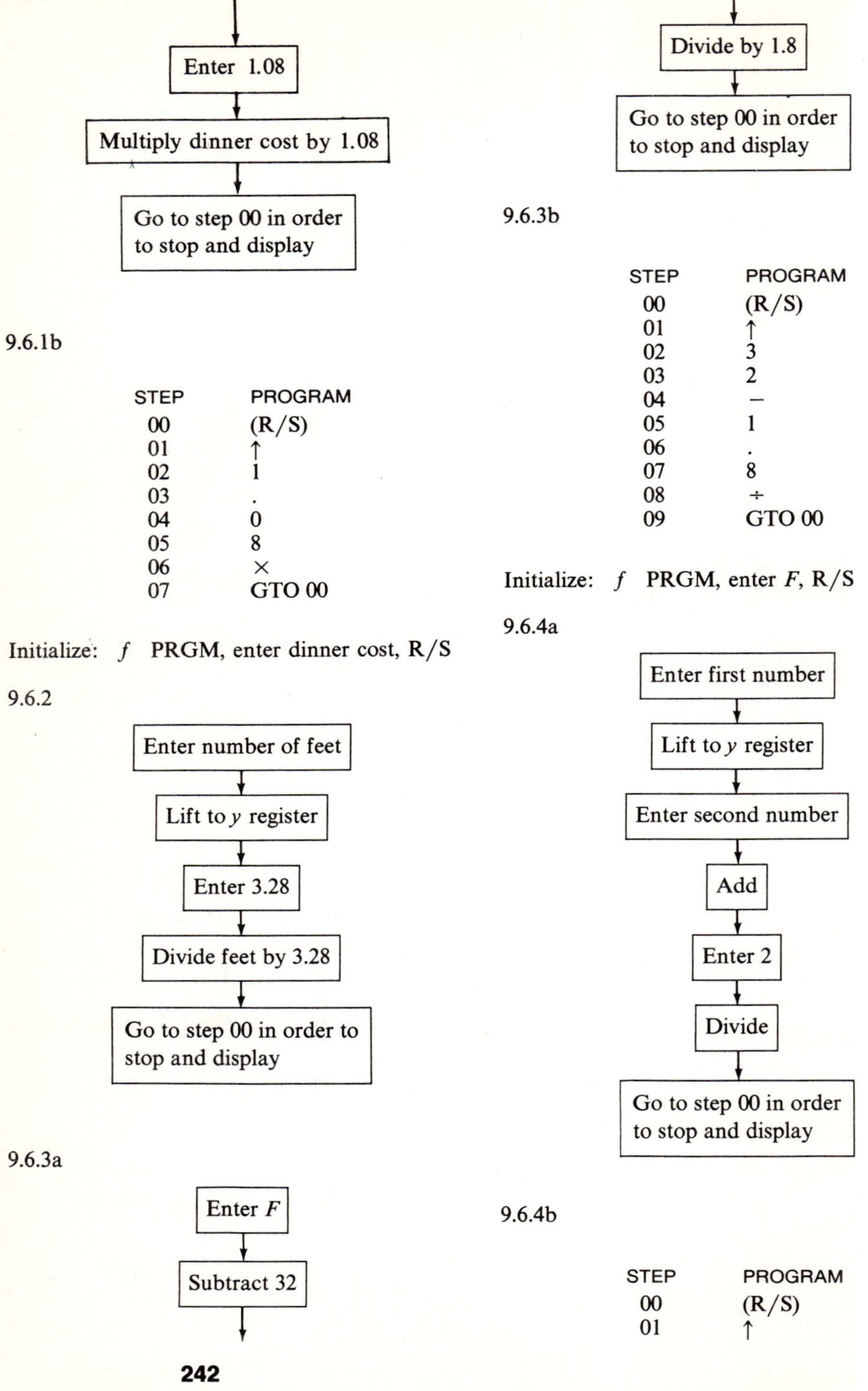

9.6.1b

STEP	PROGRAM
00	(R/S)
01	↑
02	1
03	.
04	0
05	8
06	×
07	GTO 00

Initialize: *f* PRGM, enter dinner cost, R/S

9.6.2

9.6.3a

9.6.3b

STEP	PROGRAM
00	(R/S)
01	↑
02	3
03	2
04	−
05	1
06	.
07	8
08	÷
09	GTO 00

Initialize: *f* PRGM, enter *F*, R/S

9.6.4a

9.6.4b

STEP	PROGRAM
00	(R/S)
01	↑

STEP	PROGRAM
02	R/S
03	+
04	2
05	÷
06	GTO 00

Initialize: *f* PRGM, enter first number, R/S, enter second number, R/S.

9.6.5

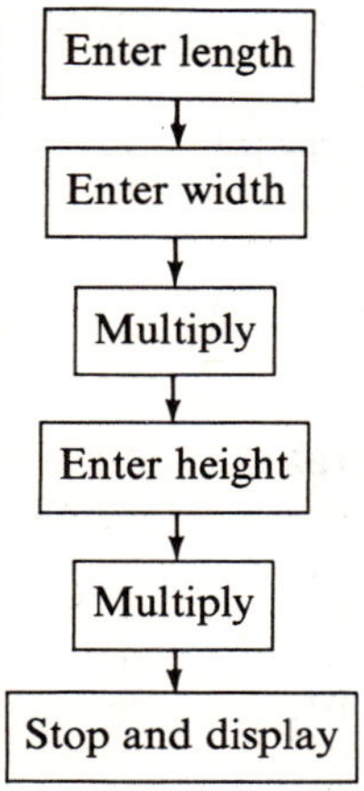

Enter length → Enter width → Multiply → Enter height → Multiply → Stop and display

STEP	PROGRAM
00	(R/S)
01	↑
02	R/S
03	×
04	R/S
05	×
06	GTO 00

Initialize: *f* PRGM, enter length, R/S, enter width, R/S, enter height, R/S

9.6.6a

STEP	PROGRAM
00	(R/S)
01	↑
02	+
03	8
04	+
05	2
06	−

STEP	PROGRAM
07	2
08	÷
09	R/S
10	−
11	GTO 00

Initialize: *f* PRGM, enter *n*, R/S, enter *n*, R/S

9.6.6b

3

9.7.1

STEP	PROGRAM
00	(R/S)
01	↑
02	.
03	6
04	2
05	÷
06	GTO 00

Initialize: *f* PRGM, enter miles, R/S
Comments: 5 mi. = 8.0645 km., 8 mi. = 12.9032 km., 31 mi. = 50.0000 km., 500 mi. = 806.4516 km., 3000 mi. = 4838.7097 km.

9.7.2

STEP	PROGRAM
00	(R/S)
01	↑
02	2
03	.
04	8
05	5
06	×
07	GTO 00

Initialize: *f* PRGM, enter hours, R/S
Comments: salaries are, respectively: \$34.20, \$51.30, \$39.90, \$62.70.

9.7.3a

STEP	PROGRAM
00	(R/S)
01	↑
02	4
03	0

STEP	PROGRAM
04	+
05	5
06	×
07	9
08	÷
09	4
10	0
11	−
12	GTO 00

Initialize: *f* PRGM, enter *F*, R/S

9.7.3b

STEP	PROGRAM
00	(R/S)
01	↑
02	4
03	0
04	+
05	9
06	×
07	5
08	÷
09	4
10	0
11	−
12	GTO 00

Initialize: *f* PRGM, enter *C*, R/S

9.7.4

STEP	PROGRAM
00	(R/S)
01	↑
02	R/S
03	×
04	.
05	0
06	3
07	×
08	GTO 00

Initialize: *f* PRGM, enter *l*, R/S, enter *w*, R/S

9.7.5

STEP	PROGRAM
00	(R/S)
01	↑
02	2
03	×
04	R/S
05	↑
06	2
07	×
08	+
09	5
10	.
11	8
12	9
13	×
14	GTO 00

Initialize: *f* PRGM, enter *l*, R/S, enter *w*, R/S

9.7.6a

STEP	PROGRAM
00	(R/S)
01	↑
02	R/S
03	+
04	R/S
05	+
06	3
07	÷
08	GTO 00

Initialize: *f* PRGM, enter *a*, R/S, enter *b*, R/S, enter *c*, R/S

9.7.6b

STEP	PROGRAM
00	(R/S)
01	↑
02	R/S
03	+
04	R/S
05	+
06	R/S
07	+
08	4
09	÷
10	GTO 00

Initialize: *f* PRGM, enter *a*, R/S, enter *b*, R/S, enter *c*, R/S, enter *d*, R/S

9.7.7

STEP	PROGRAM
00	(R/S)
01	↑
02	R/S
03	↑
04	R/S
05	+
06	×
07	2
08	÷
09	GTO 00

Initialize: *f* PRGM, enter h, R/S, enter b_1, R/S, enter b_2, R/S

9.7.8a

STEP	PROGRAM
00	(R/S)
01	↑
02	1
03	.
04	0
05	6
06	×
07	GTO 00

Initialize: *f* PRGM, enter n, R/S

9.7.8b

$100 yields $106.00

9.7.8c

Then press R/S to obtain the bank balance of $112.36 at the end of two years.

9.7.8d

Press R/S three more times to obtain the five year result of $133.82

9.7.9a

STEP	PROGRAM
00	(R/S)
01	↑
02	3
03	6
04	0
05	$x \gtrless y$ *
06	÷
07	GTO 00

Initialize: *f* PRGM, enter l, R/S

Or . . .

STEP	PROGRAM
00	(R/S)
01	↑
02	3
03	6
04	0
05	R/S
06	÷
07	GTO 00

Initialize: *f* PRGM, R/S, enter l, R/S

9.7.9b

l = 5, 8, 10, 15 give, respectively:
w = 72, 45, 36, 24.

9.7.9c

$l = 20$, $w = 18$. Find this result by the guess and check method.

10.2.1

No answer required.

10.2.2

$49.89

10.2.3

$153.25

10.2.4

$54,575,907.58

10.2.5

STEP	PROGRAM
00	(R/S)
01	EEX
02	2
03	↑
04	1

*The symbol $x \gtrless y$ represents the "x exchange y" key on the calculator.

STEP	PROGRAM
05	.
06	0
07	6
08	R/S
09	f y^x
10	×
11	GTO 00

Initialize: f PRGM, R/S, enter n, R/S

Comments: 1. For $n = 20$, $p = 320.71$.
2. Steps 01 and 02 have the effect of entering 100 in the display.

Or . . .

STEP	PROGRAM
00	(R/S)
01	↑
02	1
03	.
04	0
05	6
06	$x \gtrless y$ *
07	f y^x
08	EEX
09	2
10	×
11	GTO 00

Initialize: f PRGM, enter n, R/S

10.4.1a

Program 2

10.4.1b

Computes 0, since 34 is in the x-register (the display) and 0 is in the y-register at the time the multiplication is performed.

10.4.2

Program 2

10.4.3

Sequence 1 evaluates 10^{1+n}
Sequence 2 evaluates $1 + 10^n$
Sequence 3 evaluates $10 + n$

10.4.4

Initialization sequence (a) gives $3^5 = 243$, while sequence (b) gives $5^3 = 125$.

10.6.1

STEP	PROGRAM
00	(R/S)
01	↑
02	R/S
03	+
04	R/S
05	+
06	3
07	÷
08	GTO 00

Initialize: f PRGM, enter a, R/S, enter b, R/S, enter c, R/S

10.6.2

STEP	PROGRAM
00	(R/S)
01	↑
02	R/S
03	×
04	f $\sqrt{x}$
05	GTO 00

Initialize: f PRGM, enter a, R/S, enter b, R/S

10.6.3

STEP	PROGRAM
00	(R/S)
01	↑
02	R/S
03	×
04	R/S
05	×
06	3
07	g $1/x$
08	f y^x
09	GTO 00

Initialize: f PRGM, enter a, R/S, enter b, R/S, enter c, R/S

*The symbol $x \gtrless y$ represents the "x exchange y" key on the calculator.

10.6.4

STEP	PROGRAM
00	(R/S)
01	g $1/x$
02	R/S
03	g $1/x$
04	+
05	g $1/x$
06	GTO 00

Initialize: f PRGM, enter R_1, R/S, enter R_2, R/S

10.6.5a

STEP	PROGRAM
00	(R/S)
01	f SIN (or f COS or f TAN)
02	g $1/x$
03	GTO 00

Initialize: f PRGM, enter θ, R/S

10.6.5b

STEP	PROGRAM
00	(R/S)
01	↑
02	9
03	0
04	$x \gtrless y$
05	−
06	f TAN
07	GTO 00

Initialize: f PRGM, enter θ, R/S

10.6.6

STEP	PROGRAM
00	(R/S)
01	↑
02	2
03	$x \gtrless y$
04	f y^x
05	1
06	−
07	GTO 00

Initialize: f PRGM, enter n, R/S

10.6.7

STEP	PROGRAM
00	(R/S)
01	↑
02	3
03	2
04	−
05	g INT
06	3
07	2
08	+
09	.
10	1
11	3
12	×
13	GTO 00

Initialize: f PRGM, enter weight in ounces (even fractional parts of ounces will work), R/S

10.6.8

STEP	PROGRAM
00	(R/S)
01	↑
02	R/S
03	−
04	g ABS
05	GTO 00

Initialize: f PRGM, enter one of the years, R/S, enter other year, R/S

10.6.9

STEP	PROGRAM
00	(R/S)
01	f LOG
02	g INT
03	1
04	+
05	GTO 00

Initialize: f PRGM, enter n, R/S

10.6.10

STEP	PROGRAM
00	(R/S)
01	↑
02	3

STEP	PROGRAM
03	×
04	g π
05	÷
06	4
07	÷
08	3
09	g $1/x$
10	f y^x
11	GTO 00

Initialize: f PRGM, enter V, R/S

10.6.11a

STEP	PROGRAM
00	(R/S)
01	↑
02	R/S
03	×
04	4
05	↑
06	R/S
07	×
08	R/S
09	×
10	+
11	R/S
12	↑
13	R/S
14	×
15	+
16	R/S
17	×
18	6
19	÷
20	GTO 00

Initialize: f PRGM, enter a, R/S, enter b, R/S, enter a, R/S, enter b, R/S, enter a, R/S, enter b, R/S, enter c, R/S

Here is another program based on algebraic manipulations of the prismoidal volume formula, resulting in the familiar formula for the volume of a rectangular prism.

$$V = (ab + 4ab)\frac{c}{6}$$
$$= (6ab)\frac{c}{6}$$
$$= abc$$

STEP	PROGRAM
00	(R/S)
01	↑
02	R/S
03	×
04	R/S
05	×
06	GTO 00

Initialize: f PRGM, enter a, R/S, enter b, R/S, enter c, R/S

10.6.11b

STEP	PROGRAM
00	(R/S)
01	↑
02	2
03	÷
04	g x^2
05	g π
06	×
07	4
08	×
09	R/S
10	g x^2
11	g π
12	×
13	+
14	R/S
15	×
16	6
17	÷
18	GTO 00

Initialize: f PRGM, enter r, R/S, enter r, R/S, enter h, R/S

Comments: This program can be simplified if the prismoidal formula is first manipulated algebraically to obtain:

$$V = \pi r^2 h/3$$

10.6.11c

STEP	PROGRAM
00	(R/S)
01	g x^2
02	R/S
03	↑
04	R/S
05	+

STEP	PROGRAM
06	2
07	÷
08	g x^2
09	4
10	×
11	+
12	R/S
13	g x^2
14	+
15	R/S
16	×
17	6
18	÷
19	GTO 00

Initialize: *f* PRGM, enter *a*, R/S, enter *a*, R/S, enter *b*, R/S, enter *b*, R/S, enter *c*, R/S

10.6.12a

STEP	PROGRAM
00	(R/S)
01	g x^2
02	R/S
03	↑
04	2
05	×
06	*f* SIN
07	×
08	3
09	2
10	÷
11	GTO 00

Initialize: *f* PRGM, enter V_0, R/S, enter θ, R/S

10.6.12b

No answer required.

10.6.12c

45°, 253.1 feet

11.5.1

No answer required.

11.5.2

No answer required.

11.5.3

A corrected program for evaluating $(a - 5)/(b + 5)$ is

STEP	PROGRAM
00	(R/S)
01	↑
02	5
03	−
04	R/S
05	↑
06	5
07	+
08	÷
09	GTO 00

Initialize: *f* PRGM, enter *a*, R/S, enter *b*, R/S
Comment: Neither up arrow (↑) in steps 01 nor 05 are needed on the HP 33E. But both are needed on the HP 25 and HP 25C.

12.3.1

STEP	PROGRAM
00	(R/S)
01	STO 1
02	2
03	×
04	1
05	+
06	RCL 1
07	1
08	+
09	×
10	RCL 1
11	×
12	6
13	÷
14	GTO 00

Memory: $R_1 = n$
Initialize: *f* PRGM, enter *n*, R/S

12.3.2

STEP	PROGRAM
00	(R/S)
01	STO 1
02	1

STEP	PROGRAM
03	+
04	RCL 1
05	×
06	2
07	÷
08	$g\ \ x^2$
09	GTO 00

Memory: $R_1 = n$
Initialize: f PRGM, enter n, R/S

12.3.3

STEP	PROGRAM
00	(R/S)
01	STO 1
02	R/S
03	STO 2
04	×
05	$g\ \ \pi$
06	×
07	STO 3
08	CL X
09	RCL 1
10	$g\ \ x^2$
11	RCL 2
12	$g\ \ x^2$
13	+
14	2
15	÷
16	$f\ \ \sqrt{x}$
17	$g\ \ \pi$
18	×
19	2
20	×
21	STO 4
22	RCL 3
23	R/S
24	RCL 4
25	GTO 00

Memory: $R_1 = a$, $R_2 = b$, $R_3 =$ area, R_4 = circumference
Initialize: f PRGM, enter a, R/S, enter b, R/S, wait to see area, R/S

12.3.4a

STEP	PROGRAM
00	(R/S)
01	STO 1
02	R/S
03	STO 2
04	$g\ \ x^2$
05	×
06	1
07	8
08	0
09	RCL 1
10	÷
11	f TAN
12	4
13	×
14	÷
15	GTO 00

Memory: $R_1 = n$, $R_2 = l$
Initialize: f PRGM, enter n, R/S, enter l, R/S

12.3.4b

No answer required.

12.3.5a

STEP	PROGRAM
00	(R/S)
01	STO 1
02	R/S
03	STO 2
04	1
05	−
06	STO 3
07	4
08	0
09	0
10	÷
11	g INT
12	RCL 3
13	1
14	0
15	0
16	÷
17	g INT
18	−
19	RCL 3
20	4
21	÷
22	g INT
23	+
24	RCL 2
25	+
26	RCL1
27	+

28	7
29	÷
30	*g* FRAC
31	7
32	×
33	GTO 00

Memory: $R_1 = D$, $R_2 = Y$, $R_3 = Y - 1$
Initialize: *f* PRGM, enter *D*, R/S, enter *Y*, R/S

12.3.5b

Variable answers

12.3.5c

Saturday

12.3.6

STEP	PROGRAM
00	(R/S)
01	STO 1
02	*f* SIN
03	*g* x^2
04	RCL 1
05	*f* COS
06	*g* x^2
07	+
08	GTO 00

Memory: $R_1 = \theta$
Initialize: *f* PRGM, enter θ, R/S
Comments: For any θ, $\sin^2\theta + \cos^2\theta = 1$

12.3.7

STEP	PROGRAM
00	(R/S)
01	STO 1
02	2
03	−
04	RCL 1
05	1
06	−
07	×
08	RCL 1
09	×
10	6
11	÷
12	GTO 00

Memory: $R_1 = n$
Initialize: *f* PRGM, enter *n*, R/S
Comments: For $n = 3, 4, 5, 10$, and 100, the corresponding values are 1, 4, 10, 120, and 161,700.

12.3.8

STEP	PROGRAM
00	(R/S)
01	STO 1
02	3
03	*f* y^x
04	*g* π
05	×
06	4
07	×
08	3
09	÷
10	R/S
11	RCL 1
12	*g* x^2
13	*g* π
14	×
15	4
16	×
17	GTO 00

Memory: R_1 = radius
Initialize: *f* PRGM, enter *r*, R/S, wait to see *V*, R/S

12.3.9

STEP	PROGRAM
00	(R/S)
01	STO 1
02	R/S
03	STO 2
04	+
05	R/S
06	STO 3
07	×
08	.
09	0
10	6
11	×
12	RCL 1
13	RCL 2
14	×
15	.
16	0
17	5
18	×

STEP	PROGRAM
19	+
20	GTO 00

Memory: $R_1 = x$, $R_2 = y$, $R_3 = z$
Initialize: *f* PRGM, enter x, R/S, enter y, R/S, enter z, R/S

12.3.10a

STEP	PROGRAM
00	(R/S)
01	STO 1
02	R/S
03	STO 2
04	−
05	.
06	8
07	2
08	×
09	RCL 2
10	+
11	GTO 00

Memory: R_1 = delivery price, R_2 = transportation costs
Initialize: *f* PRGM, enter delivery price, R/S, enter transportation costs, R/S

12.3.10b

Write over step 11 with R/S and augment the program with

STEP	PROGRAM
12	STO 3
13	RCL 1
14	−
15	CHS
16	GTO 00

12.3.10c

Of course, your calculator automatically rounds to the nearest hundredth.

12.3.11

STEP	PROGRAM
00	(R/S)
01	STO 1
02	R/S
03	STO 2
04	×
05	STO 4
06	R/S
07	STO 3
08	1
09	RCL 2
10	−
11	STO 5
12	RCL 4
13	RCL 4
14	RCL 3
15	RCL 5
16	×
17	+
18	÷
19	STO 6
20	GTO 00

Memory: $R_1 = P(A|B)$, $R_2 = P(B)$, $R_3 = P(A|B')$, $R_4 = P(A|B) \times P(B)$, $R_5 = 1 - P(B) = P(B')$, $R_6 = P(B|A)$
Initialize: *f* PRGM, enter P(A|B), R/S, enter P(B), R/S, enter P(A|B′), R/S

12.3.12

STEP	PROGRAM
00	(R/S)
01	STO 1
02	R/S
03	STO 2
04	×
05	R/S
06	1
07	RCL 2
08	−
09	×
10	*f* $\sqrt{x}$
11	GTO 00

Memory: $R_1 = n$, $R_2 = p$
Initialize: *f* PRGM, enter n, R/S, enter p, R/S, wait to see E(y), R/S

12.3.13

STEP	PROGRAM
00	(R/S)
01	STO 1
02	R/S
03	STO 2
04	R/S

STEP	PROGRAM
05	STO 3
06	RCL 2
07	*f* COS
08	×
09	RCL 1
10	×
11	R/S
12	RCL 2
13	*f* SIN
14	RCL 1
15	×
16	RCL 3
17	×
18	RCL 3
19	*g* x^2
20	1
21	6
22	×
23	−
24	GTO 00

Memory: $R_1 = V_0$, $R_2 = \theta$, $R_3 = t$
Initialize: *f* PRGM, enter V_0, R/S, enter θ, R/S, enter t, R/S, wait to see x, R/S

13.3.1

Displays the sequence 10, 20, 30, 40, . . . i.e., counts by tens

13.3.2

Displays the sequence −1, −2, −3, −4, . . .

13.3.3

STEP	PROGRAM
00	(R/S)
01	↑
02	5
03	+
04	*f* PAUSE
05	GTO 02

Initialize: *f* PRGM, CL x, R/S

13.3.4

STEP	PROGRAM
00	(R/S)
01	*f* PAUSE
02	1
03	0
04	+
05	GTO 01

Initialize: *f* PRGM, CL X, R/S

13.3.5

Use the initialization *f* PRGM, enter 7, R/S.

13.3.6

STEP	PROGRAM
00	(R/S)
01	*f* PAUSE
02	EEX
03	2
04	−
05	GTO 01

Initialize: *f* PRGM, enter 1000, R/S

13.5.1

STEP	PROGRAM
00	(R/S)
01	*f* PAUSE
02	9
03	+
04	GTO 01

Initialize: *f* PRGM, enter 2, R/S

13.5.2

STEP	PROGRAM
00	(R/S)
01	*f* PAUSE
02	3
03	÷
04	GTO 01

Initialize: *f* PRGM, enter 2187, R/S

13.5.3a

STEP	PROGRAM
00	(R/S)
01	*f* PAUSE
02	2
03	×

STEP	PROGRAM
04	1
05	+
06	GTO 01

Initialize: *f* PRGM, enter 3, R/S

13.5.3b

Initialize with *f* PRGM, then enter the appropriate number, 123, −16, 2/3, or .222, then press R/S.

13.5.4a

Double each term to get the next term.

13.5.4b

Multiply each term by 2/3.

13.5.4c

Double each term, then add 1.

13.5.4d

Double each term, then subtract 1.

13.5.4e

Triple each term, then subtract 1.

13.5.4f

Square each term.

13.5.5

STEP	PROGRAM
00	(R/S)
01	*f* PAUSE
02	2
03	CHS
04	×
05	3
06	+
07	GTO 01

Initialize: *f* PRGM, enter 15, R/S

13.5.6a

Add two to the previous term.

13.5.6b

STEP	PROGRAM
00	(R/S)
01	*f* PAUSE
02	2
03	+
04	GTO 01

Initialize: *f* PRGM, enter 1, R/S

13.5.7a

STEP	PROGRAM
00	(R/S)
01	*f* PAUSE
02	2
03	÷
04	4
05	+
06	GTO 01

Initialize: *f* PRGM, enter 1 or any number, R/S

Comments: After many iterations the sequence will approach 8.0000.

13.5.7b

STEP	PROGRAM
00	(R/S)
01	*f* PAUSE
02	2
03	+
04	*f* $\sqrt{x}$
05	GTO 01

Initialize: *f* PRGM, enter any number bigger than −2, R/S

Comments: After many iterations the sequence will approach 2.0000.

13.5.8a

STEP	PROGRAM
00	(R/S)
01	*f* PAUSE
02	6
03	$x \gtrless y$ *

*The symbol $x \gtrless y$ represents the "x exchange y" key on the calculator.

STEP	PROGRAM
04	÷
05	1
06	+
07	GTO 01

Initialize: *f* PRGM, enter 6 or any number, R/S

Comments: This sequence begins 6.0000, 2.0000, 4.0000, 2.5000, . . . and tends to 3.0000. The result will be the same regardless of the first term as long as the first term is not 0, −6, or a selection of other special values near − 2.

13.5.8b

STEP	PROGRAM
00	(R/S)
01	*f* PAUSE
02	2
03	÷
04	1
05	$x \gtrless y$
06	−
07	GTO 01

Initialize: *f* PRGM, enter 5 or any number, R/S

Comments: This sequence begins 5.0000, −1.5000, 1.7500, 0.1250, , . . . , when the entered number is . Thereafter the sequence tends to 2/3. The results will be the same limiting value regardless of first term.

13.5.9a

STEP	PROGRAM
00	(R/S)
01	*f* PAUSE
02	↑
03	*g* x^2
04	$x \gtrless y$
05	−
06	GTO 01

Initialize: *f* PRGM, enter 2.1, R/S

Comments: The sequence generated is 2.1000, 2.3100, 3.0261, 6.1312, . . . and eventually grows to 9.9999999×10^{99}.

13.5.9b

The initial entry 1.9 gives 1.9000, 1.7100, 1.2141, 0.2599, −0.1924, 0.2294, −0.1768, . . . and oscillates in sign while tending to zero.

13.5.9c

The initial value 2.0 gives the sequence 2.0000, 2.0000, 2.0000, 2.0000, ...

13.5.10a

Program blinks and computes but never pauses nor stops until 9.9999999×10^{99} appears in the display.

13.5.10b

Change step 06 to GTO 01.

13.5.10c

Register R_1 is used for temporary storage of the previous term.

13.5.10d

Each term is the square of the previous term minus the previous term.

13.5.10e

The initial value of 2 yields the sequence of all twos. How does problem 5.5.10 compare to problem 5.5.9?

13.7.1a

STEP	PROGRAM
00	(R/S)
01	STO 1
02	RCL 1
03	1
04	+
05	STO 1
06	*g* x^2
07	1
08	+
09	*f* PAUSE
10	GTO 02

Memory: R_1 = term

Initialize: *f* PRGM, enter 0, R/S

13.7.1b

Initialize with *f* PRGM, enter 2, R/S. You obtain the same sequence but starting with the third term: 10, 17, 26, ...

13.7.2a

STEP	PROGRAM
00	(R/S)
01	STO 1
02	RCL 1
03	1
04	+
05	STO 1
06	g x^2
07	2
08	÷
09	*f* PAUSE
10	GTO 02

Memory: R_1 = term
Initialize: *f* PRGM, enter 0, R/S

13.7.2b

Change step 03 to read "2" and count by twos.

13.7.3

These answers assume that your programs are designed so that in each loop first 1 is added to the index, *n*, and then the *n*th term is computed.

13.7.3a

Set index at −1, compute term as 5 times the index.

13.7.3b

Set index at 0, compute term as the square of the index minus 1.

13.7.3c

Set index at 2, compute term as the square of the index minus 1

13.7.3d

Set index at 0, compute term as 2^n.

13.7.4a

STEP	PROGRAM
00	(R/S)
01	STO 1
02	3
03	RCL 1
04	1
05	+
06	STO 1
07	f y^x
08	*f* PAUSE
09	GTO 02

Memory: R_1 = term
Initialize: *f* PRGM, enter 0, R/S

13.7.4b

STEP	PROGRAM
00	(R/S)
01	STO 1
02	RCL 1
03	1
04	+
05	STO 1
06	3
07	f y^x
08	*f* PAUSE
09	GTO 02

Memory: R_1 = term
Initialize: *f* PRGM, enter 1, R/S

13.7.5

STEP	PROGRAM
00	(R/S)
01	STO 1
02	RCL 1
03	1
04	+
05	STO 1
06	RCL 1
07	f y^x
08	*f* PAUSE
09	GTO 02

Memory: R_1 = term
Initialize: *f* PRGM, enter 0, R/S
Comments: This sequence overflows the capacity of the calculator after 57 iterations.

13.7.6

STEP	PROGRAM
00	(R/S)
01	STO 1
02	RCL 1
03	1
04	+
05	STO 1
06	RCL 1
07	g $1/x$
08	f y^x
09	f PAUSE
10	GTO 02

Memory: R_1 = term
Initialize: f PRGM, enter 0, R/S

13.7.6a

$\sqrt[3]{3} = 1.442249570$ is largest

13.7.6b

$\sqrt[n]{n}$ gets smaller tending to 1

13.7.7

STEP	PROGRAM
00	(R/S)
01	STO 1
02	RCL 1
03	1
04	+
05	STO 1
06	g x^2
07	2
08	RCL 1
09	f y^x
10	−
11	f PAUSE
12	GTO 02

Memory: R_1 = term
Initialize: f PRGM, enter 0, R/S

13.7.7a

When $n = 2$ or 4, $n^2 = 2^n$; when $n = 3$, $n^2 > 2^n$; for all other n, $n^2 < 2^n$.

13.7.7b

Generate the sequence $n^3 - 3^n$. When the sequence values are negative, $n^3 < 3^n$, otherwise $n^3 \geqslant 3^n$.

13.7.8a

STEP	PROGRAM
00	(R/S)
01	STO 1
02	RCL 2
03	RCL 1
04	f y^x
05	f PAUSE
06	RCL 1
07	1
08	+
09	GTO 01

Memory: R_1 = term, R_2 = initial value
Initialize: f PRGM, 0.99, STO 2, 0, R/S
Comments: As n grows large, $(0.99)^n$ tends slowly to zero.

13.7.8b

Change the initialization to f PRGM, 1.01, STO 2, 0, R/S. As n grows large, $(1.01)^n$ grows to 9.9999999×10^{99}.

13.7.8c

Change the initialization to f PRGM, enter 1, STO 2, 0, R/S. The resulting sequence is 1.0000, 1.0000, 1.0000, 1.0000, ...

14.3.1a

96

14.3.1b

90

14.3.2a

4, 8, 16, 32, 64, . . .

14.3.2b

4, 8, 16, 32, 64, . . .

14.3.2c

Multiplied by 2

14.3.2d

Multiply the quantity in R_7 by 2.

14.3.3a

$10^5, 10^4, 10^3, 10^2, \ldots$

14.3.3b

Divide the quantity in R_5 by 10.

14.3.3c

Store 10^6 in R_5.

14.3.4

STEP	PROGRAM
00	(R/S)
01	STO 3
02	*f* PAUSE
03	4
04	STO − 3
05	RCL 3
06	GTO 02

Memory: R_3 = term
Initialize: *f* PRGM, enter 100, R/S

14.5.1

f REG clears all memory registers by filling them with 0.

14.5.2a

$1/(3^0) = 1$

14.5.2b

3, STO ÷ 4. You can check to see that this works by following the given key stroke sequence with RCL 4, *g* $1/x$, *f* PAUSE which, in a program, will show the denominator of the term.

14.5.3a

2, STO + 2, if 1 is placed in R_2 at the start.

14.5.3b

3, STO − 3, if 1 is placed in R_3 at the start.

14.5.3c

RCL 2, RCL 3, ÷

14.5.4

STEP	PROGRAM
00	(R/S)
01	*f* REG
02	*f* STK
03	1
04	STO + 3
05	RCL 3
06	RCL 3
07	1
08	+
09	×
10	2
11	÷
12	1
13	+
14	*f* PAUSE
15	GTO 03

Memory: R_3 = index
Initialize: *f* PRGM, R/S

14.8.1a

STEP	PROGRAM
00	(R/S)
01	*f* REG
02	*f* STK
03	1
04	STO + 2
05	RCL 2
06	*f* PAUSE
07	1
08	STO + 1
09	3
10	RCL 1
11	*f* y^x
12	*g* $1/x$
13	GTO 04

Memory: R_1 = index, R_2 = total, x − reg = term
Initialize: *f* PRGM, CL X, R/S

14.8.1b

The limiting value is 1.5000.

14.8.2a

STEP	PROGRAM
00	(R/S)
01	*f* REG
02	*f* STK
01	1
04	STO + 2
05	2
06	STO + 3
07	*g* $1/x$
08	STO + 1

STEP	PROGRAM
09	RCL 1
10	*f* PAUSE
11	1
12	STO + 2
13	2
14	STO × 3
15	RCL 2
16	3
17	*f* y^x
18	RCL 3
19	÷
20	GTO 08

Memory: R_1 = running total, R_2 = index, R_3 = denominator = 2^n, *x*-reg = term = $n^3/2^n$.
Initialize: *f* PRGM, CL *x*, R/S

14.8.2b

The average amount received is the limiting value of $26.00.

14.8.2c

Since $26 - 10 = +16$, the gambler's expected *profit* would be $16.00.

14.8.2d

By pressing *g* NOP at steps 16 and 17 in 14.8.2a, you can compute the limiting value of $\Sigma_{n=1}^{\infty}(n/2^n)$, which is 2.0000. Hence, $2 - 10 = -8$ and the gambler's expected *loss* is $8.00.

14.8.3a

STEP	PROGRAM
00	(R/S)
01	*f* REG
02	*f* STK
03	1
04	STO + 3
05	1
06	STO + 2
07	6
08	STO × 3
09	2
10	RCL 2
11	*f* y^x
12	3
13	RCL 2
14	*f* y^x
15	+
16	RCL 3
17	÷
18	STO + 1
19	RCL 1
20	*f* PAUSE
21	GTO 05

Memory: R_1 = running total, R_2 = index, $R_3 = 6^n$
Initialize: *f* PRGM, CL *X*, R/S

14.8.3b

The limiting value is 1.5000.

14.8.4a

STEP	PROGRAM
00	(R/S)
01	*f* REG
02	*f* STK
03	1
04	STO + 2
05	RCL 3
06	RCL 2
07	+
08	STO 3
09	6
10	×
11	1
12	+
13	RCL 3
14	3
15	*f* y^x
16	÷
17	STO + 1
18	RCL 1
19	*f* PAUSE
20	GTO 03

Memory: R_1 = running total, R_2 = index, $R_3 = T_n$
Initialize: *f* PRGM, R/S

14.8.4b

The limiting value of the series is 8.0000.

14.8.5a

STEP	PROGRAM
00	(R/S)
01	*f* REG

STEP	PROGRAM
02	*f* STK
03	1
04	STO + 2
05	RCL 3
06	RCL 2
07	+
08	STO 3
09	*g* x^2
10	2
11	0
12	×
13	RCL 3
14	1
15	0
16	×
17	+
18	1
19	+
20	RCL 3
21	5
22	*f* y^x
23	÷
24	STO + 1
25	RCL 1
26	*f* PAUSE
27	GTO 03

Memory: R_1 = running total, R_2 = index, $R_3 = T_n$
Initialize: *f* PRGM, R/S

14.8.5b

The limiting value is 32.0000.

14.8.6a

STEP	PROGRAM
00	(R/S)
01	*f* REG
02	*f* STK
03	5
04	STO + 1
05	RCL 1
06	*f* PAUSE
07	1
08	STO + 2
09	2
10	↑
11	5
12	×
13	
14	8
15	RCL 2
16	*f* y^x
17	×
18	GTO 04

Memory: R_1 = running total, R_2 = index, x-reg = term
Initialize: *f* PRGM, R/S

14.8.6b

The ball will travel 45.0000 meters.

14.8.7a

STEP	PROGRAM
00	(R/S)
01	STO 3
02	1
03	STO + 2
04	RCL 2
05	RCL 3
06	*f* y^x
07	*g* $1/x$
08	STO + 1
09	RCL 1
10	*f* PAUSE
11	GTO 02

Memory: R_1 = running total, R_2 = index, $R_3 = s$
Initialize: *f* PRGM, *f* REG, *f* STK, *f* FIX 9, enter s, R/S
Comments: Here *f* REG, *f* STK is part of the initialization rather than the program. If the sequence were at the beginning of the program, it would clear the x-register so that s would be lost.

14.8.7b

$\zeta(8) = 1.004077355$ and $\zeta(6) = 1.017343060$.

14.8.7c

For values of $s \leqslant 4$, the number of times through the loop to evaluate the function is excessive. For $s = 4$, it takes more than 200 iterations. For $s = 2$ your calculator would require more than 9 hours to calculate the correct value, $\zeta(2) = \pi^2/6$.

14.8.8

STEP	PROGRAM
00	(R/S)
01	*f* REG
02	*f* STK
03	1
04	STO 2
05	STO 3
06	STO + 1
07	RCL 1
08	*f* PAUSE
09	1
10	STO + 2
11	CHS
12	STO × 3
13	RCL 2
14	6
15	*f* y^x
16	*g* $1/x$
17	RCL 3
18	×
19	GTO 06

Memory: R_1 = running total, R_2 = index, R_3 = sign, *x*-reg = term
Initialize: *f* PRGM, *f* FIX 9, R/S
Comments: The value of the series is 0.985551092 which is the decimal form of $(31/32) \cdot (\pi^6/945)$.

14.8.9

STEP	PROGRAM
00	(R/S)
01	*f* REG
02	*f* STK
03	1
04	CHS
05	STO 2
06	STO 3
07	3
08	*f* $\sqrt{x}$
09	2
10	×
11	STO 4
12	1
13	STO + 2
14	CHS
15	STO × 3
16	RCL 2
17	2
18	×
19	1
20	+
21	3
22	RCL 2
23	*f* y^x
24	×
25	*g* $1/x$
26	RCL 4
27	×
28	RCL 3
29	×
30	STO + 1
31	RCL 1
32	*f* PAUSE
33	GTO 12

Memory: R_1 = running total, R_2 = index, R_3 = sign, $R_4 = 2\sqrt{3}$
Initialize: *f* PRGM, *f* FIX 7, R/S
Comments: The limiting value of the series is $\pi = 3.1415927$.

14.8.10

STEP	PROGRAM
00	(R/S)
01	STO 6
02	1
03	STO 5
04	RCL 6
05	RCL 5
06	×
07	*f* SIN
08	RCL 5
09	÷
10	STO + 4
11	RCL 4
12	*f* PAUSE
13	*f* PAUSE
14	2
15	STO + 5
16	GTO 04

Memory: $R_6 = x$, $R_5 = 2n - 1$, R_4 = running total
Initialize: *f* PRGM, *f* REG, *f* STK, *f* FIX 7, enter *x*, R/S
Comments: $\pi/4 = 0.7853982$ and it will take your calculator a considerable time to approach this limit.

15.4.1

STEP	PROGRAM
00	(R/S)
01	STO 1
02	2
03	0
04	0
05	RCL 1
06	f $x \leqslant y$
07	GTO 00
08	.
09	0
10	0
11	5
12	×
13	RCL 1
14	+
15	GTO 00

Memory: R_1 = balance
Initialize: f PRGM, enter balance, R/S

15.4.2

STEP	PROGRAM
00	(R/S)
01	STO 1
02	1
03	↑
04	R/S
05	f $x = y$
06	GTO 18
07	RCL 1
08	2
09	−
10	.
11	0
12	6
13	×
14	.
15	1
16	+
17	GTO 00
18	RCL 1
19	1
20	−
21	.
22	1
23	3
24	×
25	.
26	1
27	5
28	+
29	GTO 00

Memory: $R_1 = z$
Initialize: f PRGM, enter z, R/S enter class, R/S

15.4.3

STEP	PROGRAM
00	(R/S)
01	STO 1
02	R/S
03	↑
04	RCL 1
05	f $x \leqslant y$
06	GTO 02
07	R↓
08	STO 1
09	GTO 02

Memory: R_1 = number
Initialize: f PRGM, enter number, R/S
Comments: To display the smallest number in a set, continue the enter number and R/S key sequence until all the numbers have been processed.
While step 03 is unnecessary, it is included to help explain what is happening in the stack.

15.4.4

STEP	PROGRAM
00	(R/S)
01	STO 1
02	R/S
03	STO 2
04	↑
05	RCL 1
06	5
07	×
08	3
09	−
10	f $x = y$
11	GTO 14
12	0
13	GTO 00
14	1
15	GTO 00

Memory: $R_1 = x$, $R_2 = y$
Initialize: f PRGM, enter x, R/S, enter y, R/S

15.4.5

STEP	PROGRAM
00	(R/S)
01	STO 1
02	RCL 1
03	2
04	5
05	.
06	5
07	$f \quad x \leqslant y$
08	GTO 18
09	1
10	4
11	.
12	5
13	RCL 1
14	$f \quad x \leqslant y$
15	GTO 18
16	RCL 1
17	GTO 00
18	$g \quad \pi$
19	GTO 00

Memory: R_1 = number
Initialize: f PRGM, enter number, R/S

15.4.6

STEP	PROGRAM
00	(R/S)
01	STO 1
02	R/S
03	STO 2
04	R/S
05	STO 3
06	2
07	×
08	RCL 2
09	2
10	×
11	+
12	RCL 1
13	+
14	1
15	0
16	8
17	$x \gtrless y$
18	$f \quad x > y$
19	GTO 22
20	1
21	GTO 00
22	0
23	GTO 00

Memory: $R_1 = l$, $R_2 = w$, $R_3 = h$
Initialize: f PRGM, enter l, R/S, enter w, R/S, enter h, R/S

15.4.7

STEP	PROGRAM
00	(R/S)
01	STO 1
02	R/S
03	STO 2
04	R/S
05	STO 3
06	5
07	0
08	R/S
09	STO 4
10	$f \quad x > y$
11	GTO 29
12	RCL 3
13	2
14	×
15	RCL 2
16	2
17	×
18	+
19	RCL 1
20	+
21	1
22	0
23	8
24	$x \gtrless y$ *
25	$f \quad x > y$
26	GTO 29
27	1
28	GTO 00
29	0
30	GTO 00

Memory: $R_1 = l$, $R_2 = w$, $R_3 = h$, R_4 = weight
Initialize: f PRGM, enter l, R/S, enter w, R/S, enter h, R/S, enter weight, R/S
Comments: If a package can be sent by U.P.S., a "1" appears in the display, otherwise a "0" appears.

*The symbol $x \gtrless y$ represents the "x exchange t" key on the calculator.

15.4.8

STEP	PROGRAM
00	(R/S)
01	RCL 6
02	STO + 3
03	STO + 3
04	RCL 5
05	$g \quad x^2$
06	4
07	RCL 6
08	RCL 4
09	×
10	×
11	−
12	STO 2
13	$g \quad x < 0$
14	GTO 16
15	GTO 27
16	RCL 5
17	CHS
18	RCL 3
19	÷
20	R/S
21	RCL 2
22	CHS
23	$f \quad \sqrt{x}$
24	RCL 3
25	÷
26	GTO 00
27	RCL 2
28	$f \quad \sqrt{x}$
29	STO 1
30	RCL 5
31	CHS
32	RCL 1
33	+
34	RCL 3
35	÷
36	R/S
37	RCL 5
38	CHS
39	RCL 1
40	−
41	RCL 3
42	÷
43	GTO 00

Memory: $R_6 = a$, $R_5 = b$, $R_4 = c$, $R_3 = 2a$, $R_2 = d$, $R_1 = \sqrt{d}$

Initialize: *f* PRGM, *f* REG, *f* STK, enter *a*, STO 6, enter *b*, STO 5, enter *c*, STO 4, R/S, wait until you see "x_1" or "*u*," then R/S in order to see "x_2" or "*v*."

Comments: For complex roots, your calculator stops first to show *u* and then *v*. To form the roots, use $x_1, x_2 = u \pm vi$.

15.6.1

STEP	PROGRAM
00	(R/S)
01	STO 1
02	4
03	÷
04	↑
05	*g* INT
06	$f \quad x = y$
07	GTO 11
08	RCL 1
09	CHS
10	GTO 00
11	RCL 1
12	GTO 00

Memory: R_1 = year = *n*

Initialize: *f* PRGM, enter year = *n*, R/S

15.6.2a

STEP	PROGRAM
00	(R/S)
01	STO 1
02	↑
03	1
04	0
05	0
06	$f \quad x \leqslant y$
07	$f \quad x \geqslant y$
08	GTO 24
09	3
10	$g \quad 1/x$
11	$f \quad y^x$
12	↑
13	*f* LOG
14	*g* INT
15	2
16	+
17	$g \quad 10^x$
18	+
19	*f* LAST *x*
20	−
21	*g* FRAC
22	$g \quad x = 0$
23	GTO 26

STEP	PROGRAM
24	0
25	GTO 00
26	RCL 1
27	GTO 00

Memory: $R_1 = n$
Initialize: *f* PRGM, *f* REG, *f* STK, enter *n*, R/S
Comments: Notice the special key sequence in steps 12 − 20 that rounds numbers to 8 significant digits. Try the program with *g* NOP instructions in place of those steps to see that the sequence is necessary.

15.6.2b

You obtain the word "error" in the display since *f* y^x may only be used for positive numbers.

15.6.3

In problem 7.6.2 replace step 02 (which was unnecessary) with *g* ABS.

15.6.4

STEP	PROGRAM
00	(R/S)
01	3
02	STO + 1
03	RCL 1
04	*f* $\sqrt{x}$
05	↑
06	*f* LOG
07	*g* INT
08	2
09	+
10	*g* 10^x
11	+
12	*f* LAST *x*
13	−
14	*g* FRAC
15	*g* $x \neq 0$
16	GTO 19
17	RCL 1
18	GTO 00
19	RCL 1
20	*f* PAUSE
21	GTO 01

Memory: R_1 = multiple of 3
Initialize: *f* PRGM, *f* REG, *f* STK, R/S
Comments: When the calculator stops to display multiples of 3 that are perfect squares, press R/S to continue. Notice the special key sequence in steps 06–14 that rounds numbers to 8 significant digits.

15.6.5

STEP	PROGRAM
00	(R/S)
01	1
02	STO + 1
03	RCL 1
04	*g* x^2
05	2
06	×
07	RCL 1
08	2
09	×
10	+
11	1
12	+
13	*f* $\sqrt{x}$
14	↑
15	*f* LOG
16	*g* INT
17	2
18	+
19	*g* 10^x
20	+
21	*f* LAST *x*
22	−
23	↑
24	*g* INT
25	*f* $x \neq y$
26	GTO 01
27	$x \gtrless y$
28	GTO 00

Memory: R_1 = index *a*
Initialize: *f* PRGM, *f* REG, *f* STK, R/S
Comments:
1. When "*c*" is displayed, you can see "*a*" by pressing RCL 1 and compute "*b*" as $b = a + 1$.
2. The other triples are: (20, 21, 29), (119, 120, 169), and (696, 697, 985).
3. Note the use of the round-off key sequence in steps 14–22.

15.6.6

STEP	PROGRAM
00	(R/S)
01	1
02	STO + 1
03	RCL 1
04	STO + 2
05	RCL 2
06	f $\sqrt{x}$
07	↑
08	f LOG
09	g INT
10	2
11	+
12	g 10^x
13	+
14	f LAST x
15	−
16	↑
17	g INT
18	f $x \neq y$
19	GTO 01
20	RCL 2
21	R/S
22	GTO 01

Memory: $R_1 = n$, $R_2 = T_n$
Initialize: f PRGM, f REG, f STK, R/S
Comments: The first three triangular numbers that are perfect squares are 1, 36, and 1225.

Steps 07–15 use a round-off sequence.

15.6.7

STEP	PROGRAM
00	(R/S)
01	1
02	STO + 1
03	RCL 1
04	1
05	1
06	×
07	3
08	+
09	6
10	÷
11	↑
12	g INT
13	f $x \neq y$
14	GTO 01
15	RCL 1
16	1
17	1
18	×
19	8
20	+
21	R/S
22	GTO 01

Memory: $R_1 = k$
Initialize: f PRGM, f REG, f STK, R/S
Comments: The smallest is 41 and the next is 107.

16.3.1

STEP	PROGRAM
00	(R/S)
01	STO 7
02	1
03	STO 1
04	RCL 1
05	STO + 2
06	RCL 2
07	STO + 3
08	RCL 7
09	RCL 1
10	f $x = y$
11	GTO 15
12	1
13	STO + 1
14	GTO 04
15	RCL 3
16	GTO 00

Memory: $R_7 = n$, $R_1 = k$, R_2 = number of cannonballs in kth layer, R_3 = sum
Initialize: f PRGM, f REG, f STK, enter n, R/S
Comments: 10 layers use 220 cannonballs; 20 layers use 1,540 and 50 layers use 22,100.

16.3.2

STEP	PROGRAM
00	(R/S)
01	f REG
02	STO 7
03	1
04	STO 1

STEP	PROGRAM
05	RCL 1
06	1
07	−
08	RCL 1
09	×
10	3
11	×
12	1
13	+
14	STO + 2
15	RCL 1
16	RCL 7
17	f $x = y$
18	GTO 22
19	1
20	STO + 1
21	GTO 05
22	RCL 2
23	GTO 00

Memory: $R_7 = n$, $R_1 = k$, $R_2 =$ sum
Initialize: f PRGM, enter n, R/S
Comments: By inserting RCL 2, f PAUSE between steps 14 and 15, you can display each term of the sequence for any n. The sequence is n^3.

16.3.3

STEP	PROGRAM
00	(R/S)
01	STO 7
02	1
03	STO 1
04	RCL 2
05	RCL 3
06	STO 2
07	+
08	STO 3
09	RCL 2
10	f PAUSE
11	STO + 4
12	RCL 7
13	RCL 1
14	f $x = y$
15	GTO 19
16	1
17	STO + 1
18	GTO 04
19	RCL 4
20	GTO 00

Memory: $R_7 = n$, $R_1 = k$, $R_2 = f(k)$, $R_3 = f(k + 1)$, $R_4 =$ sum
Initialize: f PRGM, f REG, f STK, enter 1, STO 3, enter $n = 10$, R/S
Comments: The first ten Fibonacci numbers sum to 143.

16.3.4a

STEP	PROGRAM
00	(R/S)
01	STO 1
02	R/S
03	−
04	1
05	+
06	STO 7
07	1
08	STO 2
09	RCL 1
10	STO × 2
11	RCL 7
12	RCL 1
13	f $x = y$
14	GTO 18
15	1
16	STO − 1
17	GTO 09
18	RCL 2
19	GTO 00

Memory: $R_7 = n - y + 1$, $R_1 = n$, $R_2 =$ running product
Initialize: f PRGM, f REG, f STK, enter n, R/S, enter y, R/S

16.3.4b

5040

16.3.4c

95040

16.3.5a

STEP	PROGRAM
00	(R/S)
01	STO 1
02	R/S
03	STO 2
04	1
05	STO 3
06	RCL 1

STEP	PROGRAM
07	RCL 2
08	÷
09	STO × 3
10	1
11	RCL 2
12	$f\ \ x = y$
13	GTO 18
14	1
15	STO − 2
16	STO − 1
17	GTO 06
18	RCL 3
19	GTO 00

Memory: R_1 = numerator, R_2 = denominator, R_3 = running product

Initialize: f PRGM, f REG, f STK, enter n, R/S, enter y, R/S

Comments: For $y > n$, you will obtain 0 in the display.

16.3.5b

210

16.3.5c

210

16.3.6

STEP	PROGRAM
00	(R/S)
01	↑
02	1
03	−
04	STO 7
05	1
06	STO 1
07	STO 2
08	STO 3
09	RCL 1
10	STO ÷ 2
11	RCL 2
12	STO + 3
13	RCL 7
14	RCL 1
15	$f\ \ x = y$
16	GTO 20
17	1
18	STO + 1
19	GTO 09
20	RCL 3
21	GTO 00

Memory: $R_7 = n$, $R_1 = k$, $R_2 = 1/k!$, R_3 = running total

Initialize: f PRGM, f REG, f STK, enter $n = 20$, R/S

Comments: For $n = 20$ the sum is 2.7183 or 2.7182818 when f FIX 7 is used. What is the smallest value of n for which the sum is 2.7182818?

16.5.1

STEP	PROGRAM
00	(R/S)
01	STO 4
02	1
03	STO 1
04	RCL 1
05	RCL 1
06	$g\ 1/x$
07	$f\ \ y^x$
08	RCL 2
09	$f\ \ x > y$
10	GTO 15
11	$x \gtrless y$
12	STO 2
13	RCL 1
14	STO 3
15	RCL 1
16	RCL 4
17	$f\ \ x \leqslant y$
18	GTO 22
19	1
20	STO + 1
21	GTO 04
22	RCL 2
23	R/S
24	RCL 3
25	GTO 00

Memory: $R_1 = n$, R_2 = largest $\sqrt[n]{n}$, R_3 = best n, $R_4 = 30$

Initialize: f PRGM, f REG, enter 30, R/S, see maximum, R/S

Comments: $\sqrt[3]{3} = 1.442249570$ is maximum.

16.5.2a

STEP	PROGRAM
00	(R/S)
01	1
02	STO 1
03	$g\ \pi$
04	RCL 1

STEP	PROGRAM
05	4
06	g $1/x$
07	f y^x
08	f $x>y$
09	GTO 13
10	1
11	STO + 1
12	GTO 03
13	RCL 1
14	GTO 00

Memory: $R_1 = n$
Initialize: f PRGM, f REG, R/S
Comments: $n = 98$ is the first integer for which $\sqrt[4]{n} > \pi$.

16.5.2b

Store the new ending test value in R_2 during the initialization. Replace step 07 with RCL 2.

16.5.3

STEP	PROGRAM
00	(R/S)
01	6
02	STO 4
03	RCL 1
04	RCL 1
05	×
06	6
07	RCL 1
08	−
09	×
10	7
11	2
12	÷
13	RCL 2
14	f $x>y$
15	GTO 20
16	$x \gtrless y$*
17	STO 2
18	RCL 1
19	STO 3
20	RCL 1
21	RCL 4
22	f $x \leqslant y$
23	GTO 27
24	1
25	STO + 1
26	GTO 03
27	RCL 3
28	R/S
29	RCL 2
30	GTO 00

Memory: $R_1 = k$, $R_2 =$ best probability, $R_3 =$ best k, $R_4 = 6$
Initialize: f PRGM, f REG, Cl X, R/S, see best k, R/S.
Comments: To see the probability, press R/S or RCL 2. The maximal probability is 0.444444444.

16.5.4

STEP	PROGRAM
00	(R/S)
01	STO 7
02	1
03	STO 1
04	RCL 1
05	g x^2
06	STO + 2
07	RCL 7
08	RCL 2
09	f PAUSE (optional)
10	f $x>y$
11	GTO 15
12	1
13	STO + 1
14	GTO 04
15	RCL 1
16	1
17	−
18	GTO 00

Memory: $R_1 = k$, $R_2 =$ sum of k^2, $R_7 =$ 10,000 = end test value
Initialize: f PRGM, f REG, enter 10000, R/S
Comments: $k = 30$. Press RCL 2 to see the number of cannonballs in 31 layers, i.e., 10416; subtract 31^2 to see that there are 9455 cannonballs in 30 layers; subtract from 10,000 to see that there are 545 unused cannonballs.

*The symbol $x \gtrless y$ represents the "x exchange y" key on the calculator.

16.5.5a

STEP	PROGRAM
00	(R/S)
01	7
02	8
03	STO 4
04	0
05	STO 1
06	RCL 1
07	RCL 5
08	×
09	RCL 4
10	*f* $x \leqslant y$
11	GTO 32
12	7
13	7
14	↑
15	5
16	RCL 1
17	×
18	−
19	4
20	÷
21	STO 2
22	*g* FRAC
23	*g* $x \neq 0$
24	GTO 29
25	RCL 2
26	R/S
27	RCL 1
28	R/S
29	1
30	STO + 1
31	GTO 06
32	0
33	GTO 00

Memory: $R_1 = y$, $R_2 = x$, $R_4 = 77 + 1 = 78$

Initialize: *f* PRGM, *f* REG, Cl *X*, R/S, wait to see *x*, R/S.

Comments: $x = 18, y = 1$;
$x = 13, y = 5$;
$x = 8, y = 9$; and
$x = 3, y = 13$.
To see all solutions, continue pressing R/S.

16.5.5b

$x = 8, y = 9$ by inspection.

16.5.6

STEP	PROGRAM
00	(R/S)
01	EEX
02	2
03	STO 7
04	1
05	STO 1
06	STO 2
07	1
08	STO + 1
09	RCL 2
10	RCL 2
11	RCL 1
12	÷
13	+
14	*f* PAUSE (optional)
15	STO 2
16	RCL 7
17	*f* $x > y$
18	GTO 07
19	RCL 1
20	GTO 00

Memory: $R_1 = k$, $R_2 =$ height, $R_7 = 100$

Initialize: *f* PRGM, *f* REG, Cl *X*, R/S

Comments: The sequence of heights proceeds: 1.5000, 2.000, 2.5000, 3.0000, and so on. On the 199th day the height is 100 times the original height.

16.5.7

STEP	PROGRAM
00	(R/S)
01	RCL 2
02	RCL 4
03	RCL 1
04	×
05	−
06	RCL 0
07	÷
08	STO 6
09	↑
10	*g* INT
11	*f* $x \neq y$
12	GTO 29
13	RCL 3
14	RCL 5
15	RCL 1
16	×

STEP	PROGRAM
17	−
18	RCL 0
19	÷
20	↑
21	*g* INT
22	*f* $x \neq y$
23	GTO 29
24	R/S
25	RCL 6
26	R/S
27	RCL 1
28	R/S
29	RCL 1
30	RCL 7
31	*f* $x \leqslant y$
32	GTO 36
33	1
34	STO + 1
35	GTO 01
36	0
37	GTO 00

Memory: $R_0 = 59$, $R_1 = S$, $R_2 = 3869$, $R_3 = 2031$, $R_4 = 35$, $R_5 = 24$, $R_6 = C$, $R_7 = 100$.

Initialize: *f* PRGM, enter 59, STO 0, enter 1, STO 1, enter 3869, STO 2, enter 2031, STO 3, enter 35, STO 4, enter 24, STO 5, enter 100, STO 7, R/S, wait to see *l*, R/S see *c*, R/S.

Comments: The solution is unique: $L = 21$, $C = 46$, $S = 33$.